The Art of Voice-Acting

The Art of Voice-Acting

The Craft and Business of Performing for Voice-Over

James R. Alburger

Focal Press

Boston Oxford Johannesburg Melbourne New Delhi Singapore

Focal Press is an imprint of Butterworth–Heinemann.

 Recognizing the importance of preserving what has been written, Butterworth–Heinemann prints its books on acid-free paper whenever possible.

 Butterworth–Heinemann supports the efforts of American Forests and the Global ReLeaf program in its campaign for the betterment of trees, forests, and our environment.

Library of Congress Cataloging-in-Publication Data

Alburger, James R., 1950– .
    The art of voice-acting : the craft and business of performing for
voice-over / James R. Alburger.
        p.   cm.
    Includes bibliographical references.
    ISBN 0-240-80340-X (alk. paper)
    1. Television announcing—Vocational guidance. 2. Radio
announcing—Vocational guidance. 3. Voice-overs. 4. Television
advertising—Vocational guidance. 5. Radio advertising—Vocational
guidance. I. Title.
PN1992.8.A6A42 1999
791.45'028'023—dc21   98-38070
                                                                        CIP

British Library Cataloguing-in-Publication Data
A catalogue record for this book is available from the British Library.

The publisher offers special discounts on bulk orders of this book.
For information, please contact:
    Manager of Special Sales
    Butterworth–Heinemann
    225 Wildwood Avenue
    Woburn, MA 01801-2041
    Tel: 781-904-2500
    Fax: 781-904-2620

For information on all Butterworth-Heinemann publications available, contact our World Wide Web home page at: http://www.bh.com

10 9 8 7 6 5 4

Printed in the United States of America

To my parents, Alys & Jim Sr. You always encouraged me, had confidence in me, gave me the opportunities to make mistakes, and taught me the importance of doing my best at whatever I chose to do.
Thank you.

Contents

Foreword

I've been on both sides of the microphone for almost twenty years. Voice-acting is one of the most important ingredients of anything I do. Whether it be a television promo, a radio commercial or a sales tape, the right voice can make a good project a great one.

But turning on the microphone is just a first step in becoming a good voice actor.

Just ask James Alburger. He's a sound design wizard! Winner of countless Emmy's, Jim has created magic for many of my projects for years. He now shares his first-hand knowledge as a performer and his sound advice as an instructor and director in *The Art of Voice-Acting*.

From "Where to Start" to "Exercises to Keep Your Voice in Tip-Top Shape" to "Smart Tips on How to Successfully Complete Your First Session," this is a must read for anyone just starting out in the voice-acting business.

It's a user-friendly, step-by-step "how to" covering every aspect of this fascinating business, all put together in one simple handbook. You'll keep referring to it again and again!

Good luck.

Deborah Lawrence
Senior Producer, NBC 7/39

Preface

I've been fascinated with sound design and audio production since I was 12 years old. It always amazed me how the combination of music, voice and sound effects could create such a powerful illusion in the mind of the listener. In many ways sound can create a more vivid visual picture of what is happening than if the same scene is viewed with the eyes — simply because the listener contributes to the illusion with his or her imagination.

When performers or actors are involved, as in radio and television commercials and cartoons, the acting skills of the performers play an important role in how effectively the illusion is created. We have all heard commercials that make us feel uncomfortable because the "announcer" is shouting at us or the character we hear is not believable. We have all heard commercials that moved us to laughter or tears. The first makes us want to change the station — the second makes us want to hear more.

I once had the privilege of recording a series of luncheons at which the top commercial producers in Los Angeles presented their concepts of Visual Radio. The underlying theme was that the effectiveness of a radio (or television) commercial lies in how successfully the message is communicated on an emotional level. In other words, there must be a connection between the performer and the listener.

Words, in and of themselves, won't motivate a listener. There must be something more to it. That something more is a believable character that the listener can relate to and that becomes "real" in his or her imagination. The bottom line is how the message is perceived "in the mind of the beholder" — and the message can be anything!

When I first had the idea of writing some of my thoughts down on paper, it was for the purpose of creating some notes for my voice-over workshop. Somehow, those notes have evolved into this book, which I sincerely hope will help you more effectively reach your audience through the sound of your voice.

Introduction

"You should be doing commercials!"

"You've got a great voice!"

"You should be doing cartoons!"

If anyone has ever said any of these things to you — and you have, even for an instant, considered his or her suggestions — this may be just the book you need! If you simply enjoy making up funny character voices or sounds, or enjoy telling stories and jokes, this book will show you how to do it better and more effectively. If you are involved in any line of work in which you need to communicate any sort of message to one or more people, this book will help you make your presentation more powerful and more memorable.

This is a book about acting and performing, but it's about a kind of acting where you are not on a stage in front of thousands of people. If fact, with this kind of acting you rarely, if ever, see your audience, or receive any applause for your performance. This is a kind of acting where you will create illusions and believable images in the mind of the audience — a listening audience who might never see you, but who may remember your performance for many years.

This is a book about acting and performing for voice-over! Even though the focus of this book is on developing your talent for working in the world of voice-over, the skills and techniques you will learn can be applied to any situation in which you want to reach and motivate an audience on an emotional level.

Voice-over!

These words alone can be inspiring or intimidating. They can conjure up visions of a world of celebrity and big money. True, that can happen, but as you will learn in the pages that follow, the business of voice-over is just that — a business. It is a business that can be lots of fun and it can be a business that is, at times, very hard work. And it can be both at the same time!

Voice-over is also an art! It is a craft with skills that must be developed. The voice-over performer is an actor who uses his or her voice to create a believable character. The business of voice-over might, more accurately, be called the business of voice-acting. It is most definitely a part of show business.

I'll be perfectly honest with you right from the beginning. Working as a voice-actor is not for everyone. It requires an investment of time, energy, persistence and a little money to get started. And, perhaps, just a bit of luck. As the saying goes in show business: an overnight success is the result of 20 years of study and paying dues.

However — if you love to play, have the desire to learn some acting skills, can speak clearly, read well, don't mind the occasional odd working hours, don't take things too seriously, have a good attitude, and can motivate yourself to be in the right place at the right time — this business may be just right for you. In addition, as I mentioned earlier, the skills and techniques of voice-acting can be applied to any situation where you want your audience to connect emotionally with the message you are delivering. These skills are not limited to just doing radio and TV commercials.

This book shows you the steps to take to learn the performing skills necessary to be successful in the voice-over business. It also has the information you need to get your demo tape produced and into the hands of those who will hire you. You will get a solid foundation that you can build on to achieve lasting success in the business of voice-over.

You *don't* have to be in Los Angeles, New York or Chicago to get voice-over work. Work is available everywhere. You *do* need to have the right attitude, the right skills and a high-quality, professional presentation of your talents, or the casting people won't even give you a second look (or listen). If you master the techniques available to you in this book, you will be able to present yourself like a pro — even if you have never done anything like this before.

I began my adventure through the world of sound and voice-acting when I taught myself to edit music at the age of 12. Through my high school and college years I worked for several radio stations creating dozens of commercials as engineer, performer, writer and director. I have also performed professionally for over 30 years as a stage and close-up magician. I put my ideas about performing magic to music in my first book, *Get Your Act Together — Performing an Effective Magic Act to Music*, which has become a standard in the magic community. However, it was when I worked as a recording engineer in Hollywood that I began to realize what voice-acting was all about. In the nearly three decades since then, I have directed some of the top voice talent in the country, I have been honored as the recipient of several Emmy[1] Awards for sound design, teach voice-acting workshops and operate my own business as a voice-actor, sound designer and performance consultant.

You will notice that I refer to voice talent as the voice-over performer or voice-actor — never as "announcer." This is because that's exactly what you are — a performer (or actor) telling a story to communicate a message to an audience on an emotional level.

The term voice-over is somewhat misrepresentative of what the work? actually entails. It tends to place the focus on the voice, when the real emphasis needs to be on the performance. *Announcers* read and often focus their energy on the sound of their voice, striving to achieve a certain "magical" resonance. Effective voice-acting shifts the focus from the voice to the emotional content of the message. This requires knowledge, skill, and a love of performing. Focusing on your performance, instead of the sound of your voice, helps you become more conversational, more real and more believable.

This is why acting is such an important aspect of good voice-over work. Talking *to* your audience conversationally is much better than talking *at* them as an uninterested, detached speaker. The best communication closes the gap between the audience and the performer and frames the performance with a mood that the audience can connect with emotionally. Many people have "great pipes" or wonderfully resonant voices. But it takes much more than a good voice to be an effective communicator or voice-actor. In fact, a good voice isn't even necessary — most people have a voice that is perfectly suitable for voice-acting. What is necessary is the knowledge and skill to use your voice dramatically and effectively as part of a voice-over performance.

As you read the pages that follow, I promise that I will be straightforward and honest with you. You will find techniques and tricks of the trade that you will not find anywhere else. And, you will learn what it takes to be successful in the world of voice-over.

I wish you much luck — and please let me know when you land your first national commercial!

Acknowledgments

This book would not have been possible without the generous support and help from so many people and companies who work in the world of voice-over every day. I would like to personally thank the following:

For helping get me started with teaching my first course in voice-acting, which was the inspiration for my workshop and this book:

Deb Ingersoll and the San Diego Learning Annex.

For helping with development, proofreading and keeping me on track so my words all made sense:

Diana Fowler, Kerry and Dawne Ross, Janet Warren, Catheryn Zaro, John Turner and Jon Beaupré.

For providing scripts, copy, tricks of the trade, invaluable assistance and other materials:

The NBC Television Network, NBC 7/39 (KNSD-TV, San Diego), Pam and Vince Lubinski (Invincible Productions), Kristin Marshall Napoleon (Marshall Marketing & Communications, Inc.), Dick Orkin (DOCSI and Radio Ranch), Dennis Regan (Mainstreet Productions), Joe Sallay (LAK Advertising), Jim Staylor and Staylor Made communications, Rose Dufrense (Jefferson-Pilot Communications) and the many other talented writers and companies who contributed scripts.

For so generously sharing their time, knowledge and talents as guest speakers at my workshop, "The Art of Voice-Acting":

Deborah Lawrence (senior producer, NBC 7/39, San Diego), Catheryn Zarro (voice-actor), Laurel Murray (voice-actor), Shondra and Tom Jepperson (voice-actors, singers), Rolland Smith (television news journalist, writer, poet), Michael Klicman (actor), Dennis Regan (voice-actor), Jim Staylor (voice-actor and writer), "Shotgun" Tom Kelly (voice-actor and DJ), Clark Anthony (television news journalist, voice-actor), Pierre Charmasson (independent producer) and Jacques Albrecht (independent producer).

---

[1] National Academy of Television Arts and Sciences, Southwestern Regional Emmy awarded for outstanding sound design for television promos and programs.

1

What Is Voice~Acting?

We live in an age of information and communication. We are bombarded with messages of all types 24 hours a day. From 30-second commercials to hour-long infomercials, from documentary films, to video games, much of our time is spent assimilating and choosing to act or not act on the information we receive.

It is well known among marketing and communications specialists that the most effective way to reach an audience is to connect on an emotional, often unconscious level. This frequently involves drawing the listener (or viewer) into a story or creating a dramatic or emotional scene that the listener can relate to. In short, effective voice-over performing is story-telling and requires acting skills. The voice-over performer, in fact, can be more accurately referred to as a voice-actor.

The Voice~Actor

Voice-actors play a very important role in sales, marketing and delivery of information. It is the voice-actor's job to play a role that has been written into the script. To effectively play the role and thus sell the message, the performer must, among other things, be able to quickly determine who the intended audience is, what the key elements of the message are, and how to best communicate the message using nothing more than the spoken word. Chapters 4 through 7 will cover these subjects in detail. For the moment, you only need to know that this type of work requires more from you than simply standing in front of a microphone, reading words off a page.

Think of voice-over work as voice-acting!

Types of Voice-Over Work

When most people think of voice-over, they think of radio and TV commercials. These are only a small part of the business of voice-over. There is actually much more to it.

Let's begin with a simplified definition of voice-over. *Voice-over* can be defined as *any recording or performance of one or more unseen voices for the purpose of communicating a message*. The voice-over is the spoken part of a commercial, program or other announcement that you hear, but do not see the person speaking. The message can be anything from a simple phone message to a television commercial, sales presentation, instructional video, movie trailer, feature film or documentary narration. It may be nothing more than a single voice heard on the radio or over a stadium public address system. The production may include music, sound effects, video, computer animation or multiple voices. In most cases, the message is selling something, providing information or in some way motivating the listener to take some sort of action.

You hear voice-over messages many times every day, and you are probably not even beware of it. The following sections describe just some of the many types of voice-over work that require talented performers, like you.

RADIO

There are three basic categories of radio voice-over work:

1. **The radio DJ** — This is a specialized job that requires a unique set of skills. Most radio DJs are not considered to be voice-actors.

2. **On-air promotion** — Most radio promos are produced in-house, using DJ and station production staff. Occasionally, outside talent will be used, but not often.

3. **Commercials** — Most commercials are produced outside the station by advertising agencies. However, many radio stations do produce local commercials for their clients. Again, most in-house productions use station staff, but when the need arises, they will use outside talent.

TELEVISION

Commercials, promotion and programming all use voice-over talent in one way or another. Most television productions using voice-over talent are actually produced outside of the station. However, there are two main departments at a TV station where voice-over talent is used.

The Promotion Department handles all the station's on-air promotion — from the short "coming up next" VOCs (voice-over credits), to full :30 seconds promos. The Production Department often needs voice-over talent for locally produced commercials and in-house projects. Some TV stations have a separate unit solely for the production of commercials while other stations work with an advertising agency or outside production company.

Two other departments that use voice-over talent are the News Department and the Sales Department. Voice-over in news is part of a reporter's job in reporting a story. The Sales Department usually uses staff announcers for their projects or work with talent booked through the Production Department. In-house presentations for current and prospective clients and station marketing as well as commercials for local clients are just a few of the types of projects produced by a TV station's Sales Department.

Most TV stations have an established pool of voice-over talent on staff or readily available. Staff announcers may come to the station and record their tracks on a daily basis, or the copy may be faxed to the talent a few days before it is needed, and the announcer records it and ships the tape to the station for production. Alternatively, some projects may be recorded at a local recording studio. Some TV stations are equipped with the latest digital ISDN telephone technology that allows for a live, high-quality recording of a voice-over performer in another city, or across the country.

CORPORATE/INDUSTRIAL

There are literally thousands of locally produced audio and video presentations recorded each year for the business community. Here are just a few examples of corporate and/or industrial voice-over work:

- **Message-on-hold** — Those informative sales pitches you hear while waiting on hold.

- **In-store offers** — Usually these are part of the background music program played over a store's speaker system while you shop.

- **Sales and marketing presentations** — Video presentations that are designed to attract clients and promote vendors or products. Talent could be either on-camera or voice-over. You will often find these videos as ongoing product demos in stores like K-Mart and Home Depot or in shopping mall kiosks.

- **Convention and/or trade show presentations** — These are similar to sales and marketing presentations, but usually target potential buyers at a convention or trade show. Again, usually these are a video presentation.

- **Training and instructional tapes** — As the name implies, these tapes are designed to train personnel on anything from company policies and procedures, to the proper use of equipment. Most corporate presentations are rarely seen by the general public.

ANIMATION

This is a very specialized area of voice-over work. It's definitely not for everyone, and it is a challenging area to break into. Good animation voice-over performers usually can do a wide range of character voices and have years of acting experience. Most animation voice-over work is done in Los Angeles.

CD-ROM AND MULTIMEDIA

This market for voice-over talent developed as a result of the explosion of computer-based CD-ROM games and instructional software. Some software manufacturers produce audio tracks for these products entirely in-house, while others are produced by outside production companies.

BOOKS AND MAGAZINES ON TAPE

These are recordings of books and magazines, and fall into two basic categories: commercial tapes for sale and books or magazines on tape for the visually impaired. Commercial audio books are generally read by a celebrity to make the recording more marketable. Books and magazines on tape for the visually impaired may be produced locally by any number of service organizations or radio stations. The pay is usually minimal or nonexistent (you volunteer your talents).

Most reading services prefer their "readers" to deliver their copy in a somewhat flat tone. For example, there may be several people reading chapters from a book over a period of days. To maintain a degree of continuity in the "reading," the performers are generally asked to avoid putting much emotional spin or dramatic characterization into their reading. This type of work is excellent for improving reading skills and acquiring the stamina to speak for long periods of time, but limits your opportunities to develop characterization and emotional or dramatic delivery skills. Check your local white pages under Blind Aids and

Services or contact your local PBS radio station and ask about any reading services they might provide.

Regardless of the type of voice-over work you do, there are three things you need to have:

1. A decent speaking voice.
2. An ability to act.
3. The willingness to spend the time necessary to market and promote your talent to get auditions so that you can get the work.

Breaking into the Business of Voice-Over

Most people think voice-over work is easy. You have probably even said to yourself after listening to a commercial, "I can do that!" For some people, it is easy. For most, though, voice-over work — just like theatrical acting — is an ongoing learning process. Even experienced professionals will tell you that voice-over work can be potentially more difficult than on-camera or on-stage work. After all, the advantage of props, scenery and lighting are not available to the voice-actor. The drama, comedy or emotions of a message must be communicated solely through the spoken word. This often requires a tremendous amount of focus and concentration, plus an ability to make quick changes in mid-stream. Prior acting experience is an advantage, but these are skills you can pick up as you go, so don't let a lack of experience stop you. As long as you can use your imagination, you can do voice-over.

One of the greatest misconceptions is that you need a certain type of voice to do voice-over. You do not need a "good" voice, or "announcer" voice. You do need a voice that is easily understood. If your voice has a unique quality or sound, you can use that to your advantage, especially for animation work. But a unique voice quality can also become a limitation if that is the only thing you do. You may find you are better suited to one particular type of voice-over work — corporate/industrial, for example. If that's the case, you can focus on marketing yourself for that type of work. Still, you should consider other types of voice work when the call comes.

Variety is an important aspect of voice-over performing. By variety I mean being able to use your voice to convey a wide range of attitudes, personality, delivery, and emotions (that's why acting is so important). These are the characteristics of your voice presentation that will sell the message. And, selling is what voice-over is all about.

Many people think that because they can do lots of impersonations or make up crazy character voices, they can do voice-over work. Vocal versatility is certainly valuable, however, success in the world of voice-over also takes focus, discipline and an ability to act. When an advertiser wants to use a celebrity voice, they will either hire the celebrity, or use an impersonator who is well known and established.

Character voices are usually hired from an established pool of character voice talent — mostly in Los Angeles. These people are highly skilled actors who can create unique voice characterizations on demand and sustain the character voice over long periods of time. If you enjoy making up voices and have a talent for mimicking, this may be the place for you.

Auditions, either in person or via your demo tape, are the first step to getting work in this business. The toughest part of the business is breaking in and getting those first few jobs. Once your name gets around and you become established, the work almost seems to come to you. Remember, as with most businesses, voice-over work is a "numbers game." The more connections you can make, and the more you circulate your tape to the people who hire voice talent, the more work you will get. As for spending the time and energy necessary to get auditions, remember that voice-over work must be treated as a business if you are to succeed — and your degree of success will be directly proportional to the time you spend promoting yourself.

Just how do you break in and get yourself known as a voice-actor? That's what the rest of this book is all about. The simple answer is: get your voice recorded and get yourself known. The more complex answer is: learn everything you can about acting, communication and marketing. In this business, an old adage, "it's not what you know, but who you know," is very true. Getting work as a voice-actor is largely a numbers game — a game of networking and making yourself known in the right circles. To be successful you cannot be shy. Let every person you meet know what you do! But you must also possess the skills that qualify you as a professional, and that is what this book is really about!

A career in voice-over can be lots of fun, and it can give you lots of time for other activities. Most recording sessions last from about 10 or 15 minutes to an hour. That's it! Once your voice is recorded, you're free to do whatever you want, or you're on your way to another session.

Enjoy!

2

The Best-Kept Secret

Let's face it — if everyone were equally good at every job, there would be no need for résumés or auditions. Fortunately, in this world, every person has uniquely different talents, abilities and levels of skill. It is this variety that makes the voice-over business a potentially profitable career for anyone willing to invest the time and effort.

Voice-over is probably one of the best-kept secrets around. The job can be loads of fun and very profitable, but it is not an easy business to break into. The competition is tough, and it is easy to become frustrated when just beginning.

Voice-over work is part of "show business." As such it has all the potential excitement, celebrity status, and opportunities as the other areas of show business, as well as the long periods of waiting, frustrations in getting "booked" and problems dealing with agents and producers.

The Pros and Cons of Voice-Acting

You have probably heard most of the pros of voice-over work: big money, short hours, celebrity status (without anyone actually knowing who you are), and more. For some voice-over performers, these things are true; but it takes a long time, and constantly being in the right place, to get there. In other words, they had to work at it. Most overnight successes are the result of many years of hard work and dedication to the craft.

Like most of the performing arts, voice-acting is a hurry-up-and-wait kind of business. By that I mean you will spend a lot of time waiting: waiting at auditions, waiting for a callback, and waiting in the lobby of a recording studio. Then, once you are in the studio, things happen very fast. Even then, you may still find yourself waiting in the studio as the producer works on copy changes. If you are lucky, you will get your copy early and have a chance to read through it a few times. Most often, you will not see the copy until you walk into the studio — and you may have only a few minutes to do your best work.

Producers assume that you know what you are doing and expect you to deliver your lines professionally. Direction (coaching) from the producer or director often comes very fast, so you must listen and pay attention. Sometimes, the producer or director completely changes the concept of the reading or makes major copy changes in the middle of an audition or session — and you need to be able to adapt quickly.

The session can be over before you know it! Most voice-over sessions last from ten minutes to an hour, depending on the project, how much copy there is and, of course, the performer's ability to deliver what the producer wants. (Whether the producer actually knows what he or she wants is another issue — more about producers, writers and directors later.) Auditions will usually last anywhere from five to ten minutes — just long enough for the producers to get an impression of what you can do as a voice performer.

Your job as a voice-over performer is to perform to the best of your abilities. When you are hired, either from your demo tape or after an audition, your voice has been chosen over many others as the one most desirable for the job. Unless there is a serious technical problem that requires you being called back, you will not get a second chance after leaving the studio.

Full-Time versus Part-Time

If you think voice-over work is for you, you may have a decision to make. Not right this minute, but soon. Do you want to do voice-over work as a full-time career, or as a part-time avocation? It may not be easy to decide!

Doing voice-over work on a full-time basis is unlike just about any other job you can imagine. You must be available on a moment's notice when you are called for an audition. In addition, you must constantly market yourself, even if you have an agent.

Full-time voice-over work may also mean joining a union, and even moving to a larger city — if that's where your destiny leads you. Los Angeles, New York and many major cities are strong union towns for voice-over work, and you must be in the union to get well-paying jobs in these cities. Although the possibilities for nonunion work does exist in larger cities, it may require some additional effort to find it.

Smaller cities are a different story, however. The union for voice-over performers, AFTRA (the American Federation of Television and Radio Artists), is not as powerful in smaller towns and there is a much greater opportunity for freelance voice-over work than in bigger cities. On the other hand, major advertising agencies and big clients often use only union talent. So, if you want those jobs you need to join the union local in your area. There are also many out-of-town ad agencies that do production in smaller cities, and most of them use union talent. Nonunion work is frequently limited to lower-budget commercials written and produced by the advertiser, corporate/industrial work and some local radio and TV voice work. Unions are covered in more detail in Chapter 15.

OK — you have decided eating is still a pleasurable past-time, and you would rather not quit your day job just yet. So, how about doing voice-over work on a part-time basis? Good question!

Doing voice-over work part-time is quite possible, although you probably won't be doing the same kind of work as you would if you devoted more time to it. You will most likely do some corporate/industrial work and smaller projects for clients who have a minimal or nonexistent budget. Some of your work may be voluntary, barter, or you will do it just because you want the experience. The pay for nonunion freelance work is usually not terrific — but freelance work is a way of getting experience doing voice-over. You can gradually build up a client list and get tapes you can use later on when, or if, you decide to go full-time.

The biggest problem with doing voice-over work part-time is that you may find it difficult to deal with last-minute auditions or session calls. If you have a regular full-time job, you usually will need to arrange your voice-over work around it, unless you have a very understanding employer. If you are only working part-time, you most likely will find it easier to make the auditions and sessions. Voice-over work can be an ideal opportunity for the homemaker who is not working a 9 to 5 job and wants to do something creative, for a retired person with good performing skills, or for the self-employed individual who has a flexible schedule.

As a part-time performer, you can (and should) market your talent and get an agent. As your skills improve and you get more work, you may eventually join the union. If your agent knows you are only doing this part-time, he or she may be reluctant to send you out on many auditions. The image of a performer who is only available part-time is not one that agents particularly like. On the other hand, agents do understand that you need to eat, so they may be willing to work with you.

Doing voice-over work can be very satisfying, even if you only do an occasional session. Generally, the more you work, the more skilled you become — and the greater your skills, the more you can charge for your talent. The day may come when you decide to do voice-over full-time and go for the "big money" in Los Angeles, Chicago, New York or some other major voce-over market. In the meantime, don't be in a hurry — make the best of every opportunity that comes along and create your own opportunities whenever possible. Networking — telling people you meet what you do — is extremely important. You never know when you might be in just the right place to land that important national spot that changes your entire life!

In the chapters that follow, you will learn the skills you need to acquire to become an accomplished voice-over performer. You will also learn how to prepare for your demo tape, and you will be guided step-by-step through the process of producing your demo. Once you know how to get your demo ready, you will learn some methods of marketing your talents.

3

Where to Start:
Voice-Over Basics!

When you stand in front of a microphone as voice talent, your job is to effectively communicate the message contained in the words written on the paper in front of you. You are a storyteller. You are an actor! The words in your script, by themselves, are nothing but ink on a page. As a voice-actor, your job is to interpret those words in such a way as to effectively tell the story and meet the perceived needs of the producer or director.

The Voice-Over Performer
as Actor and Salesperson

I use the words "perceived needs" because many producers or writers only have an idea in their head. The producer may think he knows what he wants, when, in reality, he hasn't got a clue as to the best way to deliver the message. You may find yourself in the enviable position of solving many of your producer's problems simply by performing the copy in a way that you feel effectively communicates the message. In other words, your acting abilities are the vital link between the writer and the audience.

YOUR ROLE AS A VOICE-ACTOR

You are the actor playing the role of the character written in the script. Unlike stage performers, who may have several days to define and develop their characters, you may have only a few minutes. You must use your best acting skills to deliver your best interpretation of the copy. Your job is to breathe life into the script, making the thoughts of the writer become real.

You need to be able to quickly grasp the important elements of the script, understand your character (even if your character is simply an announcer), find the key elements of the copy, and choose what you believe to be the most effective delivery for your lines. In most cases, the producer or director will be coaching you into the read that gets you as close as possible to his or her vision. Sometimes you will be on your own. Every script is written for a purpose and you must be able to find and give meaning to that purpose.

One mistake made by many beginning voice-over performers is that they get nervous when they approach the microphone. They are focused on their voice, not their performance. When they get "on mic," they fidget, stand stiff as a board, cross their arms or put their hands behind their backs or in their pockets. It is impossible to perform effectively under those conditions.

What is needed, is to get into the flow of the copy, breathe properly, relax, have fun, and let the performance take you where it needs to go. Discover your character and let that character come into you so that you can "become the character."

UNDERSTAND YOUR AUDIENCE

Every message has an intended (or target) audience. Once you understand who the audience is and your role in the copy, you will be on your way to knowing how to perform the copy for the most effective delivery. Figure out who you are talking to. Narrow it down to a single individual and relate to that person on an emotional level. This is the first step to creating an effective performance and a believable character.

Chapter 7, The Character in the Copy, goes into greater detail about analyzing the various kinds of copy and creating characters.

WHAT TO LOOK FOR IN A SCRIPT

Here's an example of some of the things to look for in a script. This is copy for a single voice :15 TV promo. Dialog copy has some additional requirements, but this will give you the idea. Read it through once to get a feel for the copy.

> This is Yosemite. Before the traffic. Before the floods. Before it became a national disgrace. Will Yosemite make a miraculous comeback or be a paradise lost forever? You'll see, on "Yosemite: Treasure or Tragedy?" Tonight only at 5, only on NBC 7/39.

Now, read it a second and third time, looking for the following points. Finally, read it out loud for time, to see how close you can come to 15 seconds.

- Who is the audience this copy is trying to reach?

- What is the single primary message in the copy (what are you selling)?

- What are the supporting statements for the primary message?

- What is your role (character) in the copy?

- What is the emotional hook in the copy (if any)?

- What sort of delivery do you think would be the most effective — strong, hard-sell, happy, smiling, mellow, soft-sell, fast, slow?

- What is your attitude as the character in this spot — serious, comfortable, happy, sad and so on?

- What visual images come into your mind as you read the copy?

OK, how did you answer the questions? This spot was a TV promo for a news feature series, so there are visuals that go with the copy. You would normally know that at the session and would most likely have access to a storyboard that would describe the visual action your words would play against. Sometimes, however, you will not have anything more than the words on the page. Here's an interpretation of this copy:

- The target audience is men and women who are concerned about the environment. The focus is primarily on adults who are outgoing, enjoy traveling or camping and may have had the first-hand experience of traveling through the once pristine beauty of Yosemite.

- The message is *not* what Yosemite once was. Rather, it is an offer to answer the question of what will happen in the future. To have the question answered, the viewer must watch the program.

- The copy uses some emotionally charged words such as "traffic," "floods," "disgrace" and "miraculous." These words (along with the visuals) are intended to create a response in the audience. Each viewer's response to these words will be unique, but the intent is to create an impact in the viewers mind as to how tragedies created by humans and nature affect beautiful places.

- The character here is telling the story of Yosemite, a once beautiful place that is now ravaged or threatened by people and nature. Each of the first four sentences is delivered with a different attitude, all leading up to the question that is posed. To effectively deliver this copy, it is helpful to set a mental picture of each of the four scenes: a beautiful woodland park, traffic congestion, the aftermath of a flood, and the ugliness of a disaster area. The mental image changes at "miracle comeback" and shifts again to an appropriate image of a "paradise lost."

- The overall delivery is sincere, compassionate and concerned, with a serious tone. The emphasis for each of the first four sentences is on the first word, to provide punctuation for the emotion that follows. A secondary emphasis is on the emotion word. The end of the copy is delivered in a more matter-of-fact manner, but still keeping the tone of compassion about the story.

All these answers combine to provide the information you need to effectively deliver the copy. The visual image is important because it sets a solid framework for your character and helps establish the attitude of the spot. As an actor, you need to know these things. Otherwise, you are just reading words on a page — and that's boring!

With experience, you can get a complete analysis in a matter of seconds, just from a single reading of the script. Trust your instincts and use what you have learned from your interpretation to give depth to your character and life to the copy. Above all, bring your unique personality into the copy and everything else will come naturally.

THE VOICE-ACTOR AS A SALESPERSON

The message — or sell — is the most important part of all copy, and virtually all voice-over copy is selling something. Commercials usually sell products or services, or try to get an emotional response from the audience and motivate action; instructional tapes sell procedures; books on tape sell entertainment; and so on. Acting is the means by which any of these messages can be effectively communicated, the story told and the listener motivated to take action. So, you are not only a performer, but you are also a salesperson. For the time you are in the recording studio, you are an employee of your client's business. In fact, you are the advertiser's number one salesperson and must present yourself as a qualified expert.

Your acting job may only last a few minutes in the studio, but that performance may be repeated thousands of times on radio or TV. The credibility of the product or advertiser — and the success of an advertising campaign — may be directly related to the effectiveness and believability of your performance.

Getting the Skills You Need

The bottom line here is to get experience — as much as you can, wherever you can, any way you can! Take classes in acting, voice-over, and marketing. Get as much experience as you can reading stories out loud. Read to your children. Read to your spouse. Practice telling stories with lots of variety in your voice.

Analyze the characters in the stories you read. Take more classes. Ask the basic journalism five "Ws": who, what, when, where and why. Read the same copy in different ways, at different speeds and with different feelings or emotional attitudes — loud, soft, slow, fast, happy, sad, compassionate, angry. If possible, record yourself and listen to what you did to see where you might improve. Take some more classes. You can't take enough classes!

One of the best ways to acquire skills as a voice-actor is to constantly be listening to what other voice-over performers are doing. Mimicking other performers can be a good start to learning some basic performing techniques. But to really get an understanding of communicating on an emotional level, listen to how they deliver the lines:

- How do they interpret the message?

- How do they reach you emotionally?

- How do they use inflection, intonation, pacing and express feelings?

- Is their delivery conversational or screaming?

- What is your reaction?

In short, do they sound as if they are reading or do they sound natural and believable? Use what you learn from studying others and adapt that information to your own voice and style. One of the keys to successful voice-acting is to "make the copy your own." This simply means that you bring to the performance something of yourself to give the character and copy truth and believability. That's good acting! Chapters 4 and 7 discuss techniques for doing this.

A TWIST OF A WORD

You will notice that the better commercials and voice-over work do not sound like someone doing voice-over work. They sound like your best friend talking to you — comfortable, friendly, and most of all, not "announcery." A good performer can make even bad copy sound reasonably good, and what can be done with good copy is truly amazing.

Create an emotional, visual image in the mind of the audience with a twist of a word. A slight change in the delivery of a word can change the entire meaning of a sentence. Speaking a word softly or with more intensity, or perhaps sustaining a vowel, making the delivery crisp or taking the inflection up or down can all affect the meaning of a sentence, and its emotional impact in the mind of the listener. These are skills that are acquired over time and are all basic acting techniques that help to create an emotional connection with the audience.

To be an effective voice performer you need to discover the qualities and characteristics of your voice that will make you different from all those other voices out there. Keep trying new techniques. Keep practicing and studying the work of others in the business. Find your unique qualities and perfect them. Learn how to make any piece of copy your own, and you will be in demand.

CLASSES

You can never take enough classes! There is always something new to be learned. Even if you leave a class with only one small piece of useful information, that small piece may someday pay big dividends. The same is true of books and articles. You will be amazed at where you can find a tip or trick that will help you create a believable performance.

There are three types of classes that are most valuable for the voice-over performer: acting, voice-over and improvisation. Acting classes will give you opportunities to learn about directing, dramatic structure, comedic timing, stage presence, emotional delivery, and innumerable other fine points of performing. Voice-over classes will give you opportunities to practice your skills on-mic and get some coaching. Improvisation in voice work is most common with dialog or multiple voice copy. This type of training helps improve your spontaneity and ability to adapt quickly. You will also learn skills that can be applied to character development and copy interpretation. Take some classes! I promise you will learn a lot, and you might actually have fun. Here are some of the places you can find classes:

- Community theater groups are constantly in need of volunteers. Even if you are working on a crew, you will be able to study what goes on in the theater. Watch what the director does, and learn how the actors become their characters. Don't forget that voice-acting is theater of the mind — without props, scenery or lighting.

- Most community colleges offer continuing education classes, often in the evenings or on weekends. Tuition is usually reasonable and the skills you can learn will pay off later on. Suitable courses can also be found in most college theater arts curriculums.

- The Learning Annex has classes in many cities across the country and offers a variety of classes in voice-over, acting, comedy, improvisation and other subjects that can give you opportunities to acquire the skills you need. Check your local Learning Annex or other adult education office for classes offered in your area.

- Many cities have private acting and voice-over courses. They are usually not advertised in the phone book, so they may be somewhat difficult to locate. Check the classifieds of your local paper, or the Reader in your area. You can also call the drama department at high schools and colleges for any referrals they might be able to make.

- For voice-over classes, try calling some of the recording studios in your area. Many recording studios work with voice-over performers every day and can offer some valuable insights or give you some good leads. Some studios offer classes or do the production work for a class offered by someone else. Or they might be able to simply point you in the right direction by suggesting local workshops or refer you to a local talent agent who might be able to give you some direction.

A WORD OF CAUTION

Larger cities, such as Los Angeles and New York, have many voice-over workshops and classes available. Most are reputable and valuable resources. Be careful, though, because some classes are little more than scams designed to take your money. Usually the scam classes will provide you with "teaser" information. They tell you just enough to get you excited — usually conveniently underplaying the negatives of the business. Then they tell you they will produce and market your demo for a fee — usually $500 to $1,500. You may even be required to take their class if you want them to produce your demo. Demo fees are usually in addition to the fees you pay for the class, although some will include a demo as part of the tuition. You may get a demo from these classes, but the quality may be poor, and their promises of marketing the tape or sending it out to agents are usually worthless.

Many legitimate classes will also offer their services to assist with your demo. The difference is that you will not be pressured into buying their services and the demo will not be a condition of taking the class. An honest voice-over instructor will not encourage you to do a demo until you are ready. When they do assist with your demo, the production quality is generally high. Regardless of who you hire to produce your demo, be sure to check them out. Get copies of some demos they have done and get a list of former clients. If they are legitimate, they will be happy to help you. Some will even give you a free consultation.

Be aware that it is highly unlikely that any demo producer will be able to guarantee that your demo will be heard. No matter what they tell you, you will be much better off making the calls to the agents yourself to get your demo out there. Do not rely on someone else to do it for you. See Chapter 13, Your Demo Tape, for more about demos.

4

Voice-Acting 101

A voice-over performer is an actor — period. It doesn't matter what the copy or script is for. It doesn't matter if the copy is well-written or poorly written. It doesn't matter if you are delivering the copy alone or with others. You are an actor when you stand in front of the microphone.

Acting is an art. Acting skills take time to learn and master. Acting is not difficult, it's just that as we've grown, we've simply forgotten how to play. As a child, you were acting whenever you pretended to be someone you were not. That's really all acting is — pretending!

It's All About Pretending

Voice-over performing — or voice-acting — is your chance to bring out the child inside. You may be pretending to be a specific character, an inanimate object that talks, or just pretending to be a spokesperson providing information. Regardless of the copy you are reading, there will always be some sort of character in those words. To be believable, that character must be brought to life. To do that effectively, you must become a master at pretending.

There are many ways to discover a character and bring it to life. The process is very much like telling a bedtime story to a young child. You simply figure out who is speaking and decide what physical attitude and vocal characteristics the character has. Chapter 7, The Character in the Copy, explains in detail how to break down a script for character and story.

Learning how to bring the character to life is the first step of interpreting the copy. Before you can effectively interpret the copy, however, you need to know how to set the physical and mental attitudes of your character.

19

Use Your Body – Use Your Mind

The two most valuable tools you have in voice-over (besides your voice) are your body and mind. This may sound a bit odd, but the fact is that moving your body — using facial expressions, physical exertion and even the way you stand — can be of immense value in creating and delivering an effective character.

Your imagination is another critical ingredient in creating your character and communicating the message. Your imagination helps you visualize the story and bring your past experiences to the script; that's how you make the copy your own.

These two important tools are fundamental to theatrical acting. If you learn to use them as a voice-over performer, you will become much more effective with your script interpretation and character performance. However, body movement and imagination are just two of the many skills you need to develop as a voice-actor.

Basic Keys to Successful Voice-Acting

There are many things you can do to improve the effectiveness of your delivery. As you begin to master these techniques, you will find your delivery becoming increasingly effective. You will also discover that you will become more versatile and better able to handle a wider range of delivery styles. The following sections describe concepts and performing techniques that are basic to theatrical acting, and any or all will be of tremendous value to you as a voice-over performer.

BE IN THE MOMENT

This is basic acting. You need to be focused on your performance. You cannot be thinking about what you are doing later that afternoon and expect to give a good performance. You also cannot be in the moment if you are struggling to get the words right. As long as you are focused on the copy, you will sound as though you are reading. To be in the moment, you must become comfortable with the words to the point where they become yours.

Being in the moment means that you understand your character, who your character is speaking to and the message in the script. It also means that you speak the words in the script with a truth and honesty that comes from the heart of the character. A good way to be and stay in the moment is to practice the following techniques.

LISTEN AND ANSWER

Be aware of what is going on in the copy. Don't just read words off the page — listen to your character, and to the other performers if you are doing dialog copy. Interact with what is being said. Be real! Respond to the message emotionally and physically. Remember that acting is reacting. Listen to yourself as you deliver the lines. Listen to how you deliver the lines, and your internal response to the words you are saying, then react accordingly. This technique can give life to an otherwise dull script.

KNOW YOUR AUDIENCE

Decide on who will be hearing the message. You would not talk to a ten- year-old with statistics, numbers and facts. By the same token, you should not talk to adults in the same way you talk to kids. Different styles of delivery are appropriate for different audiences. By knowing your audience, you will be able to figure out the most effective way to reach them.

In most cases, the copy alone will give you a good idea of who the audience is. At other times, it may be helpful to ask the producer who he or she is trying to reach. The more you can learn about the intended audience, the better you will be able to act your part.

ALWAYS TALK TO JUST ONE PERSON

Every voice-acting performance is a conversation between the performer and the listener. It is impossible to effectively communicate a message if you try to reach several people at the same time. Focus your attention on just a single person and talk to that individual as though he or she is your closest friend. Attempting to shotgun your performance, by trying to connect with many people at once, may result in the listening audience losing their interest and becoming uneasy with you as a performer.

MAKE IT THE FIRST TIME EVERY TIME

Be spontaneous, every time! Use your acting and imagination skills to keep the copy fresh. Each performance (or take) should be as though the character is experiencing the moment for the first time. You may be on take 24, but your character in the copy needs to be on take 1. Using your imagination to visualize a scene, character or situation can help make your performance real and believable take after take.

TELL THE STORY EFFECTIVELY

Don't just read the words off the page. Play the storyteller — no matter what the copy is. Search for an emotional hook in the copy. Find a way to close the gap between the performer and the audience. Find a way to connect with that one person you are talking to, on an emotional level.

Your emotional connection may be in the softness of your voice. Or it may be in the way you say certain words. It may be in the way you carry your body as you speak your lines. Or it may be in the smile on your face. Make that connection, and you will be in demand.

Don LaFontaine, one of the top voice-actors in the country, was once asked what he did as he performed. His answer was, "I create visual images with a twist of a word." It is the little shift of inflection or subtlety in the delivery of a word or phrase that makes the difference between an adequate voice-over performance and an exceptional one. Effective storytelling is using the subtleties of performance to reach the audience emotionally and create strong, memorable visual images.

BE YOUR OWN DIRECTOR

A part of you needs to be able to look at your performance objectively, as if observing from a distance. This director in your mind will give you the cues to keep your performance on track. Directing yourself is a valuable skill that you can use constantly — even when there is a director on the other side of the glass.

When you are wearing your "director" hat, you need to be listening for all the little things in your delivery that are not working. Look for the important words in the copy that need to be emphasized. Look for the parts that need to be softened. Look for places to pause — a half-second of silence can make all the difference. Listen for the rhythm, the pace, and the flow of the copy. As the director, you are your own critic. Your goal is to constructively critique your performance to increase your effectiveness in communicating the message.

The process of looking at your performance objectively can be quite difficult if you are working by yourself. You would be wise to work with a voice coach or take some classes to learn what directors look (or listen) for and how they work with performers to get the delivery they want. Watch and learn as others are directed. Observe how the director focuses the performer on the particular part of the copy that needs improvement.

Record your practice sessions and have a skilled director listen to your tapes to give you suggestions on what you can do on your own. As you gain experience, your performance and self-direction become as one, and you will instinctively know how to deliver a piece of copy.

USE YOUR BODY

Be physical! Body movement is an expression of emotion, and your expression of emotions or feelings will communicate through your acting and will be heard through the tone of your voice. Move your body in whatever manner works for you to effectively get to the core emotion of the message.

Try the following: Find a short paragraph in a book or magazine, preferably with some emotional content. Read the paragraph once or twice to get a basic understanding of its content. Stand straight and stiff, feet together, head up, looking straight ahead with an expressionless face. Hold the book or magazine in front of you at about eye level. Now, read the words out loud — without moving your body or face — and listen to the sound of your voice. Listen to the lack of expression in your voice. Listen to how totally boring you sound.

While keeping the same physical attitude — and still without moving, read the same copy again and try to put some emotion into your reading. You will find it extremely difficult to put any emotion or drama into a reading without moving. When you begin to communicate emotions, your body instinctively wants to move.

Now, relax your body, separate your feet slightly, loosen up and put a big smile on your face. Read the same copy again — this time moving your arms and body, keeping the smile on your face. Listen to how your physical attitude and facial expression changes the sound of your voice. Try this with different physical positions and facial expressions and you may be amazed at the range of voices you will find. A big smile will add brightness and happiness to the sound of your voice. A frown or furrowed brow will give your voice a more serious tone. Tension in your face and body will communicate stress through your voice.

It's a mistake to stand in front of the microphone with your hands hanging limp at your sides or stuffed in your pockets — unless that physical attitude is consistent with your character in the copy. Keep you hands at about chest level and your elbows bent. This allows you the freedom to move your hands as you speak.

The way you stand can also affect your voice performance. Although body stance primarily communicates information visually, it can also be very important when creating a character. Body language, just as facial expression, translates through the voice. For example, to make a character of a self-conscious person more believable, you might roll your shoulders forward and bring your arms in close to the body, perhaps crossing the arms at certain points in the copy.

Physical changes help to create a believable character who is somewhat self-conscious, a bit defensive, perhaps unsure of the situation and who may even be shy and focused on how she or he is perceived by others. Your body posture assists in framing the attitude and personality of the character. The following are some typical body postures that will help you understand how body stance can affect your performance. If used unconsciously, these postures can have an adverse affect on your performance because they will have a direct impact on your speaking voice. However, if consciously applied to a character or attitude, these and other body postures can be used to enhance any voice performance:

- **Arms behind back ("at-ease" stance)** — This body posture reflects nervousness and implies that the speaker doesn't know what to do with his or her hands or is uncomfortable in the current situation. Clasping the hands in back or in front of the body tends to minimize other body movement and can block the flow of energy through your body. This in turn may result in a "stiffer" sound with a restricted range of inflection and character.

- **Straight, stiff body with hands at the side ("attention" stance)** — Standing straight and tall, with chest out, head held high and shoulders back implies authority, control and command of a situation. This projection of power and authority can be real or feigned. This stance is sometimes used as a bluff to create an outward image of authority to cover for an inward feeling of insecurity. This body stance can be useful for a character who is to project power, authority or dominance over a situation.

- **Arms crossed in front of the body ("show me" stance)** — Crossed arms often represent an unconscious feeling of self-consciousness and insecurity, creating an attitude of defiance or being defensive. Crossed arms can also imply a certain level of dishonesty.

- **Hands crossed in front of the body ("Adam and Eve" stance)** — As with the at-ease stance, this posture implies that the speaker doesn't know what to do with his or her hands. This stance, with the hands crossed like a fig leaf, is commonly perceived as an indication that the speaker has something to hide. This stance can be useful in helping create a character who projects suspicion.

- **Hands on the hips ("mannequin" stance)** — This posture makes the speaker appear inexperienced or unqualified. Hands on the hips also blocks the flow of energy through the body and limits the performer's ability to inject emotion and drama into a performance. This stance can be used to create an attitude of arrogance.

FIND THE RHYTHM IN THE COPY

Consider voice-over copy in terms of a musical composition. Music has a range of notes from high to low, being played by a variety of instruments (the voices). The tempo of the music may be generally fast or slow (the pace), and the tempo may fluctuate throughout the composition. The music also has a range of loud-to-soft (dynamics). These elements combine to create interest and attract and hold the listener's attention. Voice-over copy works the same way.

All copy has a rhythm, a tempo, and a flow. Rhythm in voice-over copy is much the same as rhythm in music. There are many pieces of music that run two minutes, but each has a unique rhythm. Many times, the rhythm changes within the composition. Rhythm in voice-over copy is as varied as it is in music. Some copy has a rhythm that is smooth, classy and mellow. Other copy has a choppiness that is awkward and uncomfortable.

Some of the factors that affect rhythm in voice-over copy are pacing, pauses, breaths, the subtle emphasis of key words and even diction and intonation. In dialog copy, rhythm also includes the timing of the interaction between characters. Find the rhythm in the copy and you will win auditions.

Rhythm is something that can only be found by making the copy your own. You cannot get into a rhythm if you are just reading words off a page. Make the words your own by knowing your character, and you will be on your way to finding the rhythm. You might find it interesting to record yourself in a conversation. You may discover that you have a rhythm in the way you speak, which is quite different from the rhythm of others in the conversation.

A conversation has several things going on at once: There is a rhythm to the words, a tempo or pacing and the interaction between the people having the conversation. Listen for pauses, people talking at the same time, the energy of the conversation, and the way in which certain words are emphasized. Observe how they move their bodies, especially when expressing an emotion or feeling. All these elements, and more, go into creating the rhythm of a conversation.

UNDERSTAND THE PLOT OR STORY

Look for the basic dramatic elements of a story in the copy — who, what, when, where, why and how:

- Who is your character?

- Who are the other characters (protagonist, antagonist) in the story?

- What does your character want or need at this moment in time?

- What is the plot of the story?

- What is the relationship between the characters?

- What is the conflict?

- What complications arise?

- What is the environment?

- When does the story take place?

- When does the peak moment happen?

- Where is the story taking place?

- Why is the character in the situation he or she is in, and what prior events have brought the character to this moment in time?

- How is the conflict resolved, or not resolved?

- How is the message expressed through the resolution or nonresolution of the conflict?

By understanding the story line, you will know your role in the story. A dramatic story structure with a definite plot is most often found in dialog scripts. However, many single voice scripts have a plot structure that evolves through the course of the story.

Unfortunately, most small-market and lower-end copy is written solely to provide information. Information-based copy, also known as spokesperson copy, rarely has a story or plot, and thus there is no conflict. With no conflict to be resolved, it is much more challenging to find an emotional hook. With spokesperson copy, you still need to determine the audience and your character, and you need to find a way to bridge the gap between performer and audience. With spokesperson copy, this can be a much greater challenge than it is with a plot-based story script. However, an emotional connection can still be made with the audience through effective characterization, and a "twist of a word."

FIGURE OUT THE BACK-STORY

The back-story (the moment before) is what happened before the first line of copy. What occurred in the lives of the characters that brought them to the point of talking about what they are now discussing? What is the situation they now find themselves in, and how did they get there?

In some scripts, the back-story, or moment before, is pretty obvious. In others, you'll have to make up something. Either way, the back-story is essential to the development of your character. Without knowing what happened the moment before the copy, you cannot know how your character will react to other characters in the copy as it is written.

A back-story can be found for any type of copy. To discover the back-story, look for clues in the script that reveal specific details about what is taking place. Use these clues to create your own idea of what took place *before* the story in the script. This is your back-story, and this is what brought your character to this moment in time. Learn how to find the back-story and you will learn how to understand the motivation of your character.

MAKE UP A LEAD-IN LINE

A lead-in line is simply a short statement of a possible back-story. Before delivering your first line, you say something that would be a logical introductory statement, or lead-in. You can say it silently, or out loud. If you say the line out loud, be sure to leave a slight pause before your first line of copy so that the editor can remove the unwanted lead-in line.

For example, if you are reading copy for a spokesperson commercial, you might want to have a lead in line that sets up who you are talking to. Let's say you have determined that your audience is men and women in their thirties and forties, self-employed and financially well off. You have set your character as someone who is equal to the audience, so you won't be patronizing; however, you will be conveying some important information.

Here's the copy:

> Health care. It's on everyone's mind. If you're looking for health care that really works, get to know FHP, in San Diego. For over 33 years, FHP has offered a variety of flexible health plans. FHP, an idea who's time has come.

For a lead-in line, you might set up the copy by putting yourself in the position of talking to your best friend, John. Rather than starting cold, set a visual image in your mind of a conversation between you and John. Deliver your lines starting with:

> *(Silently: I learned something really interesting today, and you know, John . . .)*
> Health care. It's on everyone's mind. . . .

Your lead-in line sets up a conversational delivery that helps you to close the gap and communicate your message on an emotional level. This same approach works for all types of copy in any situation. The lead-in line can be anything from a few short words to an elaborate story leading into the written copy.

LOOK FOR LOGICAL PLACES TO BREATHE

You need to breathe, and you will sometimes be working a script with extremely long, complicated sentences. Breath points in most copy usually occurs after a portion of a thought has been stated. Listings provide natural break points between each item. You probably won't want to breathe or pause between each item, but there usually is an opportunity if you need it. To make lists more effective, try to make each item in a list unique by altering your delivery or inflection.

LOOK FOR KEY WORDS YOU CAN EMPHASIZE FOR EFFECT

Personal pronouns — I, we, our, and your — are all words that listeners tune in to. These are *connecting words* that help the voice-actor reach the audience on an emotional level. Use these words to your advantage. Don't rush past them. Take your time with these words.

In some copy, you will want to give these words a special emphasis for greater impact. At other times, you may want to underplay the personal pronouns and give extra emphasis to words that are the subject of a sentence. For example, the sentence — "It's what you're looking for!" — could have emphasis placed on any of the five words, or a combination of two or more. The contractions — "it's" and "you're" — could even be separated into "it is" and "you are." Each variation gives the sentence a unique meaning. Read the line out loud with different emphases to see how the meaning changes.

LOOK FOR TRANSITIONS IN THE COPY

A copy transition can take many forms. It may be a transition of a character's mood or attitude. Or it may be a transition in the rhythm or pace of delivery. It might be a transition from a question asked to an answer given. It could even be a transition between concepts or products within a list. Transitions help "hook" the audience and keep their attention. Look for transitional phrases in the script and decide how you can make the transition interesting. Avoid keeping your delivery the same through all the transitions as you read a script. Give each transition a unique twist. Change your physical attitude, mental picture, or use some other device to let your audience know that something special has happened, or that you have moved on to a new idea.

Script Analysis

The process of studying a script for information about the message, the intended audience, and your character is called a *script analysis*. As you begin working with voice-over copy, you may find that it will take you a few minutes to make the choices about your character and other aspects of the copy. However, as you gain experience, you will be able to do a thorough script analysis in the time it takes you to read the copy a few times.

The Script Analysis Worksheet on pages 30 and 31 can be used when working with any piece of copy. By answering the questions on the worksheet, you can quickly learn everything you need to know about a script and your character. If an answer is not clear from the copy, then make it up. You won't be graded on your answers, I promise. The answers you come up with are a tool for you to use in developing effective characters and delivery.

For you to maintain a consistent performance, it is important that you stick with the choices you make in your script analysis. If something isn't working for you, of course, you can change your mind. But any new choices or changes should only be made to make your performance and your character more real and believable.

Physical Attitudes to Help Delivery

Don't be afraid to be physical in the studio. I have seen voice-over performers do some of the strangest things to get into character. The basic rule is "whatever works — do it." I once worked with a voice-actor who arrived at the studio wearing a tennis outfit and carrying a tennis racket. Throughout the session, he used that tennis racket as a prop to help with his character and delivery. I've seen other voice-actors go through a series of contortions and exercises to set the physical attitude for the character they are playing. Your analysis of the copy can give you a starting point for your physical attitude. When you've decided on your physical attitude, commit to it and use your body to express yourself.

Many people are self-conscious when just starting in this business, and that's normal. However, when you are in the "booth," you really need to leave any judgments you may have about your performance outside. If you

Script Analysis Worksheet

Answering the following questions, based on the copy, will help you discover the audience you are speaking to, your character, and any special attitude you need to incorporate into your performance.

Who is the advertiser or client? _____

_____

What is the product or service? _____

_____

What is the delivery style?

☐ Hard-Sell (fast and punchy) ☐ Single Voice ☐ Corporate/Narrative
☐ Medium-Sell (mellow) ☐ Dialog, multiple
☐ Soft-Sell (relaxed) ☐ Character/Animation

Who is the advertiser/client trying to reach (target audience)? Determine the age range, income, sex, buying habits and any other specific details that become apparent from the way the script is written. Who is the "other person" you are talking to? Visualize this individual as you perform the copy.

_____

_____

_____

Find important words or phrases in the copy that you can emphasize using dynamics of loudness or emotion. These include the advertiser's name, product, descriptive adjectives and an address or phone number. These elements of the copy need special attention in your performance. Underline or highlight the words or phrases you want to emphasize.

What is the message the advertiser/client wants to communicate to the target audience? What is the story you are telling through your performance? What is the USP (Unique Selling Proposition)?

_____

_____

_____

How does the story (plot) develop? For dialog copy, find the setup, the conflict, and how the conflict is resolved or not resolved? Discover how the plot flows. Are there any attitude changes with your character or others? Plot development is critical to effective dialog copy. Determine your role in the plot and how your character develops.

_____

_____

Use arrows ↗ ↘ to indicate copy points for changes in inflection or attitude.

What is your role (your character in the story) in terms of how the story is being told? Do a basic character analysis to define your character's age, life style, clothing, speaking style, attitude toward the product or situation in the script, etc. What are your character's motivations? What are your character's WANTS and NEEDS at *this moment in time*? What happened to your character in the moment immediately before the copy? Be as detailed as necessary in order to discover your character.

_____

_____

_____

How does your character relate to any other characters in the script, or to the audience in general. Is your character an active player in telling the story (as in a dialog commercial), or is your character that of a narrator imparting information to a captive audience (as in a single-voice "spokesperson" commercial)? What can you do to create a bond between your character, other characters in the script and the audience?

_____

_____

What can you do to make your character believable? Any special vocal treatments or physical attitudes?

_____

_____

Does your character have any unique or interesting attitudes or speaking characteristics? (Speaks slowly, fast, with an accent, squeaky voice, etc.) If so, identify these.

_____

_____

Study the copy for pauses that might be used to provide emphasis, and for places to breathe. This is especially important in industrial copy which frequently contains long, run-on sentences with technical terminology. Mark breaths and pauses with a slash mark (**/**).

Find the rhythm of the copy. All copy has a rhythm, a beat and timing. Discover the proper timing for the copy you are reading. Dialog copy has a separate rhythm for each character as well as an interactive rhythm.

Look for transitions in the script (similar to attitude changes). These may be transitions from asking a question to providing an answer (common in commercial copy), or a transition between attitudes of your character.

Look for words you can emphasize and that will connect you with the audience. Personal pronouns, such as "you," "our," "my" and "I," may be written into the script or simply implied. If connecting words are implied, find a way to make that implied connection through your performance (without actually saying the words).

are concerned about what the people in the control room think about *you* as you are performing (rather than what they think about *your performance*), you will not be able to do your best work. It comes down to taking on an attitude of "I don't care" when walking into the booth or studio. It's not that you don't care about doing your best, or making the character in the copy real and believable. You must care about these things. But you cannot afford to care about what others think of you and what you are doing as you perform to the best of your abilities.

If getting to your best performance means that you are moving your entire body and waving your arms wildly, that's what you need to do. You can't afford to worry that the people in the control room might think you are crazy. The engineer and producer certainly don't care! They are only interested in recording your best performance as quickly as possible, and they have seen it all anyway.

Usually you can perform better if you are standing, but in some cases, being seated may help with your character. If you sit, remember that a straight back will help your breathing and delivery. If possible, use a stool rather than a chair. Sitting in a chair tends to compress the diaphragm, while a stool allows you to sit straight and breathe properly. If a chair is all that's available, sit forward on the seat rather than all the way back. This helps you keep a straight back and control your breath. Most studios are set up for the performers to stand in front of the microphone. Standing allows for more body movement and gives you a wider range of motion without being restricted.

Your physical attitude is expressed through the relaxation and tension of your face and other muscles. All human emotions and feelings can be communicated vocally by simply changing physical attitudes. Often, the copy expresses a specific emotion or attitude. Find a place in your body where you can feel the tension of that emotion or attitude — and hold it there. Holding tension in your body contributes to the realism and believability of your character. Focus on centering your voice at the location of the tension in your body and speak from that center. This helps give your voice a sense of realism and believability.

A tense face and body will communicate as anger, frustration or hostility. A relaxed face and body results in a softer delivery. Try reading some light copy with a tense body; you will find it very difficult to make the copy believable. You can make your delivery more friendly and personable simply by delivering your lines with a smile on your face. Turning your head to the side and wrinkling your forehead will help convey an attitude of puzzlement. Wide-open eyes will help create an attitude of surprise. Practice reading with different physical attitudes and you will be amazed at the changes you hear. Your physical attitude comes through in your voice.

Your Clothes Make a Difference

Wear comfortable clothes when performing voice-over. Tight or uncomfortable clothing can be restricting or distracting. You do not want to be concerned with shoes that are too tight when you are performing in a high-priced recording studio. Stay comfortable. The voice-over business is a casual affair. Remember that voice-actor who came into the studio in his tennis outfit?

Another note about clothing: The microphone in the studio is very sensitive and will pick up every little noise you make. Be careful not to wear clothing that rustles or "squeaks." Nylon jackets, leather coats, and many other fabrics can be noisy when worn in a recording studio. If you insist on wearing noisy clothing, it may be necessary for you to restrict your movement while in the studio, which can seriously affect your performance.

Commit to Your Choices

As you work with a piece of copy, you will be making decisions and choices about who your audience is, who your character is, what the back-story is, and many other aspects of your performance. It is important to commit to these choices in order to be consistent throughout the recording session.

Of course, as new choices are made to enhance your character, you must commit to these also. In some cases, you may find that the choices you have committed to are not working as well as you or the producer might like. You may find it necessary to change or revise some of your choices. As new choices are made, commit to them to maintain a consistent character. As you commit to choices that develop the character and strengthen the delivery or emotional impact of the performance, you will be creating realism and believability in your performance.

The Magic of Your Mind:
If You Believe It, They Will!

Believability is one of the secrets of success in voice-acting. One of your objectives as a voice-over performer is to lead the audience to action. The most effective way to do that is to create a suspension of disbelief during the time you are delivering your message. You suspend disbelief whenever you go to a movie or to the theater and allow yourself to be drawn into the story. In reality, you are fully aware that the people on the stage or screen are just actors, and that life really isn't that way. However, during the time you are experiencing the performance, you suspend your disbelief and momentarily accept the appearance of the reality of what is happening in the story.

Suspension of disbelief in voice-over is essential for creating a sense of believability in the message. The audience must believe you, and for that to happen, *you* must momentarily believe in what you are saying.

Use your imagination to create a believable visual image in your mind for the message you are delivering. The more visual you can make it, the more believable it will be for you and for your audience. On a subconscious level, your mind does not know the difference between illusion and reality. So, it follows that if you create a strong enough visual illusion in your mind, your words will be believable. Just as your physical attitude affects the sound of your voice, your mental attitude helps make your performance believable.

Creating a visual illusion is a technique used by most great actors and virtually all magicians. For a magician to make the audience believe that a person is really floating in the air, he must momentarily believe it himself. The performer's belief in what is taking place contributes to establishing the suspension of disbelief in the audience. If the magician is focused on the mechanics of his illusion, he will not give a convincing performance.

Any performer focused on the technical aspects of the performance cannot possibly be believable. This is every bit as true for a voice-over performer as it is for a theatrical performer. The technical aspects and techniques of your work must become completely automatic to the point where you are not even aware of them. The words on that script in front of you must come from within you — from the character you create. Only then will you be able to successfully suspend disbelief. This is what's meant by the phrase "making the words your own."

Creating visual images is a good technique to use when you are delivering dialog copy and single-voice or industrial copy that is technical or difficult. If you create the visual mental illusion of being an expert in the area you are talking about, that attitude of authority will communicate through your voice.

Read your script a few times to get an understanding of what you are saying. Then, set your visual image and let your character come in and be the storyteller, the expert, the spokesperson, the salesperson, the eccentric neighbor, the inquisitive customer, and so on. By allowing your character to take over, you automatically shift your focus from the technical aspects of reading the copy to the creative aspects of performing.

Creating a visual image helps give life to your character, reason for its existence, an environment for it to live in and motivation for its words. Visualization helps make the character in the copy believable to you. If the character is believable to you, its words become true, and the message becomes believable to the audience. To put it another way: If you believe it, the listener will.

5

Techniques

A technique is something you might think of as homework — there are always new techniques to study and learn. The application or use of any technique is something that becomes very personal over a period of time as the process of the technique evolves into something that is uniquely yours.

A voice-over technique is really nothing more than a skill that allows you to become a better performer. Sure, you can do voice-over without learning any skills, or you may already have an innate ability with many of them. However, having an understanding of basic acting and voice-over techniques gives you the knowledge necessary to work efficiently under the pressure of a recording session — and to make your performance more real and believable.

As a voice-actor, you job is to give life to the words written by the copywriter. The writer had a vision — a sound in mind — when writing the script. You must make the words real and believable. Technique is the foundation for your performance. It is the structure on which your character, attitude and delivery are built. Technique must be completely unconscious. The moment you begin thinking about technique, the illusion is broken and the moment is lost.

As you begin to study and learn the techniques that follow, you will find yourself thinking about what you are doing. However, as you gain experience and become more comfortable, your technique will become automatic, and you will be able to adapt quickly to changes without having to think. Voice exercises can help you develop and perfect your acting techniques. Chapter 6, Taking Care of Your Voice, includes many exercises, tips and suggestions for improving your voice and developing your skills.

Style

It is interesting to note that using the voice is the only art form in which an individual style may be developed out of an inability to do something. It may be an inability to form certain sounds, or it may be a cultural affectation of your speaking pattern that results in a quality uniquely your own.

One person's vocal style might emphasize lower frequencies, creating an image of strength and power. Someone else may not be able to reach those low tones, and his or her style might be based on a somewhat warped sense of humor expressed through attitude as he or she speaks. Each of us has developed a unique vocal style for speaking in our everyday lives.

Your fundamental speaking style is a reflection of how you perceive yourself. And your style may change from moment to moment as you move from one situation to another. When you are confident of what you are doing, you might speak with determination and solidarity. But when your insecurities take over, your voice might become weak, breathy and filled with emotion.

Your style as a voice-actor comes first from knowing who you are, and then expands on that by adding what you know about human nature, personality, character development and acting. Chapters 6 and 7 cover these aspects of voice-acting in detail.

Developing your style as a voice-actor is an on-going process. You start with your voice as it is now, and as you master new acting and performing skills your style will begin to develop. The tools you use to learn new skills are called Techniques.

The Road to Proficiency

Acquiring a skill, and becoming good at that skill, is called *competency*. Becoming an expert with the skill is called *proficiency*. You must first be competent before you can become proficient. Sorry, but it just doesn't work the other way around.

BECOMING COMPETENT

Your degree of competency with any skill actually falls into the following four distinct levels. Each person works through these levels at his or her own pace and with varying degrees of success.

LEVEL #1: *Unconscious Incompetence.* At this level you are not even aware that you don't know how to do something. You have absolutely no skill for the task at hand.

LEVEL #2: *Conscious Incompetence.* You become aware that there is something you don't know or understand, and you begin to take steps to learn what you need to know.

LEVEL #3: *Conscious Competence.* You have acquired the basic skills necessary to accomplish the task. However, you must consciously think about what you are doing at each step of the process.

LEVEL #4: *Unconscious Competence.* When you reach this level, you have mastered the skills necessary to accomplish the task without thinking about what you are doing.

THREE STAGES TO PROFICIENCY

There are three stages to acquiring a proficient level of skill to become an expert that must be worked through regardless of the skill that is being learned. Playing the piano, building a table, or performing in a recording studio all require the same three stages of learning and perfecting the skills needed to achieve the end result.

STAGE #1: *Understand the underlying mechanics.* Every skill requires an understanding of certain basic mechanical techniques that must be learned before any level of expertise is possible. In the craft of voice-acting, some of these mechanics include: breath control, pacing, timing, rhythm, inflection, and effective use of the microphone.

STAGE #2: *Understand the theory and principles that are the foundation for using the skill effectively.* In voice-acting, these principles include script analysis, character development, audience psychology and marketing.

STAGE #3: *Apply the knowledge learned in the first two stages and continually improve on the level of skill being achieved (practice and rehearsal).* For the voice-actor, this means constantly studying acting techniques, taking classes and workshops, studying performances by other voice-actors (listening to commercials, etc.), following the trends of the business and working with what you learn to find the techniques that work best for you.

Three Steps to Creating a Successful Performance

In all areas of performing, there are three steps to creating an effective performance; the end result of any task can be considered as a performance. For example, when building a table, you are performing a series of tasks required to result in a finished table. Your degree of proficiency (expertise) at performing the various tasks will determine how sturdy your table is and what it looks like when you are finished.

The following three basic steps to performing any task are necessary in the business of voice-acting as well:

1. Practice — learning the skills and techniques

2. Rehearsal — perfecting and improving techniques and skills

3. Performance — the end result of learning and perfecting

The steps must be done in that order. You, no doubt, have heard the phrase "practice makes perfect." Well, guess what! It's is a misnomer. Even *perfect* practice may not make perfect, because it is possible to practice mistakes without realizing it — only to discover too late that the end result is ineffective — and you may not understand why.

PRACTICE

Practice is the process of learning what is needed to achieve the desired result — acquiring the skills and applying the basic mechanics and techniques to achieve proficiency. In voice-over work, the practice phase begins with the initial read-through; having any questions answered by the producer; doing a character analysis; doing a script analysis; working on timing, pacing and delivery; locking in the correct pronunciation of complicated words; and possibly even recording a few takes to determine how the performance is developing. To discover problems in the copy or character, and correct them, practice is an essential step in voice-over .

If problems are not corrected quickly, they will need to be addressed later during the rehearsal phase. In the real world of voice-over, there are two aspects to the practice phase. The first is when you are practicing on your own to learn basic skills and techniques, and the second is the initial practice read-through at a session. Personal practice should be a life-long quest of learning new skills and techniques. The practice phase at a recording session generally lasts only a few minutes.

REHEARSAL AND PERFORMANCE

Rehearsal begins once all the details of the performance are worked out. The character's attitude, voice, delivery and timing are set during practice. You have committed to your choices of attitude, character, vocal texture, and so on. Rehearsal in voice-over work begins as tracks are recorded. The choices you have committed to are polished, tweaked, tuned and perfected. Every rehearsal (read as: recorded take) has the potential of being used as the final performance, either in whole or in part.

The process of perfecting the performance progresses through a series of takes. Each take is subject to refinement by direction from the producer, director or engineer. Once an aspect of the performance is set, it should be rehearsed in the same manner, as much as possible, until adjusted or modified by the director. When the delivery on a line is set, don't vary it too much in the following takes. Set the tone of the delivery in your mind so that you can duplicate it in the takes that follow as you polish the rest of the copy.

Eventually, every line of copy will be set to the liking of the producer. In some cases, a producer may actually have the voice-actor work line-by-line, getting just the right timing and delivery on one line before moving on to the next line. Later, the engineer will assemble each line's best take to create the final track.

Theatrical actors practice their lines as they work on their blocking and staging. The director gives them some basic instruction, but for the most part, actors are in the practice phase as long as they are working with a script and learning what they are doing and where they need to be at any point in time during a scene. By the time they are ready to put down their scripts, they are at a point where they know what they are doing on stage — and rehearsal begins.

As they rehearse, the director makes adjustments and polishes the performance. Finally, there is a dress rehearsal where all the ingredients of the show — music, scenery, props, lighting, special effects, actors and so on — are brought together. The dress rehearsal is normally the final rehearsal before opening night and usually is considered to be the first complete performance. There is no such thing as a dress-practice! Some theatrical directors even consider the entire run of a show as a series of rehearsals with an audience present.

Never assume you have perfected a technique. There will always be something new, more or different that you can learn to expand your knowledge. There will always be new techniques for you to try and use. There will always be a different way you can approach a character or piece of copy. There will always be new trends in performance style that require learning new techniques. To be an effective and versatile voice-actor, you need to be aware of the trends and willing to learn new techniques.

All About Breathing

To do any voice-over work, it is essential that you know how to breathe. Proper breathing provides support for your voice and allows for emotional expression. It allows you to speak softly or with power, and to switch between the two styles instantly. Proper breathing is what makes possible the subtleties of communicating a broad range of information and emotion through the spoken word.

Breathing comes naturally, and it is something you should not be thinking about while performing. From the moment we are born, we are breathing. However, during our formative years, many of us were either taught to breathe incorrectly, or experienced something in our environment that left us with an improper breathing pattern. It may be that we learned to breathe from our chest, using only our lungs. Or perhaps, we adapted to our insecurities and created a mental block that inhibits our ability to breathe properly.

YOUR VOCAL PRESENTATION

Arthur Joseph, a voice specialist and creator of Vocal Awareness, describes vocal presentation as the way in which others hear and respond to you and that it is directly related to your perception of yourself. If you perceive yourself to be outgoing, strong, forceful and intelligent, your voice reflects these attitudes and perceptions with a certain loudness and assertiveness. By the same token, if you perceive yourself to be weak, helpless and always making mistakes, your voice reflects your internal beliefs with qualities of softness and insecurity. How you breathe is an important factor in your individual vocal presentation because breath control is directly related to the loudness, tonality and power behind your voice.

Your perception is your reality. So, if you want to change how you are perceived by others, you must first change how you perceive yourself — and that requires awareness. In most cases, a problem with vocal presentation is a habit directly related to a lack of vocal awareness — and habits can be changed. Changing a habit requires an extreme technique — discipline, conscious diligence and constant awareness. A number of vocal presentation problems, and exercises for correcting them, are discussed in Chapter 6, Taking Care of Your Voice.

Many of the exercises in this book will help you discover things about yourself and your voice, of which you might not have been aware. They will also help you improve or change your breathing technique and vocal presentation, and maintain the new qualities you acquire. The lessons you learn about your voice from this and other books will help give you awareness of your voice and will be of tremendous value as you proceed on your voice-acting journey.

Arthur Joseph's *The Sound of the Soul* (1996) is an excellent book devoted to the subject of achieving vocal awareness through a series of twelve rituals. Another book on this subject is *Change Your Voice, Change Your Life* by Dr. Morton Cooper (1984). Both are available at most bookstores and are a good starting point for developing good breathing habits to effectively use your voice.

BREATH CONTROL FOR THE VOICE-ACTOR

The first lesson you must learn before you can begin mastering the skills of voice-acting is how to breathe properly. Take a moment to observe yourself breathing. Is your breathing rapid and shallow? Or, do you inhale with long, slow, deep breaths? Observe how you breathe when you are under stress or in a hurry, and listen to your voice under these conditions. Does the pitch of your voice rise? When you are comfortable and relaxed, is the pitch of your voice lower and softer? Feel what your body is doing as you breathe. Do your shoulders rise when you take a deep breath? Does your chest expand? Do you feel tension in your shoulders, body or face? Your observations will give you an idea of how you handle the physical process of breathing that we all take for granted.

Of course, the lungs are the organ we use for breathing, but in and of themselves, they cannot provide adequate support for the column of air that passes across your vocal cords. The diaphragm, a muscle situated below the rib cage and lungs, is the real source of support for proper breathing.

Allowing your diaphragm to expand when inhaling allows your lungs to expand more completely and fill with a larger quantity of air than if a breath is taken by simply expanding your chest. When you relax your mind and body, and allow a slow, deep, cleansing breath, your diaphragm expands automatically. Contracting your diaphragm, by pulling your lower abdominal muscles up and through your voice as you speak, gives a constant means of support for a column of air across your vocal cords. For a performer, correct breathing is breathing from the diaphragm, not from the chest.

Good breath control for a performance begins with a relaxed body. Tense muscles in the neck, tongue, jaw and throat, usually caused by stress, constrict your vocal cords and causes the pitch of your voice to rise. Tension in other parts of your body also has an affect on the quality of your voice and your ability to perform. Relaxation exercises reduce tension throughout your body and have the additional benefit of improving your mental focus and acuity by providing increased oxygen to your brain. Chapter 6, Taking Care of Your Voice, has several exercises for relaxing your body and improving your breathing.

Good breath control and support can make the difference between a voice-actor successfully transcending an especially unruly piece of copy or ending up exhausted on the studio floor. A voice-actor must be able to deal with complex copy and sentences that seem to never end, and to make it all sound natural and comfortable. The only way to do it is with good breath control and support.

The following piece of copy must be read in a single breath in order to come in at :10, or "on-time." Even though the words will go by quickly, it should not sound rushed. It should sound effortless and comfortable, not strained or forced. Allow a good supporting breath and read the following copy out loud:

> Come in today for special savings on all patio furniture, lighting
> fixtures, door bells and buzzers, including big discounts on hammers,
> shovels, and power tools, plus super savings on everything you need
> to keep your garden green and beautiful.

How did you do? If you made it all the way through without running out of air, congratulations! If you had to take a breath, or ran out of air near the end, you need to increase your lung capacity and breath support. Long lists and wordy copy are commonplace and performing them requires a relaxed body, focus, concentration and breath support. You need to start with a good breath that fills the lungs with fresh air.

Check your breathing technique by standing in front of a mirror. Place your fingers just below your rib cage, with thumbs toward the back and watch as you take a slow, deep breath. You should see and feel your stomach expand and your shoulders should not move. If your hands don't move and your shoulders rise, you are breathing from your chest.

As the diaphragm expands, it opens the body cavity, allowing the rib cage to open and the lungs to expand downward as they fill with air. If you breathe with your chest, you will only partially fill your lungs. It is not necessary for the shoulders to rise in order to obtain a good breath. In fact, rising shoulders indicates that the breath is getting caught in the chest or throat. Tension, fear, stress and anxiety can all result in the breath getting caught in the chest or throat, causing the voice to appear weak and shaky and words to sound unnatural.

Breathing from your diaphragm gives you greater power behind your voice and can allow you to read longer before taking another breath. This is important when you have to read a lot of copy in a short period of time, or when the copy is written in long, complicated sentences.

Do the following exercise and then go back and read the copy above again. You should find it easier to get through the entire piece in one breath.

- Begin by inhaling a very slow, deep, cleansing breath. Allow your diaphragm to expand and your lungs to completely fill with air. Now exhale completely, making sure not to let your breath get caught in your chest or throat. Rid your body of any remaining stale air by tightening your abdominal muscles after you have exhaled. You may be surprised at how much air is left in your lungs.

- Place your hands below your rib cage, lower your jaw and allow two very slow preparatory breaths, exhaling completely after each one. Feel your diaphragm and rib cage expand as you breathe in and contract as you exhale. Your shoulders should not move. If they do, you are breathing from your chest and are getting only a "shallow" breath.

- Allow a third deep breath and hold it for a few seconds before beginning to read. Holding your breath before starting allows you to get a solid start with the first word of your copy and gives stability to your performance.

A slow, deep, cleansing breath is a terrific way to relax and prepare for a voice-acting performance (see Exercise 1 on page 59). It will help center you and give you focus and balance. However, working from a script requires a somewhat different sort of breathing. You will need to find places in the copy where you can take a breath. For some scripts you will need to take a silent catch breath. At other times you might choose to vocalize a breath for dramatic impact, or take a completely silent breath so as not to give away a punch line or in some other way telegraph the moment.

If you breathe primarily from your chest, you will find that breathing from your diaphragm makes a difference in the sound of your voice. Your diaphragm is a muscle and, just as you tone other muscles in your body, you may need to tone your diaphragm.

Here's an exercise that will help you see if you are using your diaphragm and that will help you develop this very important muscle:

- Lay on your back on the floor or a hard surface. You may also want to put a pillow under your head.

- Bend your knees and place a fairly heavy book on your stomach. The book should be heavy enough for you to feel its weight but not so heavy as to make breathing difficult. A thick telephone book works quite well.

- As you breathe, you should see the book rise and fall. If the book doesn't move much, you are probably breathing from your chest.

• Practice using your diaphragm by expanding your stomach as you breathe. In time, you will find that you will become aware of how you are breathing throughout the day. Practice consciously using your diaphragm in everyday situations and soon you will find yourself using your diaphragm without even being aware of it.

The Elements of a Voice-Acting Performance

There are many aspects to voice-over performing, and as with any skill, a certain level of proficiency is needed before a person is considered to be working at a professional level. Working at a professional level means that a performer has a thorough understanding of the many intricacies of the craft and is a master of many skills and techniques. A voice-actor working at this level can make any character believable by unconsciously bringing together the many elements of a performance.

LESS IS MORE

Extreme accuracy with pronunciation or an obvious presentation does not necessarily create the highest level of believability. You will find that you can often create a greater level of truth and honesty in a character by simply holding back a little. It may be that speaking a bit slower, a bit softer, or being somewhat more relaxed might be just the thing to make that emotional connection with the listener. If your character has a specific regional sound or accent to his or her voice, you may find that softening the edge makes your performance more effective. If your character is intended to be an exaggeration, the less is more philosophy probably won't apply, and to be effective you may actually have to go overboard on the characterization.

Less is more is a technique often used by filmmakers to create tension and suspense or as a form of misdirection to set the audience up for a surprise. For example, in the Steven Speilberg film *Jurassic Park*, the initial appearance of the T-Rex was not accompanied by a huge roar. Instead, the tension of the moment was created by ripples in a simple cup of water, implying the approach of something huge and menacing.

The same technique of minimalizing in your voice performance can create a moment of dramatic tension, or wild laughter. It often has to do with the character's attitude, the twist of a word, the phrasing of a word or sentence, the pace of the delivery or simply a carefully placed pause.

Understanding and applying the principle of less is more is an acquired skill. As your performing skills improve and you gain experience, you begin to learn how this technique apples to voice-acting. However, before less is more can be used effectively, you must have a solid foundation in the basics of proper speech.

VOCAL RANGE AND DYNAMIC RANGE

Vocal and dynamic range are two aspects of voice-acting that directly relate to the believability of a performance. Both can be easily misused, forced or overdone. The trick to understanding vocal range and dynamic range is in the interpretation of a script. What is the writer's objective? Who is the intended audience? How should the words be spoken to achieve the maximum emotional and dramatic effect? The dynamics of a performance depend on variations in loudness, pacing, pitch and emotional expression.

Vocal range refers to the performer's ability to put variety into the performance. You've undoubtedly experienced a seminar or lecture at which the speaker spoke in a monotone — no vocal range, resulting in the audience tuning out and losing interest. Vocal range is the degree of variety in a performance and is achieved through changes in pacing, rhythm, timing and phrasing. Listen to the way people talk to each other and you will notice a wide range of speaking styles. Excitement, enthusiasm, awe, sarcasm, pity, wonder, sorrow, cynicism, and sadness are all expressed in different ways by different people. The variations in the way a person expresses herself or himself reflects that individual's vocal range.

Dynamic range, on the other hand, is directly related to attitude and tone. This is the difference between your loudest and softest sounds. Dynamic range is expressed as variations in the volume (loudness) of your voice as your speak — from a whisper to a shout.

Combined, the vocal and dynamic range aspects of voice-acting serve to help create drama, humor and tension in a performance. When effectively used, they go hand-in-hand to result in a performance that inspires, motivates and is believable.

ARTICULATION

Complex sentences and awkward word combinations are an everyday occurrence that every voice-actor must deal with. Words must be spoken clearly and concepts communicated in a way that can be understood. Unless a specific speech affectation is called for in a script, it is generally unacceptable to stumble through words or slur through a piece of copy. *Articulation* refers to the clarity with which words are spoken. Most common problems with articulation are the result of *lazy mouth*, or the tendency to not fully use the muscles of the tongue, jaw and mouth when speaking.

Good articulation can be especially tricky when copy must be read quickly. Read the copy from page 42 again, this time making sure that your articulation is crisp and clear. Don't worry about getting it in "on-time," just focus on making every word clear and distinct.

Come in today for special savings on all patio furniture, lighting
fixtures, door bells and buzzers, including big discounts on hammers,
shovels, and power tools, plus super savings on everything you need
to keep your garden green and beautiful.

When the same letter is back-to-back in adjacent words such as the "s"
in "hammers, shovels" and "plus super," it's easy to slide through the words
sounding the letter only once. It is also easy to drop the letter "d" from
words like "and" and "need," especially when the next word begins with a
"t," "d," "g" or "b." The letter "g" on words, such as "big," can sometimes
be swallowed resulting in the phrase "big discounts" sounding like "bih
discounts." The suffix "ing" can often be modified when in a hurry, causing
words, such as "lighting" and "everything," to sound like "lightin" and
"everythin." With good articulation, the ends of words are clearly heard,
but not overenunciated and suffixes are properly pronounced.

The "s" and "z" sounds should be clearly distinct. The "s" in "door
bells" should have a different sound from the "z" in "buzzers." The
consonant "s" should sound like the end of the word "yes." The "z"
consonant is a bit more complex to form than the "es" sound. To properly
pronounce the "z" sound, the tip of the tongue starts in the "es" position
and is then arched slightly back toward the roof of the mouth. Say the word
"buzz" and hold the "z." You should feel a distinct vibration of your tongue
and teeth.

Plosives are another articulation problem area. *Plosives* are caused by
excessive air rushing out of the mouth when speaking letters such as "P,"
"B," "G" and "K." When this sudden rush of air hits a microphone's
diaphragm, the result is a loud "pop." Plosives can be corrected by turning
slightly off-axis of the microphone or by using a foam windscreen or nylon
"pop filter" in front of the mic. To feel the effect of plosives, place your
hand directly in front of your mouth and say the letter "P" several times.
Turning your hand to the side will show you how the blast of air is reduced
when turning off-mic.

To achieve a conversational and believable delivery, it is often
necessary to violate some of the basic rules of crisp articulation. However,
it is important to understand and to master the correct way to do something
before you can effectively do that thing incorrectly and make it believable.
In other words, you've got to be good before you can do bad, good.

DICTION

Diction is defined as the accent, inflection, intonation and speaking
style dependent on the choice of words. Diction is directly related to
articulation, the clarity of your delivery, the correct pronunciation of words
and the sound of a character's voice. Diction is important in all voice-over

performances — you really do want to say the client's name correctly and clearly. One of the best ways to improve your diction is simply to slow down as you speak and focus on your enunciation and clarity.

If you are creating a character voice, your diction becomes even more important. A character voice may be a dialect or specific speaking style, and it is vital that your words be understood. Listen to yourself closely to make sure you are speaking clearly and at the correct pace for the character. Exercise 8, the cork (or pencil), on pages 61 and 62, can help with diction.

PACING

Pacing refers to the speed of your delivery. It is closely related to the rhythm and timing of the copy. Within two or three read-throughs, you should be able to find the pace that will allow you to read the copy within the allotted time. Some directing cues that relate to pace are: "pick it up" (speed up), "stretch" (slow down), "fill" (you have extra time), and "tighten" (take out breaths or pauses between words).

RHYTHM AND TIMING

All voice-over copy has a built-in rhythm. It is very important for you to find the rhythm in the copy — especially in dialog copy. *Rhythm* is the flow of the words, the way the words are organized in sentences, and the placement of emphasis on certain words. Poetic copy has an obvious rhythm (or meter). The rhythm of narrative copy is a bit more challenging to find, but it is there.

Dialog copy has a definite rhythm, which often includes a sort of verbal syncopation, gradually building to a punch line. Dialog copy also involves timing. *Timing* refers to the interaction between characters, and is directly related to rhythm. How quickly does one character speak after another finishes a line? Do the characters step on each other's lines? Is there a long silence before a character speaks? These are all aspects of timing.

If you have a natural sense of timing, you are ahead of the game. If not, the producer will direct you into the timing, and you will get a sense of what is needed as the session progresses. As you become comfortable with your character, timing becomes automatic.

Watch TV sitcoms to study timing. Study the interaction between characters and how they deliver their lines. Listen for the jokes, and how a joke is set up and delivered. Watch the physical characteristics of the actors as they work together. What are their gestures? What facial expressions do they use when they deliver a joke? What expressions do they have when they react to something? How do they express emotion? Use what you learn to help develop your rhythm and timing.

Another thing to notice is the difference in rhythm and timing between radio copy and TV copy. The "radio rhythm" is generally a bit quicker than the "TV rhythm." Television has a visual aspect, which is almost always the primary focus of a commercial. For this reason, TV copy is written to be paced a little bit slower than the same copy used for a radio commercial. Because radio uses only one of the senses, the rhythm, timing and pace are set a bit faster. The faster tempo of radio helps grab the listener's attention and hold it while the message is delivered.

PHRASING

Phrasing in voice-over copy is very much like phrasing in music. It refers to the flow of your delivery, the variations in tempo as you speak, and the subtle nuances of your tone of voice. More specifically, phrasing relates to the way you say certain words or sentences. For example, a short statement — "I don't want to go" — can be phrased in several different ways. The first word "I" can be emphasized as the sentence is spoken rapidly to give personal emphasis. By the same token, the word "don't" can receive the emphasis to give an entirely different meaning. Putting a bit of a whine in the voice, and a frown on your face will create a clear image that "going" is something you really do not want to do. Another way of phrasing this sentence would be to stretch out the word "don't," sustaining the word and those that follow while adding natural vocal sounds and pauses as the phrase is spoken more slowly and deliberately. This technique, called *pulling lines*, adds realism and believability to the character. A pulled version of this line would read like this: "I, uh . . . dooon't . . . mmm . . . waaant tooo goooo."

Phrasing is closely related to pacing, rhythm and timing in that it refers to how quickly words are spoken within a sentence or paragraph. But, even more than that, phrasing allows you to make the words more real and believable by adding emotional content.

ATTITUDE

What is it that you, as an actor, bring to the performance of voice-over copy? Are you happy? Sad? Angry? What is the mood of the copy? How do you visualize the scene? What is there — in your personal history — that you can tap into to help make the words real and your performance believable? Answer these questions and you will have your attitude.

Attitude is the mind-set of the character in the copy. It gives a reason for the words, and motivation for the character's existence. When you read through copy for the first time, find something in the words that you can relate to. Find an emotional hook. Bring something of yourself to the copy as you perform and you will create more effective characters, a strong suspension of disbelief and a believable illusion of reality.

One of the keys to an effective performance is making the copy your own. Every moment of our lives is stored in our memory. Think back through your life to a time, experience, sensation or feeling that is similar to what your character is experiencing and hold that memory in your mind as you perform the copy. In acting, this is called *sense memory*, a concept developed by Stanislavski and taught by many famous acting schools.

SUBTEXT

All commercials have an attitude. In fact, all copy has an attitude. Your job is to find it and exploit it. One way to find the attitude is to uncover the subtext. The thought or feeling behind your words is commonly known in theater as *subtext*. Subtext is what sets your attitude and establishes, or shades, the meaning of what you are saying. It is the inner motivation behind your words. Subtext allows you to breathe life into the words in a script and into the character you create.

Using your sense memory to unlock emotional hooks is a technique for setting attitude. Now take that process a step further and define the attitude in words to arrive at the subtext. For example, let's say you have this line: "I really like your perfume." If the thought behind your words is "What is that disgusting odor? You smell like something that's been dead for a week!" the perceived meaning will be quite different than if your thought and/or feeling is "Wow! You smell amazing! That perfume you're wearing makes me want to be close to you." Each of these subtexts results in a completely different mental and physical attitude that comes through in your voice.

What you are thinking and feeling as you deliver your lines makes a tremendous difference in the believability of your character. You have a subtext in your everyday conversations and interactions with others. The idea here is to include a subtext in your performance. Decide how you want the listener to feel or respond to your character — what emotional response do you want to produce? To get the desired response, all you have to do is think the appropriate thoughts and feel the appropriate feelings as you perform.

TONE

Closely related to attitude and subtext, *tone* is the volume of your voice, and the overall delivery of your performance. It is important to be consistent throughout your performance. Do not change your tone in mid-copy. If you are doing a soft delivery, maintain that tone from beginning to end. If your copy is fast-paced and hard-sell, keep the attitude and tone throughout.

If you change tone as you read, your levels on the audio console will fluctuate, and you will drive the engineer and producer crazy. To maintain a consistent tone, do not drift off-mic. Stay in the same position relative to the microphone from start to finish. Working close to the mic gives a warm, soft tone, while backing off as little as a few inches gives a cooler tone for straighter, more direct reads.

Occasionally a script is written that calls for a complete change of attitude and tone in mid-copy. If there is a logical motivation for your character to change attitude, then it would be out of character to maintain a consistent tone throughout the copy.

IMITATION

It has been said that imitation is the sincerest form of flattery. This may be true, but as a voice-over performer, you want to be unique. You can learn a lot from imitating techniques. But do not imitate other voice-over performers. Be yourself, and find the uniqueness of your voice.

Study the work of other performers and actors, and only mimic what they do to learn their techniques. Then adapt what you learn to your personality and performing style. If you insist on imitating other performers, it could take a long time for you to find your unique voice-over personality.

Microphone Techniques: Using the Microphone

Microphone technique is a subtle but powerful way of enhancing your character or the emotional impact of your delivery. The following sections describe some things you should know about microphones that will affect your performance in the studio.

MICROPHONE PLACEMENT

In a recording studio environment you will generally be standing in front of a music stand (copy stand) with a microphone on a boom at about head level. Studio microphones are very sensitive and often have a "pop" screen positioned between the mic and your mouth. The pop screen prevents blasts of air from hitting the microphone's diaphragm. Most engineers position the mic off to the side of the performer's mouth, or perhaps in front of the performer, above the copy stand at about forehead level. Studio microphones are usually *cardioid* — directional — and are aimed toward the performer's mouth. The acoustics of the voice booth are *dead*, meaning there are no reflected echoes. The result is a very clean sound.

Microphone placement is simple for a single performer, but becomes more critical when there are several performers in the same studio, each with his or her own mic. In this case, the engineer strives to obtain maximum separation from each performer to minimize how much of each actor's voice is picked up by the other microphones.

WORKING THE MICROPHONE

As you physically move closer to a studio microphone, your voice increases in lower frequencies (bass) and the overall tone of your voice will be more intimate. This phenomenon is called *proximity effect* and is a common characteristic of all directional microphones. As you move away from a studio mic, the mic picks up more of the natural ambience of the room. This results in a more open sound, which is cooler and less intimate. Don't be afraid to experiment, but do let the engineer know what you are doing because he or she will need to adjust recording levels accordingly.

NEVER BLOW INTO OR TAP A MICROPHONE

Studio microphones are delicate and *very* expensive. Blowing into a microphone can cause severe damage. When testing a mic or giving a level to the engineer, always speak in the actual volume of your performance. When the engineer asks you to read for levels, consider it an opportunity to practice or rehearse your performance.

Tapping the mic, although not usually harmful, is annoying to most engineers. It's good to keep engineers on your side; they control how you sound and have complete power in the control room. Remember basic studio etiquette — don't touch the equipment!

LET THE ENGINEER POSITION THE MIC

Always let the engineer adjust the mic to where you will be standing or sitting. Do not move or adjust the mic yourself. The same goes for the pop stopper. After positioning your mic and returning to the control room, the engineer will ask for your level, and may ask you to physically change your position relative to the mic. You may be asked to *move in* on the mic (move closer to the mic), or *back off* a bit (move an inch or so away from the mic). These physical adjustments should be minor, and are intended to help produce the right sound for your voice. If you are popping, you may be asked to change the angle of your face in relation to the mic, or to turn slightly off-mic to prevent your breath from hitting the mic.

HOLDING THE MICROPHONE

You will rarely need to hold the mic during an actual session. However, it may be necessary for some auditions. If it ever happens to you, you need to know how to properly hold the mic for the best sound.

The correct hand-held mic technique is to hold it vertically or at a slight angle, with the top of the mic at chin level, about an inch below the lips and slightly away from the chin, not touching the face. In this position, you will be speaking across the top of the mic rather than directly into it. Talking across the mic minimizes breath pops. You can test for proper mic placement by pursing your lips and blowing straight ahead or saying "puh, puh." Slowly raise a finger from below your chin up to your lips and you will know where to position a mic to avoid being hit with your breath.

If you need to hold the mic, do not play with the cord. Just let the cable hang from the end of the mic. Wriggling the cable can cause noises in the mic that can affect how your performance is heard. You may not hear anything as you perform, but cable noises can be heard by the producer later on, and may cover up parts of an otherwise good audition.

Acting Classes

You can never take enough classes. You've heard it before, and you will hear it again. Acting classes are where you can learn a wealth of techniques for analyzing copy, developing character, delivering lines, discovering motivation, using body language, interacting with other characters and much, much more.

Even if you have no desire to perform on stage, the techniques you learn in an acting class will be invaluable to you as a voice-over performer. Even if you repeat the same class or workshop a second or third time, you will learn something new. You might learn a new technique or you may find that simply observing the other students in the class gives you a new insight into your own performance.

Acting classes are available at most colleges, as well as from local community theater groups and other sources. Many cities have an actor's studio that offers ongoing workshops. Improvisation workshops are another useful class for the voice-actor. Improvisation in voice-over is important because it gets your creative juices flowing and helps with your interaction with other characters in multiple-voice scripts. In an improv class, your creative talents will be expanded and you will discover things about yourself you never knew.

Take classes — you won't be sorry.

6

Taking Care
of Your Voice

As a voice-actor, the tool of your trade is your voice. Just as any other craftsperson must know how to care for the tools of his or her trade, you should know how to care for your voice. So, with that in mind, this chapter includes some simple exercises and tips, most of which you will probably find helpful, others merely interesting, and some perhaps totally weird.

Be Easy on Yourself

My first recommendation is for you to record yourself reading copy every chance you get. I guarantee that you will most likely not care for the way you sound, and what you hear may surprise you. There is a good reason why most people are uncomfortable listening to their recorded voice. When you speak, you are not actually hearing your own voice in the same way others do. Much of what you hear is actually resonance of vibrations from your vocal cords traveling through your body and bones to your inner ear. When other people hear you, they don't get the advantage of that nice resonance. The way your voice sounds to other people is what you hear when your voice is played back from a tape recorder.

I suggest you get a portable cassette recorder — one that you can use wherever you are to record your voice. Some are made with a built-in microphone, while others need a mic that plugs in. A small micro cassette recorder can be used, but the quality is usually not very good. You can also use your home stereo cassette machine if it has a mic input jack — check the owner's manual. Another option is to use the sound recording capabilities of a computer if you have the proper hardware and software.

With the proper equipment, you can even use a VCR. Radio Shack has inexpensive microphone mixers that can be hooked up to most audio and video cassette recorders. Be sure to properly connect a microphone to the equipment's line input. Video cassette recorders need a video source in order to properly record audio. So, if you use a VCR, make sure it has a mode that allows you to record a picture along with your audio. A basic tip: A typical microphone connector for consumer equipment is one-quarter inch. The RCA connectors on the back of most stereo equipment are for line-level inputs or outputs and won't work for a microphone — you need a microphone mixer with a line-level output to connect to the RCA line-level input of the recorder. If you have any questions about the type of connector you have, or how to hook it up, any stereo store salesperson can help you.

Practice reading out loud the newspaper, magazine ads, and pages from a novel — anything that tells a story. Record yourself reading a few short paragraphs with different styles of delivery and different emotions. Create different characters and read the copy with their attitudes. Change the pitch of your voice — make your voice louder or softer — and vary the dynamics of pacing, rhythm and emotion. Practice looking for, and emphasizing, the key elements of the copy.

By now you are probably listening to other voice-over work at every opportunity. How do you compare? Try to adapt your style to imitate the delivery of someone you have heard on a national radio or TV commercial. Don't try to be that other performer, but rather imitate the techniques and adapt them to your style. If you are still looking for your style, the exercises in this chapter will help you find it.

Listen to your tapes to evaluate what you are doing, but don't be too hard on yourself. Don't be concerned about what your voice sounds like. Focus on what it feels like as you work on your reading. Listen to where you are breathing and if your delivery indicates an understanding of the copy. Listen for your pace, rhythm and overall believability. Be as objective as you can and make notes about the things you hear that you would like to correct. Practice the exercises and techniques in this book that apply. Recording and listening to yourself can be an enjoyable process and a great learning experience that helps give you an awareness of what you are doing with your voice.

Exercising Your Voice

Two things are essential when exercising your voice: (1) a deep breath with good breath control and (2) making a sound. Your vocal cords are muscles, and as with all other muscles in your body, proper exercise and maintenance will provide greater endurance and stronger performance. The vocal cord muscles are little more than flaps that vibrate as air passes over them. Sound is created by a conscious thought that tightens the vocal folds enabling them to resonate as air passes by. Overexertion and stress can cause the vocal cords to tighten too much, resulting in hoarseness and an impaired speaking ability. A sore throat, cold, flu or other illness can also injure these muscles. If injured, your vocal cords will heal more rapidly if they are allowed to stay relaxed.

The manner in which we speak — how we breathe and use our vocal and facial muscles — can often be traced to our childhood. Cultural and regional speech patterns have a major influence on how we speak, as do family attitudes and speaking habits and the way in which our parents spoke to us. From the time we first began to talk, we developed speaking habits and attitudes that remain with us today. We became comfortable with these habits because they worked for us as we learned to communicate with others. Some of these habits might include a regional accent, rapid speech, slurred speech, not thinking thoughts through before speaking, a lack of confidence in our ability to communicate, and improper breathing. These and many other speech habits can be corrected through exercise and technique.

Changing a habit will take approximately 21 days and 200 or more repetitions. For most people, it takes about seven days of repetition of a new behavior pattern before the subconscious mind begins to accept the change. It takes another 14 days, more or less, for a new habit pattern to become established in the mind. This time frame is true for changing just about any habit. As much as we might wish otherwise, it does take a concentrated effort and constant awareness to achieve the desired results.

Discover which of the exercises in this chapter are most helpful and do them on a regular basis, setting aside a specific time each day for your voice exercises. A daily workout is especially important if you are correcting breath control or a specific speaking habit.

Correcting Speech Problems and Habits

As you do these exercises, it is very important for you to observe what is happening with your voice, diaphragm, body and facial muscles. Awareness of what is happening physically is vital to improving your ability to experience yourself as you work on changing a habit, and later during a performance. Self-awareness helps you discover and correct problems with your speech. Without it, you will not be able to recognize the characteristics you need to work on.

It is often helpful to have another set of ears listening to you as you work on correcting a problem or speaking habit. A speech therapist or voice coach can be invaluable to improving your speaking voice. You can also get constructive criticism designed to improve your communication skills from acting classes and workshops.

There are many common speech problems that can be corrected by simple exercise and technique. However, all these problems have an underlying cause that requires self-awareness to correct them. Cicely Berry, in her book *Voice and the Actor* (1973)[1] discusses the human voice and methods to improve a vocal performance in great detail. She also explains some of the following common speech problems and how to correct them.

UNCLEAR DICTION OR LACK OF SPEECH CLARITY

Usually, unclear diction or lack of speech clarity is the result of not carrying a thought through into words. A lack of focus on the part of the performer or an incomplete character development can affect diction. This problem can be heard in the voice as a lack of clarity or understanding, often communicated through inappropriate inflection or attitude.

To correct this problem, work on getting a clear understanding of each thought before you speak. Then, speak more slowly than what might feel comfortable to you. Speaking slowly forces you to stay focused on what you are saying.

Stuttering can be classified in this problem area. Although the actual cause of stuttering is still not known, research has shown that it may have different causes in different people and is generally a developmental disorder. Even though research has found three genes that appear to cause stuttering, there is no evidence that all stutterers have these genes or that stuttering is an inherited trait.

There are two traditional therapies to correct stuttering. The first is *stuttering modification therapy,* focusing on reducing fears and anxieties about talking. It can be done with a self-therapy book or with a speech pathologist. The second is *fluency shaping*. This therapy teaches the stutterer to talk all over again by beginning with extremely slow, fluent speech and gradually increasing the speaking rate until speech sounds normal. This therapy is normally done at a speech clinic.[2]

OVEREMPHASIS, EXPLOSIVE CONSONANTS AND OVERENUNCIATION

The source of overemphasis or overenunciation usually derives from the actor's insecurity or lack of trust in his or her ability to communicate. As a result, the tendency is to push too hard to make sense and start to explain. The moment you begin to overemphasize, you lose the sense.

To correct this problem, don't worry about the listener understanding what you are saying. Stay focused on your thought and just tell the story. Don't explain it, just tell it. It may help to soften the tone of your voice and slow down, or simply to focus on talking to a single person. If you find yourself overemphasizing, you may be trying too hard to achieve good articulation.

Sibilance, the overemphasis of the "s" sound, is often caused by not differentiating between the "s," "sh" and "z" sounds. It can also be the result of dental problems, loose dentures or missing teeth. Minor sibilance problems can be corrected in the studio with a "de-esser," but serious problems can only be corrected with the help of a speech therapist or perhaps a good dentist.

LOSING, OR DROPPING, THE ENDS OF WORDS

A habit common to many people who are just starting in voice-over and acting is to simply not pronounce the ends of words. Words ending in "b," "d," "g," "p," "t" and "ing" are especially vulnerable.

The cause of this problem is simply not thinking through to the end of a thought. The brain is rushing from one thought to another without giving any thought an opportunity to be completed. This is usually due to a lack of trust in ones abilities, but can also be the result of a lack of focus or concentration.

One way to correct this problem is to force yourself to slow down — speaking each word clearly and concisely as you talk. Think each thought through completely before speaking, then speak slowly and clearly, making sure that the end of each word is spoken clearly. You may find this difficult at first, but stick with it and results will come. Awareness of this problem is critical to being able to correct it.

LACK OF MOBILITY IN THE FACE, JAW AND LIPS

A person speaking with lack of mobility is one who speaks with only minimal movement of the mouth and face. This can be useful for certain types of characterizations, but is generally viewed as a performance problem. Lack of mobility can be due in part to insecurity or a reluctance to communicate; however, it can also be a habit.

To correct this problem, work on the facial stretching exercises. Practice reading out loud in front of a mirror. Watch your face as you speak and notice how much movement there is in your jaw, lips, forehead and face. Work on exaggerating facial expressions as you speak. Raise your eyebrows, furrow your brow, put a smile on your face, or frown. Stretch your facial muscles. Go beyond what feels comfortable.

CLIPPED VOWELS

Many people think in a very logical sequence. Logical thinking can result in a speech pattern in which all parts of a word are treated equally. This often results in a monotone delivery with vowels being dropped or clipped. There is little emotion attached to the words being spoken even though an emotional concept may be the subject.

Vowels add character, emotion and life to words. To correct the problem of monotony, search for the emotion in the words being spoken and commit to the feeling you get. Find the place in your body where you feel that emotion and speak from that center. Listen to your voice as you speak and strive to include emotional content and a variety of inflections in every sentence. For someone who is in the habit of speaking rapidly or in a monotone, this problem can be a challenge to overcome, but the rewards are well worth the effort. Once again, slowing down as you speak can help you overcome this problem.

BREATHINESS AND DEVOICING CONSONANTS

Breathiness is the result of exhaling too quickly, or exhaling before starting to speak. Improper breath control, resulting from nervousness or an anxiety to please, is the ultimate cause. Consonants and ends of words are often dropped, or unspoken, and breaths are taken at awkward or inappropriate places within a sentence.

To correct this problem, work on breathing from your diaphragm. Take a good breath before speaking and maintain a supporting column of air as you speak. Also, be careful not to rush, and think each thought through completely.

EXCESSIVE RESONANCE OR AN OVEREMOTIONAL QUALITY

This problem arises from an internal involvement with an emotion. It is usually the result of becoming more wrapped up in the emotion than understanding the reason for the emotion.

Correcting this problem may involve developing the skill of looking at things a bit more objectively. People who exhibit this problem are generally reactive and live life from an emotional center. For them life is drama. Work on looking at situations from a different angle. Try to be more objective and less reactive. When you feel yourself beginning to react, acknowledge the feeling and remind yourself to step back a bit from your emotional response.

Voice and Body Exercises

A variety of methods to use to care for your voice are covered later in this chapter. But first, let's begin with some ways to create a relaxed body and mind. That will be followed by a variety of exercises designed to tune your voice and exercise the muscles of your face. When doing breathing or relaxation exercises, it is important for you to breathe correctly. Most of us were never taught how to breathe as children — we just did it. As a result, many of us have developed bad breathing habits. See the All About Breathing section in Chapter 5, for breathing techniques and exercises to help you become comfortable breathing from your diaphragm.

You will find it much easier to get into the flow of a script if you are in a relaxed and alert state of mind. This makes it easier for you to concentrate on your performance. The exercises that follow will help you relax and serve to redirect your nervous energy to productive energy that you can use effectively as you perform.

These relaxation exercises will be most effective when you allow yourself to take slow and deep breaths. Take your time with these and allow yourself to feel and experience the changes that take place within your body.

EXERCISE 1: RELAX YOUR BODY AND MIND

This exercise is best done while sitting in a quiet place. Begin by allowing a very slow, deep breath through your nose. This is the basic breathing technique used for vocal awareness described in Chapter 5. Expand your diaphragm to bring in as much air as you can, then expand your chest to completely fill your lungs. Hold your breath for a few seconds, then slowly exhale through your mouth — breathe out all the air. As you do this, think calm thoughts, or simply repeat the word "relax" silently to yourself. Take your time. Do this about ten times and you will find that your body becomes quite relaxed, and your mind will be much sharper and focused. You may even find yourself becoming slightly dizzy. This is normal and is a result of the increased oxygen going to your brain.

If you are nervous going into an audition or session, this exercise is an excellent way to convert your nervous energy into productive energy. Do this in your car before entering the studio.

EXERCISE 2: RELAX YOUR NECK

A relaxed neck helps keep the vocal cords and throat relaxed. Begin by relaxing your entire body with the technique described in Exercise 1. If you want to close your eyes for this one, feel free. As with Exercise 1, I do not recommend doing this while driving.

This exercise should be done very slowly and it can be done sitting or standing. Do *not* do this if you have a neck injury. If, at any time, you feel any pain in your neck, stop immediately. There may be a neck injury present that your doctor should know about. Begin by sitting or standing up straight. Slowly tilt your head forward until your chin is almost resting on your chest. Allow your head to fall forward, slightly stretching your neck muscles. Slowly rotate your head to the left in a circle until your left ear is over your left shoulder; then move your head back and to the right. Inhale as you move your head back. Begin to exhale as you continue moving your head around until your chin returns to its starting point. Keep breathing. Now rotate your head in the opposite direction. This exercise will help loosen your neck and throat muscles, which will help keep you relaxed.

EXERCISE 3: RELAX YOUR ARMS

This exercise helps remind you to keep your body moving and converts locked-up nervous energy into productive energy you can use. When you are in a session, it often can be helpful to simply loosen up your body, especially if you have been standing in front of the mic for a long time. Remember that moving your body is a very important part of getting into the flow of the script. Loosen your arms and upper body by letting your arms hang loosely at your side and gently shake them out. You can do this before or after any of the other exercises. This relaxation technique works quickly and can be done inconspicuously. You can also expand your shake out to include your entire upper body.

EXERCISE 4: RELAX YOUR FACE

A relaxed face allows you to be more flexible in creating a character. You can use your facial muscles to add sparkle and depth to your delivery. Your face is one of the best tools you have as a voice-actor.

To relax your face, begin by relaxing your body. Then, scrunch up your face as tight as you can and hold it that way for a count of ten. Relax and stretch your face by opening your eyes as wide as you can. Open your mouth wide and stretch your cheeks and lips by moving them while opening and closing your jaw. You can also use your fingers to help stretch your checks and forehead. The process of stretching increases blood flow to your face and gives a feeling of invigoration.

EXERCISE 5: RELAX YOUR TONGUE

This may sound odd, but your tongue can get tense too. A simple stretching exercise can relax your tongue, and also helps relax the muscles at the back of your mouth. You may want to do this exercise in private.

Begin by sticking out your tongue as far as you can, stretching it toward your chin. Hold for a count of five, then stretch toward your right cheek. Do the same toward your left cheek and finally up toward your nose.

Another tongue stretch that also helps open up the throat is to gently grasp your extended tongue with your fingers. You might want to use a tissue or towel to keep your fingers dry. Begin with a deep breath and gently stretch your tongue forward as you slowly exhale and vocalize a "HAAA" sound, much like the sigh you make when yawning. In fact, this exercise may very well make you feel like yawning. If so, good. Yawning helps open your throat.

EXERCISE 6: HORSE LIPS

Take a long deep breath and slowly release air through your lips to relax them. Let your lips "flutter" as your breath passes over them. This is a good exercise to do alone in your car on your way to a session. By forcing the air out of one side of your mouth or the other, you can also include your cheeks as part of this exercise.

EXERCISE 7: YAWNING

There is a good chance that all this stretching will result is a big yawn. If that happens, enjoy it. Yawning is a good thing. It stretches your throat, relaxing it and opening it up. More important, yawning helps you take in more air, increasing the flow of oxygen to your brain, improving your mental abilities. It also helps lower the pitch of your voice and improves resonance.

To increase the feeling of relaxation, vocalize your yawn with a low pitch "HAAA" sound, concentrating on opening the back of your throat. It is also important that you allow yourself to experience what happens to your body as you yawn.

EXERCISE 8: THE CORK (OR PENCIL)

You will probably find this a little odd at first, but the results will most likely amaze you. Trust me, this one may seem weird, but it works! If a cork is too large or awkward for this exercise, you will find it much easier with a pencil. Using a cork will be a tougher workout, and it may also be a bit messier.

Get a wine bottle cork — save the wine for later, or have it first (your choice). Now, find a few good paragraphs in a book or newspaper. Before doing anything with the cork (or pencil), begin by recording yourself reading the copy out loud. Stop the recorder. Now place the cork in your mouth horizontally so that it is about one-quarter inch behind your front teeth. If you use a pencil, place it lengthwise between your teeth so you are gently biting it in two places. Don't bite hard enough to break the pencil, and don't place the pencil too far back — it should be positioned near the front of your mouth.

Now read the same paragraphs out loud several times. Speak very slowly and distinctly, emphasizing every vowel, consonant and syllable of each word. Don't cheat and be careful not to drop the ends of words. In a very short time your jaw and tongue will begin to get tired.

After you have spent a few minutes exercising your mouth, remove the cork, turn the recorder back on and read the copy one more time. Stop the tape and play back both recordings. You will notice a remarkable difference in the sound of your voice. The *after* version will be much crisper and easier to listen to.

The cork (or pencil) is a good exercise you can do anytime you feel the need to work on your clarity or enunciation. You can even do this in your car, singing to the radio, as you drive to an audition or session. Although a pencil is a suitable substitute for a cork, using a cork will give you quicker results simply because is forces you to work your muscles harder.

EXERCISE 9: THE SWEEP

Vocal range is important for achieving emotional attitudes and dynamics in your performance. By vocal range, I am referring to the range from your lowest note to your highest note. Start this exercise by taking a deep breath, holding it in and releasing slowly with a vocalized yawn. This will help to relax you. Now fill your lungs with another deep breath and release it slowly, this time making the lowest note you can with a "HAAAA" sound. Gradually increase the pitch of your voice, sweeping from low to high.

Probably, you will find one or two spots where your voice breaks or "cracks." This is normal and simply reveals those parts of your voice range that need some work. Over time, as you practice this exercise, your vocal range will improve. This is also a good breathing exercise to help you with breath control. If your recordings reveal that you take breaths in mid-sentence or that the volume (overall loudness) of your voice fluctuates, this exercise will help. Practicing this regularly will improve your lung capacity and speaking power, as well as vocal range.

EXERCISE 10: ENUNCIATION EXERCISES

Some of the exercises just described and many of the phrases in this section are used by permission from a small but excellent book titled *Broadcast Voice Exercises* by Jon Beaupré (1994)[3].

To improve diction and enunciation, repeat the phrases that follow. Speak each syllable clearly and precisely, stretching your lips and cheeks as you read. Make sure all sounds are being heard, and don't cheat on the ends of words. Watch yourself in a mirror as you do these exercises. Listen to yourself carefully and be aware of what you are feeling physically and emotionally. Do the exercises slowly and deliberately making sure that each consonant and vowel is spoken clearly and distinctly. Remember that consistent repetition is necessary to achieve any lasting change. For an extra challenge, try these with the cork or pencil.

Specific Letter Sounds — do each four times, then reverse for four more. Make a clear distinction between the sounds of each letter.

Gudda-Budda (Budda-Gudda)
    [Emphasize the "B" and "G" sounds.]

Peachy-Weachy (Weachy-Peachy)
    [Emphasize the "P" and "W" sounds.]

Peachy-Neachy (Neachy-Peachy)
    [Emphasize the "P" and "N" sounds.]

Peachy-Leachy (Leachy-Peachy)
    [Emphasize the "P" and "L" sounds.]

Fea-Sma (Sma-Fea) [pronounce as FEH – SMA]
    [Emphasize the difference between the "EH" and "AH" sounds.]

Lip-Sips (Sip-Lips)
    [Make the "P" sound clear and don't drop the "S" after lips or sips.]

TTT - DDD (Tee Tee Tee, Dee Dee Dee)
    [Emphasize the difference between the "T" sound and the "D" sound.]

PPP - BBB (Puh Puh Puh, Buh Buh Buh)
    [The "PUH" sound should be more breathy and have less vocalizing than the "BUH" sound.]

KKK - GGG (Kuh Kuh Kuh, Guh Guh Guh)
[Emphasize the difference between the "K" and "G."
Notice where the sounds originate in your mouth
and throat.]

Short Phrases — make sure every syllable is spoken clearly and that the ends of words are crisp and clear.

Flippantly simpering statistics, the specifically Spartan
strategic spatial statistics of incalculable value
[This one works on "SP" and "ST" combinations. Make sure
each letter is clear.]

She stood on the steps
Of Burgess's Fish Sauce Shop
Inexplicably mimicking him hiccuping
And amicably welcoming him in.
[Make each word clear — "Fish Sauce Shop" should be
three distinctly different words and should not be run
together. Once you've mastered this, try speeding up
your pace.]

TONGUE TWISTERS

Tongue twisters are a great way to loosen up the muscles in your face and mouth. Go for proper enunciation first, making sure all letters are heard and each word is clear. Speak each tongue twister slowly at first, then pick up speed. Don't cheat on the end of words. For an extra challenge, practice these using your cork. You will find that after working these with your cork, they will be a bit easier to do.

I slit a sheet; a sheet I slit, upon the slitted sheet I sit.

A proper cup of coffee in a copper coffee pot.

A big black bug bit a big black bear, and the big black bear bled blood.

The sixth sick sheik's sixth sheep's sick.

Better buy the bigger rubber baby buggy bumpers.

Licorice Swiss wrist watch.

Tom told Ted today to take two tablets tomorrow.

The bloke's back brake block broke.

Most Dr. Seuss books can provide additional tongue twisters, and can be lots of fun to read out loud in a variety of styles. Some excellent tongue twisters can be found in *Fox in Sox* and *Oh, Say Can You Say* (1979). Another good book of tongue twisters is *You Said A Mouthful* by Roger Karshner (1993).

Tips and Suggestions for Maintaining Your Voice

Keeping your voice in good condition is vital to keeping your performing abilities at their peak. Some of the following tips may seem obvious, and you may already be aware of others. Some of the tips here were taken from the private files of some top professional voice-actors. None of them are intended to be a recommendation or endorsement of any product, and as with any remedy, if you are unsure please consult your doctor.

TIP 1: SEEK GOOD TRAINING

A good performer never stops learning. Take classes in acting and voice-over. Even classes in improvisation and singing can be helpful. Learn the skills you need to become the best you can be. Study other performers. Watch, listen and learn from television and radio commercials. Observe the trends. Practice what you learn to become an expert on the techniques. Then, rehearse regularly to polish your performing skills. Take more classes.

TIP 2: NO COFFEE, SOFT DRINKS, SMOKING, ALCOHOL OR DRUGS

Coffee contains ingredients that tend to impair voice performance. Although the heat from the coffee might feel good, the caffeine can cause constriction of your sinuses or throat. Coffee is also a diuretic. The same is true for some soft drinks. Soft drinks also contain sugar that can cause your mouth to dry out.

Smoking is a sure-fire way to dry out your mouth quickly. Smoking over a long period of time will have the affect of lowering your voice by damaging your vocal cords, and the other potential risks are not worth it. Besides, in this age of digital audio, if the pitch of your voice needs to be changed, the engineer can do that electronically.

Alcohol and drugs both can have a serious affect on your performance. You cannot present yourself as a professional if you are under their influence. Using alcohol and drugs can have a serious negative influence on your career as a voice-actor. Word can spread quickly among talent agents, studios and producers affecting your future bookings. I have also seen sessions cancelled because the voice talent arrived at the studio "under the influence."

TIP 3: KEEP WATER NEARBY

Keep a bottle of room temperature water with you whenever you are doing voice work. Water is great for keeping the mouth moist and keeping you hydrated. You can tell when your mouth is getting dry because you will start to hear little clicking noises that drive engineers crazy.

As your mouth dries out, tiny saliva bubbles begin to form, and as you speak, the bubbles are popping. Swishing water around in your mouth from time to time will greatly reduce the dreaded "dry mouth" and eliminates "mouth clicking." Your water should be at room temperature because cold liquids may constrict your throat.

TIP 4: HAVE SOME JUICE

Some juices can be helpful in keeping your mouth moist and your throat clear. Any of the Ocean Spray brand juices do a good job of cleansing your mouth. A slice of lemon in a glass of water can also help. Grapefruit juice, without pulp, can help strip away mucus and cleanse the mouth. Any juice you use to help clear your mouth and throat should be a clear juice that contains no pulp. Be careful of fruit juices that leave your throat "cloudy" or that leave a residue in your mouth. Orange juice, grape juice, carrot juice and others can be a problem for many people.

TIP 5: THE GREEN APPLE THEORY

A trick used by some voice-actors is to keep a green apple with them whenever they go to a session. Taking a bite of a Granny Smith or Pippin green apple tends to help cut through mucous buildup in the mouth and clear the throat. Lip smacks and mouth noise are the nemesis of the voice-actor, and a green apple can help with this problem. This only works with green apples. Red apples may taste good, but they don't produce the same effect.

TIP 6: AVOID DAIRY PRODUCTS

Dairy products, such as milk and cheese, can cause the sinuses to congest. Milk will also coat the inside of the mouth, affecting your ability to speak clearly. Stay away from milk and cheese products when you know you are going to be doing voice-over work.

TIP 7: CLEARING YOUR THROAT

When you need to clear your throat, do it gently with a mild cough rather than a hard, raspy throat clearing, which can actually hurt your vocal cords. Try humming from your throat, gradually progressing into a cough. The vibration from humming often helps break up phlegm in your throat. Always be sure to vocalize and put air across your vocal cords whenever you cough. Building up saliva in your mouth and swallowing before a mild cough is also beneficial. Be careful of loud yelling or screaming and even speaking in a harsh, throaty whisper. These can also hurt your vocal cords.

TIP 8: AVOID EATING BEFORE A SESSION

Eating a full meal before a session can leave you feeling sluggish and often leaves your mouth in a less-than-ideal condition for performing. If you do need to eat, have something light and be sure to rinse your mouth with water before performing. Avoid foods that you know will cause digestive problems. I know of one voice-actor who had to avoid eating anything for several hours before a session. Even the smallest amount of food resulted in her saliva glands working overtime, causing her speaking to be very "slurpy."

TIP 9: AVOID ANYTHING THAT CAN DRY
OUT YOUR THROAT

Air conditioning can be very drying for your throat. Be careful not to let cold, dry air be drawn directly over your vocal cords. Smoke and dust can also dry out your throat.

TIP 10: BE AWARE OF YOURSELF AND YOUR ENVIRONMENT

Get plenty of rest and stay in good physical condition. If you are on medication (especially antihistamines), be sure to increase your intake of fluids. If you suspect any problems with your voice, see your doctor immediately. Be aware of dust, smoke, fumes, pollen and anything in your environment that may affect your voice. If you have allergies, you need to know how they will affect your performance, and what you can do about them.

TIP 11: USE A THROAT LOZENGE TO HELP KEEP
YOUR MOUTH MOIST

Allowing a throat lozenge or cough drop to slowly dissolve in your mouth can help keep your throat and mouth moist. However, most lozenges are like hard candy and contain sugar that can actually dry your mouth. Exceptions to this are Ricola Pearls natural mountain herbal sugar free throat lozenges and breath mints and Grether's Red Current or Black Current Pastiles lozenges. These are soft lozenges and contain ingredients which are soothing to the vocal folds. The best time to use a lozenge is about 30 minutes before a session. Do not hold the lozenge in your mouth when speaking.

TIP 12: DON'T USE SPRAYS OR LOZENGES TO COVER
UP THROAT PAIN

Covering up throat pain will not improve your performance and may even result in serious damage to your vocal cords. If you feel you cannot perform effectively, the proper thing to do would be to advise your agent or client as soon as possible so that alternative plans can be made. The worst thing you can do is to go to a session when you are ill. If you must attend a session when your voice is not in top form, be careful not to overexert yourself or do anything that might injure your vocal cords.

TIP 13: LEARN TO BREATHE FROM THE DIAPHRAGM

Proper breathing technique is essential for good voice-acting. Practice breathing slowly from your diaphragm rather than from your chest. Standing and sitting with good posture will help with your breathing. See All About Breathing in Chapter 5.

TIP 14: PRACTICE CREATING VISUAL MENTAL PICTURES

Visual images will help you express different emotional attitudes through your voice. Close your eyes and visualize the scene taking place in the copy or visualize what your character might look like. Lock the image in your imagination and use it as a tool to help feel and experience whatever it is that you need to express in the copy. Visualization will also help create a sense of believability as you read your lines.

TIP 15: KEEP YOUR SINUSES CLEAR

Clogged or stuffy sinuses can seriously affect your performance. They can be appropriate at times, if they are consistent with a character, or if they are part of a style that becomes something identified with you. Usually, however, stuffy sinuses are a problem.

Many performers use a decongestant to clear their sinuses. Nasal sprays tend to work more quickly than tablets or capsules. Be careful when using medications to clear your sinuses. Although they will do the job, they can also dry your mouth and can have other side effects. Even over-the-counter decongestants are drugs and should be used in moderation.

When used over a period of time, the body can build up an immunity to the active ingredient in decongestants, making it necessary to use more to achieve the desired results. Once the medication is stopped, sinus congestion can return and may actually be worse than before. Also, some decongestants can make you drowsy, which can be a problem if you are working long hours.

An alternative to decongestants is a saline nasal rinse, technically known as Buffered Hypertonic Saline Nasal Irrigation[4]. Rinsing the nasal passage with a mixture of warm saline solution is a proven method for treating sinus problems, colds, allergies, and post-nasal drip and for counteracting the effects of environmental pollution.

There are a variety of ways to administer the nasal wash, including a syringe, bulb and water pik. However, one of the easiest to use, and most effective, is a Neti™ Pot. This is a small lead-free ceramic porcelain pot with a spout on one end. Although the nasal wash can be done using only a saline solution, some studies have shown that the addition of baking soda (bicarbonate) helps move mucus out of the nose faster and helps the nose membrane work better.

The following recipe for a saline nasal wash can be an effective method of clearing stuffy sinuses.

THE BUFFERED HYPERTONIC SALINE NASAL IRRIGATION
(Otherwise known as: Rinsing the nose with salt water)

The Benefits:

• Rinsing the nose with this salt water and baking soda
solution washes out crusts and other debris and helps the mucus
membrane in your nose function properly.

• Salty water pulls fluid out of swollen membranes. Washing the inside
of the nose decongests it and improves air flow. It will help keep your
sinus passages clear and open and make breathing easier.

The Recipe[4]:

• Carefully clean and rinse a one-quart glass jar. Use the Neti Pot to fill
the clean jar with 16 ounces of bottled water (the Neti Pot holds about
8 ounces). DO NOT use tap water because it contains many chemicals
and undesirable contaminants. It is not necessary to boil the water.

• Add one slightly rounded teaspoon of noniodized salt such as Kosher
salt. DO NOT use regular table salt because it has unwanted additives.
Kosher salt can be found at the grocery store.

• Add half a rounded teaspoon of baking soda (pure bicarbonate).

• If the mixture is too strong, use less salt. A properly mixed solution
should not burn or irritate the sinus membrane.

Instructions[5]:

• Pour half of the mixture into the Neti Pot or a small bowl. If you
prefer the solution to be slightly warm, place the bowl in a microwave
oven for a few seconds. Before using, be sure the water is warm, but
NOT hot.

• If you use a syringe, bulb or water pik, do not put the used syringe or
bulb back into the storage container because this will contaminate the
mixture.

• Stand over the sink or in the shower so that you are looking directly
down, then rotate your head to one side so one nostril is directly above
the other. The forehead should be level with the chin, or slightly
higher.

• Gently insert the spout of the Neti Pot into the upper nostril so it forms
a comfortable seal. Keep your mouth open as the solution enters the
upper nostril and drains out the lower. If using a bulb or water pik,
gently pour or squirt the mixture into your nose. Aim toward the back

of your head, NOT the top of your head. If your forehead is higher than your chin, the solution will drain into your mouth. If you get some on the solution in your mouth, spit it out. It will not hurt you if some is swallowed.

• After rinsing both sides, exhale vigorously through both nostrils while holding your head over the sink. Do not pinch your nostrils.

• If you use a nasal steroid such as Flonase, Vancenase, Beconase, or Nasacort, you should always use this mixture first. Steroid sprays work best and will reach deeper into the nose and sinuses when applied to nasal membranes that have been cleaned and decongested with this salt water and soda solution.

• You can put this mixture into a small spray container, such as a decongestant nasal spray bottle. This is a good way to use the mixture with children. Squirt the solution many times into each side of the nose.

The Neti™ Pot is inexpensive, easy to use and perhaps the best way to apply a nasal wash. You can obtain yours by contacting the Himalayan Institute at their address, Web site or by phone at:

Himalayan Institute   Toll-free: (800) 822-4547
RR1 Box 400   Direct: (717) 253-5551
Honesdale, PA 18432-9706   Fax: (717) 253-9087

Internet: www.himalayaninstitute.org
E-mail: Himalaya@epix.net

TIP 16: IF YOU HAVE A COLD

You know what a cold can do to your voice and sinuses. If you feel a cold coming on, you should do whatever you can to minimize its effects. Different precautions work for different people. For some, taking Alka Seltzer changes their blood chemistry and helps to minimize the effects of a cold. For others, decongestants and nasal sprays at the first signs of a cold help ease its onset.

Lozenges and cough drops can ease the symptoms of a cold or sore throat, but be aware that covering up the soreness may give you a false sense of security and that your vocal cords can be more easily injured in this condition. You can't prevent a cold, but if you can find a way to minimize its affect on your voice, you will be able to perform better when you do have a cold.

If you have a cold and need to perform, it will be up to you to decide if you are fit for the job. Many performers find that they can temporarily offset the effects of a cold by drinking hot tea with honey and lemon. The heat soothes the throat and helps loosen things up. Honey is a natural sweetener and does not tend to dry the mouth as sugar does. Lemon juice cuts through the mucus, thus helping clear the throat. The only problem with this mixture is that tea contains caffeine, which may constrict the throat.

TIP 17: LARYNGITIS AND REMEDIES

There can be many causes of laryngitis, but the end result is that you temporarily lose your voice. Frequently this is the result of a cold or flu infection that has moved into the throat and settled in your larynx. When this happens to a voice-over performer, it usually means a few days out of work.

The best thing to do with laryngitis is nothing. That is, *don't* talk and get lots of sleep! Your vocal cords have become inflamed and need to heal. They will heal faster if they are not used. Also, the remedy of drinking hot tea with honey and lemon juice will often make you feel better.

A classic bar remedy (I'll give the nonalcoholic version here) is a mix of hot water, Collin's mix and fine bar sugar. This is similar to hot tea, lemon juice and honey with the benefit of no caffeine. The idea is to create a hot lemonade that can be sipped slowly. Many performers have reported this mixture actually helped to restore their voice.

Another remedy that is said to be effective is to create a mixture of honey, ground garlic cloves and fresh lemon juice. This doesn't taste very good, but many have reported a quicker recovery from laryngitis after taking this remedy. Garlic is known to strengthen the immune system, which may be a factor in its effectiveness.

Similar to hot tea with honey and lemon is a remedy popular in the eastern United States. This was given to me by one of my voice students and seems to work quite well. Boil some water and pour the boiling water into a coffee cup. Add 1 teaspoon of honey and 1 teaspoon of apple cider vinegar. The mixture actually tastes like lemon tea, but with the benefit of having no caffeine. Slowly sip the drink allowing it to warm and soothe your throat.

TIP 18: ILLNESS

The best thing you can do if you have a cold or laryngitis or just feel ill is to rest and take care of yourself. If you become ill, you should let your agent, or whoever cast you, know immediately and try to reschedule. However, there are times when you must perform to the best of your abilities, even when ill.

These can be difficult sessions, and the sound of your voice may not be up to your usual standards. In situations such as this, be careful not to force yourself to the point of causing pain or undue stress on your voice. In some cases, it is possible to cause permanent damage to your vocal cords.

If you are ill, use your good judgment to decide if you are capable of performing. Talent agents and producers are generally very understanding in cases of illness.

TIP 19: RELAX, AVOID STRESS AND HAVE FUN

Use the exercises in this chapter to stay relaxed before and during auditions or sessions.

Working as a voice-over performer can be like getting paid to play. The more you enjoy what you do, the easier it will be for you to give a believable performance. If you begin to get stressed during a session, practice some of the relaxation exercises in this chapter. Above all, keep breathing.

---

[1] Berry, Cicely. *Voice and the Actor*. New York: Macmillan, 1973.
[2] Kehoe, Thomas David. *Stuttering: Science, Therapy and Practice*. Boulder: Casa Futura Technologies, 1997.
[3] Beaupré, Jon. *Broadcast Voice Exercises*. Los Angeles: Broadcast Voice Books, 1994.
[4] Buffered Hypertonic Saline Nasal Irrigation recipe provided in part by John H. Taylor, M.D., Inc., and Patrick G. McCallion, M.D., La Mesa, CA.
[5] Neti Pot instructions provided by the Himalayan Institute.

7

The Character in the Copy

When you read copy as a voice-actor you are performing a character. The character may be well defined by the manner in which the words are written, or you may need to discover it. Scripts written for specific or stereotyped characters occasionally have some directions written on the script. The directions may be something like: "read with an English accent," or "cowboy attitude." Many times, producers or writers will be able to give you additional insight into their vision of the character. It will then be up to you to create an appropriate voice for that character.

The character you create may be defined as simply an "announcer" or spokesperson doing a hard-sell sales pitch or, perhaps, a "friendly neighbor" telling the story about a great new product he has discovered. In other cases, the character you need to define may have a complex personality with a range of emotions.

Reading through a script once or twice usually gives you an idea of what you need to do to bring your character to life. However, there will be times when the attitude or personality of your character is not clear, and you might need some help in figuring out the best way to perform the copy.

In theater, this process of defining the attitude and personality of a character is called a *character analysis*, which can be as detailed as you like. The more details you include in your character analysis, and the more you understand your character, the better you will be able to take an attitude and personality to "become" that character for your performance. Or, to put it another way, the more you understand the character in your copy, the easier it will be for you to find those emotions, attitudes and personality traits within you that you can use to create your character and bring life to the words in the script.

Let's review some of the key elements of copy that can help determine your character. For a more complete explanation, please refer to Chapter 4, Voice-Acting 101.

- **The structure of the copy** (the way it is written) — Is the copy written in a dialect style? Is the wording "flowery" or expressive in one way or another? Is the copy a straight pitch? What is the pace of the copy? What is the mood of the copy? What is the attitude of the character?

- **The audience** — Knowing the target audience is a good way to discover your character. Experienced copywriters know that most people fit into one of several clearly defined categories. The words they choose for their copy will be carefully chosen to target the specific category of buying public they want to reach. Specific words and phrases will be used to elicit an emotional response from the target audience. Your character may be defined in part by the words spoken to convey a thought, or his or her attitude may be clearly expressed within the context of the copy.

- **A back-story** (the moment before) — What happened before the first word of copy? The back-story is the sequence of events that brought your character to this moment in time. This may or may not be obvious in the script. All dialog copy has a back-story. There can also be a back-story for single-voice copy. If a back-story is not defined, make one up.

- **Other characters** (in a dialog script) — How do other characters interrelate with your character and each other. This interaction can give solid clues about your character.

- **Conflict** — What happens in the copy to draw the listener into the story? Where is the drama in the story? How is conflict resolved or left unresolved? Is the conflict humorous or serious? How is the product or message presented through the resolution or nonresolution of conflict?

There are many other clues in the copy that will lead you to discovering the character. As the performer, you may have one idea for portraying the character, and the producer may have another. If there is any question about your character, discuss it with the producer.

Your Best Tool Is Your Own Personality

The best tool you have to define a character is your own personality. When you know yourself, you can tap into parts of your personality to give life to the character in the copy.

Personality analysis is a subject that has been studied for thousands of years. Hippocrates developed a system of defining personality traits, which placed individuals into four separate personality types with dominant and recessive traits. The extrovert types were called Sanguine and Choleric, and the introvert types were Melancholy and Phlegmatic. The Hippocrates system of personality analysis was very restrictive in its definitions of personality types but it did provide a basic structure within which people could be placed.

More recently the psychologists of our world have developed highly refined methods of determining specific personality types. Some of their studies have shown that personality is largely a result of the chemical makeup of the brain. Cultural upbringing and conditioning further contribute to personality development.

There are several excellent books available that will help you discover some fascinating aspects of your personality. Many of these books are written as aids to improving relationships. Three excellent personality ones are: *Please Understand Me — Character and Temperament Types* by David Keirsey and Marilyn Bates (1984), *Are You My Type, Am I Your Type* by Renee Baron and Elizabeth Wagele (1995) and *Dealing with People You Can't Stand* by Dr. Rick Brinkman and Dr. Rick Kirschner (1994). These books look at personality types from different points of view and offer some fascinating reading.

An advertiser's understanding of who buys the company's products is crucial when it comes to a marketing campaign. Your understanding of yourself is equally necessary when it comes to creating a character that will effectively communicate the message in the advertiser's copy. The best way for you to learn more about yourself is to ask questions and find the most appropriate answers. Based on your answers, you will be able to determine some of your dominant and recessive personality traits.

Most studies of personality type start with several basic categories, then divide those into subcategories. Every person has characteristics in several categories, but certain areas are dominant, and others are in the minority.

The books referred to earlier can help give you an in-depth analysis. In addition, the following simple questions will give you an idea of some basic personality differences.

- Do you respond to problems emotionally, or do you think about them before responding?

- Do you have a strong need to express yourself creatively, or do you prefer quiet activities?

- Do you avoid unpleasant emotions (including fear), or are you inclined to take risks?

- Do you rely on your instincts for information, or do you rely on what you see and hear?

- Do you seek approval from authority figures, or do you rebel?

- Do you play the role of a nurturer, or do you treat others in a detached manner?

- Do you express anger readily, are you accommodating and out of touch with your anger, or do you see anger as a character flaw?

- Do you prefer literal writing or a more figurative writing style?

- Are you more realistic or speculative?

- Do emotions impress you more, or do principles?

- Are you attracted to creative, imaginative people, or to more sensible, structured people?

- Do you tend to arrive at events early, or are you generally late?

- Do you do things in the usual way, or do you do things in your own way?

- Do you feel better having made a purchase or having the option to purchase?

- Do you operate more from facts or from principles?

- Do you find it easy to speak to strangers, or is this difficult?

- Are you fair-minded or sympathetic?

- Do you prefer planned activities or unplanned activities?

Your answers to these and other questions will only scratch the surface of your personality. When you gain an in-depth understanding of who you are, you will be ahead of the game when it comes to creating a believable character. With an understanding of yourself, you will be able to tap into some of the core elements of your own personality as you create a unique character.

Sociocultural Awareness

You should also know that the corporate business world uses highly refined methods of personality and social analysis to define the demographics (statistical data) of the marketplace for selling products and services. These studies define the buying attitudes and purchasing habits of consumers and aid advertisers in reaching their desired market.

There are several companies whose entire business is based on analyzing the buying trends of different types of people. By understanding what motivates a person to buy, an advertiser can write in specific words and phrases, or a particular style. For TV commercials and print advertising, editing techniques and use of color, type style, and other visual elements are used — all of which are "hot" buttons designed to trigger a buying impulse in the listener, viewer or reader. In radio commercials, similar hot buttons are triggered through the careful choice of words and phrases, the use of appropriate music and various production techniques. In any case, the desired result is to reach the audience on an emotional level and to motivate the audience to take action.

Today, advertisers are faced with a marketplace of "occasional" consumers who are no longer characterized by predictable buying habits and who no longer exhibit strong brand loyalty. The key objective of marketing sociocultural research is to identify the links between personal motivations and buying behavior in order to understand the consumer and why he or she is attracted by certain propositions and not by others. Simply studying consumer behavior is not adequate, nor is analyzing buying habits in terms of age or class. To understand modern society, it is necessary to look much deeper at the sociocultural diversity of society and find the trends and characteristics that can make the difference between commercial success or failure.[1]

Marshall Marketing & Communications, Inc. (MM&C) is one of the leaders in sociocultural analysis for the purpose of marketing on a local and regional basis. MM&C, in association with the International Research Institute on Social Change (RISC), which has operated nationally in the United States since 1987 and internationally since 1978, uses a program called RISC AmeriScan[2] to help advertisers understand and adjust to purchasing behaviors of present and future consumers. The RISC AmeriScan program is quite extensive and could be the subject of a book of its own, so only those aspects that relate to voice-acting are included here.

Through a series of studies, both on national and local levels, a probability sample of people is surveyed with a carefully developed questionnaire. The questions don't ask for opinions, but rather register relevant preferences and facts about the individual. The results of the survey capture the person's sociocultural characteristics.

To more easily view the results, a chart is created that takes on the basic appearance of a compass. The first axis (pointing north and south) is linked to attitudes of change. At the north are people who see change as a positive force in their lives (Exploration). To the south are people who prefer stability, structure and consistency (Stability). The other axis of the compass (east-to-west) relates to the balance between the individual and society. To the east are those who are more independent and seek immediate pleasure (Individual); to the west are people with strong ethics and more community oriented (Social).

Respondents are scored on each of approximately 40 sociocultural characteristics. Their scores result in a specific placement on the compass, and can be represented as a "cloud of dots" in multidimensional diagrams (Figures 7-1 and 7-2).[3] The diagram is then divided into ten territories to result in the RISC AmeriScan map (Figures 7-3 and 7-4). Individuals positioned close to each other tend to have shared values and similar preferences, while those at opposite extremes have little in common.[4]

A basic understanding of how advertisers target their message will be beneficial to you as a voice-actor. Knowing what the cultural and social norms are for any specific demographic group will give you some much-needed information to aid in the development of a believable character. For example, let's say that, based on the copy you are given, you can determine that your audience is outgoing, youthful, interested in experiencing new things and likes to live on the edge. You make this determination based on your interpretation of the words and phrases in the copy. With this information you can now make reliable choices and adapt your character and performance energy to something your audience can relate to, thus creating a sense of believability.

For the audience described here, you would most likely need to perform with considerable energy and excitement in your voice. A slow, relaxed delivery probably would not be an effective way to reach the audience, unless the script was specifically written for that attitude.

THE TEN CULTURAL TERRITORIES

Each of the ten segments on the RISC AmeriScan map (Figure 7-4), represents a cultural territory with specific attitudes, beliefs, preferences, motivations and buying habits. Advertisers use these cultural territories to aid in targeting their advertising and marketing plans. All aspects of a campaign, including words, visuals, colors, music and sound effects are carefully chosen to match the characteristics of the territory being targeted. The closer the match, the more likely it is that the message will reach the target audience.

These ten RISC AmeriScan cultural territories can also be useful in developing a believable character. Understanding the motivations, attitudes

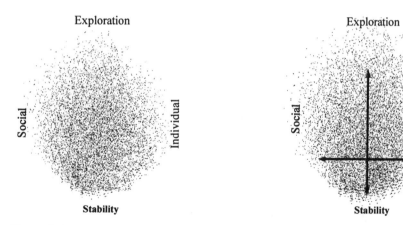

Figure 7-1: Respondents' scores create a "cloud of dots."

Figure 7-2: Respondents are placed on the compass based on sociocultural characteristics.

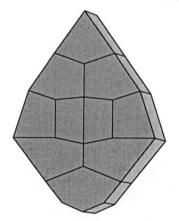

Figure 7-3: The multidimensional diagram is divided into ten territories.

and belief system of your audience will enable you to tap into those parts of your own personality and bring them into the character you are creating. When you create a believable character, an emotional connection can be made with the audience, giving the message a stronger impact.

The following pages separate the ten cultural territories into their sociocultural profiles, key attributes as defined by RISC, and other useful information to help you understand your audience and create a believable character. As an exercise to develop your acting skills, use these territory charts as a guide to create a variety of characters with different attitudes. Find a paragraph in a book or newspaper and read the same copy from the attitude of a character in each of the ten territories. Allow your mind and body to take on the characteristics, belief system and attitudes in each territory and observe how each character can be unique.

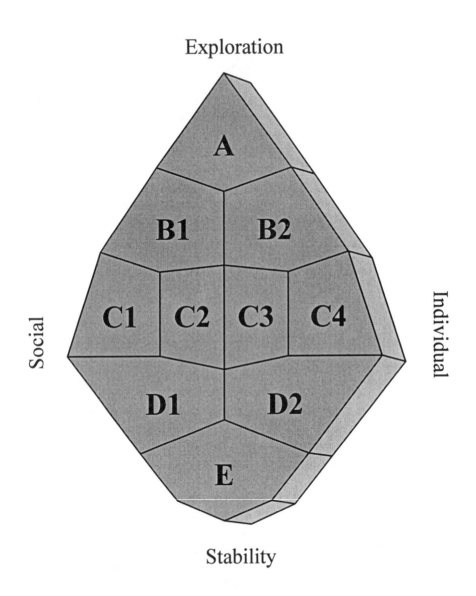

Figure 7-4: RISC AmeriScan ten cultural territories map.

TERRITORY A — Personal Growth, Socially Involved, Connected

TONE OF VOICE CONSUMER WILL BEST RESPOND TO: Persuade

Key Attributes	Sociocultural Profile	Motivations
• Exploring human potential • Community ties • Networking • Empathy • Personal growth • Social commitment • Coping with uncertainty • Social fexibility • Well-being	• Integrate society and- the self • Combine traditional and modern ideas • Active involvement in the growth and change of society • Social and personal development important	• Belongings, culture, novelty • Rely on own sense of style and instinct • Interest in newness, curiosity and the unusual • Acceptance of ambiguity and paradox • Interaction, experience, and diversity are important

© RISC, 1997

TERRITORY B1 — Community, Spirituality, Social Responsibility

TONE OF VOICE CONSUMER WILL BEST RESPOND TO: Legitimize

Key Attributes	Sociocultural Profile	Motivations
• Exploring human potential • Community ties • Spirituality • Social commitment • Order and vigilance • Integrity • Global world • Empathy • Well-being	• Comfort and well-being of others is most important • Caregivers and nurturers • Family values • Concern for others • Religious tolerance • Uphold tradition while also creating new rituals for special occasions • Focus daily life on family and social gatherings	• Belongings, culture, novelty • Rely on their own sense of style and instinct • Interest in newness, curiosity and the unusual • Acceptance of ambiguity and paradox • Interaction, experience, and diversity are important

© RISC, 1997

TERRITORY B2 — Independent, Experimental, Interest in New

TONE OF VOICE CONSUMER WILL BEST RESPOND TO: Seduce and Enliven

Key Attributes	Sociocultural Profile	Motivations
• Exploring human potential • Coping with uncertainty • Personal growth • Networking • Pleasure • Risk-taking • Strategic opportunism • Emotions	• Intense and eager to explore • Open and optimistic • Invigorated by diverse, multiple connections • Active and involved • Always push their limits • Strongly individualistic yet open to a broad view of community • Uncertainty equals a challenge	• Culture, novelty, understanding, independence • Fascinated by the avant-garde and unexpected • Will pay more for what they want • Intrigued by the one-of-a-kind and impossible and the experiences that come with it

© RISC, 1997

TERRITORY C1 — Rituals, Loyalty, Duty, Conventional

TONE OF VOICE CONSUMER WILL BEST RESPOND TO: Build on Trust

Key Attributes	Sociocultural Profile	Motivations
• Order and vigilance • Spirituality • Community ties • Organized life • Well-being • Clear-cut principles	• Defined by duty, morality, family and community • Lead principled and routine lives • Seek reassurance and stability • Adhere to a firm moral code and a strong sense of values • Observe traditional rituals	• Belongings, understanding, nurturance, stability • Good deeds equals goodwill • React to community involvement • Primary concern is family • Always defined in relation to others • Comforted by the familiar

© RISC, 1997

Source: RISC AmeriScan Sociocultural Territories, copyright RISC, 1997.
Reprinted by permission of Marshall Marketing & Communications, Inc.

TERRITORY C2 — Rules, Principles, Need for Recognition

TONE OF VOICE CONSUMER WILL BEST RESPOND TO: Inform and Position

Key Attributes	Sociocultural Profile	Motivations
• Clear-cut principles • Organized life • Social fairness • Environment • Competitive drive • Integrity • Roots	• Tentative and unsure • Mediate the needs of the family and the individual • Less willing to sacrifice for the common good • Not certain among those outside of family circle • Unbalanced in desire to explore their individuality • Simple and collective enjoyment for well-being	• Recognition, understanding, nurturance, stability • Need positive reassurance from others • Driven by commitment to provide comfort for family • Simple, straightforward messages and symbols are important keys

© RISC, 1997

TERRITORY C3 — Achievement, Exhibition, Trend Setters, Self-Indulgent

TONE OF VOICE CONSUMER WILL BEST RESPOND TO: Inform and Position

Key Attributes	Sociocultural Profile	Motivations
• Strategic opportunism • Risk-taking • Emotions • Pleasure	• Rely on others to promote their own achievement • Focus on short-term gains and personal risk-taking • Indulge in the pleasures of immediate gratification • Lack a strict moral code • Materialism important • Unconcern for community • In constant pursuit of being "number one"	• Thrills, accomplishment • Identity is reflected in the display of awards, status symbols and possessions • Need to succeed and to have success recognized • Live life to the fullest • Seek immediate advantages from products and services

© RISC, 1997

Source: RISC AmeriScan Sociocultural Territories, copyright RISC, 1997.
Reprinted by permission of Marshall Marketing & Communications, Inc.

TERRITORY C4 — Materialism, Seek Pleasure, Need for Recognition

TONE OF VOICE CONSUMER WILL BEST RESPOND TO: Stimulate and Flatter

Key Attributes	Sociocultural Profile	Motivations
• Strategic opportunism • Risk-taking • Emotions • Pleasure • Social flexibility • Blurring of the sexes	• Point of view is pleasure • Put themselves first • Willing to take social and personal risks • Tend to be the fashion leaders • Driven by impulse and immediate gratification • Intense and self-centered • Live life in the present, moment by moment	• Thrills, diversion, exhibition, sexuality • Highly attracted to "new" • Want to be entertained • Seek ways to express their uniqueness • Sexual innuendo and overt eroticism hook their interest in being cutting edge

© RISC, 1997

TERRITORY D1 — Need for Structure, Control, Respect for Authority

TONE OF VOICE CONSUMER WILL BEST RESPOND TO: Demonstrate

Key Attributes	Sociocultural Profile	Motivations
• Organized life • Roots • Security • Clear-cut principles	• Strong beliefs in duty and clearly defined rules • Unquestioning respect given to authority figures • Routine balances the uncertainty of life • Brand loyalty is more habit than conviction • Basic pleasures and familiarity shape their structured lifestyles	• Control, stability, dependence • Abundance is a sign of prosperity • Not particularly selective about purchases • Promotions, gimmicks, price incentives are key • Basic benefits more important than image and style

© RISC, 1997

Source: RISC AmeriScan Sociocultural Territories, copyright RISC, 1997.
Reprinted by permission of Marshall Marketing & Communications, Inc.

TERRITORY D2 — Personal Style, Spontaneous, Concern About Future

TONE OF VOICE CONSUMER WILL BEST RESPOND TO: Gratify

Key Attributes	Sociocultural Profile	Motivations
• Security • Status • Pleasure • Aimlessness • Blurring of the sexes • Risk-taking • Fear of violence	• Pleasure is a feeling of power • Aspire to set themselves apart from the masses • The "wannabe's" of the Rich and Famous • They are both whimsical and spontaneous • Fashionably antiestablishment • Resist tradition	• Nonconformity, sexuality, exhibition • Need options that allow them to be different • Resist the persuasions of mass culture • Developed sense of style • Appreciate parodies of conventional values, norms, and status

© RISC, 1997

TERRITORY E — Need for Security, Worriers, Suspicious of Change

TONE OF VOICE CONSUMER WILL BEST RESPOND TO: Reassure

Key Attributes	Sociocultural Profile	Motivations
• Aimlessness • Fear of violence • Security	• Security is the prevailing tendency • Yearning for stability makes them suspicious of change and reluctant to be a part of it • Resist pleasure • Fearful outlook on world • Strong preoccupation with health problems • Possessions equals security	• Security, dependence • Need to feel free of the threat of harm • Want the comfort of knowing that they and loved ones are protected • Expect immediate results from products and services • Long-term or preventive benefits seen as misleading

© RISC, 1997

Theater of the Mind

Voice-acting is theater of the mind. You do not have the advantage of props, flashy lighting or scenery. All you have are the words on a piece of paper — and your individual creativity. From the words, you must create an illusion in the mind of your audience. In order for you to create a believable illusion, you need to know what is going on in the mind of the character you are playing. You also need to know the relationships of the characters in the script to the *unique selling proposition* (USP) — the advertisers message or unique product benefit. To learn what is going on in the character's mind, and to understand the USP, you need to analyze the script.

Analyzing a voice-over script is very much like reducing a play to its essential parts. The more information you can discover in the copy, the easier it will be to create a believable performance. Single-voice spokesperson copy is frequently information-based and may not require much analysis. However, dialog copy and plot scripts are short theatrical pieces and must be understood to be effectively performed.

Although analyzing a script is helpful in understanding its component parts, it is important to realize that *overanalyzing* a script can kill spontaneity and cause the voice-actor to place too much focus on technique and thinking about what he or she is doing. Remember, to be effective, technique must become automatic and occur without any conscious effort. Study a script just long enough to discover what you need to know, then put the script down and let your instincts do the rest.

To create effective theater of the mind, your performance must reflect real-life, exhibit some sort of tension, contain something the listener can relate to, and have a sense of honesty and a ring of truth. These are all elements of good theater and should be incorporated into any voice-acting performance, regardless of the type of copy or the length of the project.

When creating a character for your performance, keep in mind the following basic elements of good theater:

- Interesting characters with wants and needs "at this moment in time"

- A story or sequence of events that leads to a climax

- Conflict in one or more forms

- Resolution or nonresolution of the conflict, usually in an interesting or unexpected manner

- Closure in which any loose ends are satisfactorily resolved

Uncover these elements in a voice-over script and you will better understand your character.

Creating a Performance Road Map: Analyzing and Marking a Script

One of the first things you should do as you begin working with a script is to quickly analyze it, searching for clues to help you create a believable character and effective delivery. Look for words and phrases that describe the attitude and emotion. Notice the context of the copy and how the message is presented. Look for places where you can add variety by using the dynamics of pacing, energy, attitude, tone of voice and emotion. Look for natural breaks and transitions in the copy.

By the time you read a script once or twice, you should be able to make some solid choices on how you intend to perform it. You should know who you are speaking to (the audience), who you are as the speaker (your character) and why you are speaking the words in the script at this moment in time (your motivation).

Mark the copy and make notes to create a map of how you will deliver it. These markings are your personal cues to guide you through an effective performance of the copy.

Practice marking magazine or newspaper articles or short stories and you will quickly find a system that works for you. In a short time, you will refine your system to a few key markings which you can use regularly to guide you through almost any script.

Here are a few suggested markings and possible uses. Adapt, modify and add to them as you like:

- Underline (_____) — emphasize a word, phrase or descriptive adjectives

- Circle (O) — key elements of conflict in the script

- Box (□) — the peak moment in the copy — put a box around the words or phrase at that point in the copy

- Highlight (▓▓▓) or different color underline — resolution or nonresolution of conflict

- Arrow pointing UP (↗) — take inflection on a word up

- Arrow pointing DOWN (↘) — take inflection on a word down

- Wavy line (~~~) — modulate your voice or inflection

- Slash or double slash (//) — indicate a pause

Discovering Your Character

Just as you have a personality, so does the character written into every script. The character for a single-voice script is often simply that of an announcer or spokesperson delivering a sales pitch of some sort, or communicating basic information. But, even this announcer has a personality that is appropriate to the copy. Scripts written for dialog or comedy have multiple characters that are often more easily defined. For all types of copy, finding the personality of the character allows you to give the character life and helps make your performance believable. Remember, making your performance believable is what voice-acting is all about.

CHARACTER ANALYSIS

As you have seen, there are many clues in copy that will help you discover the character and his or her personality. The target audience, the mood or attitude of the copy, the writing style, and any descriptive notes all give you valuable information. The sociocultural data in the RISC AmeriScan map can be another useful tool in helping to uncover a character's personality.

The process of analyzing, or discovering, your character is something that will become automatic in time. Once you know what to look for, you will soon be able to define your character after reading through the copy once or twice.

Voice-over performing does not require the same sort of in-depth, detailed character analysis that might be necessary for a theatrical performer. However, to be believable, you do need to have a good idea of the character you are portraying. Refer to the RISC AmeriScan territories earlier in this chapter to get a clear picture of the attitudes and motivations of the character you are creating.

Here are some things to look for and consider as you read through your copy to discover and define your character:

- Who is this character talking to? (Target audience)

- What is the environment for the copy? (Mood)

- What is the character's age? (Young, old, middle-age)

- How does the character stand? (Straight and tall, hunched over, arms crossed, hands on hips, etc.)

- Where is the character from? (Geographic region, country)

- Does the character speak with an accent or in a dialect? (If so, what would be the country of origin? A poorly done dialect or accent can have negative results unless done as a parody or characterization.)

- How would the character dress? (Well dressed, high-end business suit, or casual)

- What would you guess to be the character's economic status? (Financially well off, struggling, etc.)

- What is the overall mood or attitude of the copy? (Fast-paced, slow and relaxed, romantic feel, emotional, aggressive, etc.)

- What is the pace of the copy? (Slow-paced copy often calls for a relaxed type of character while fast-paced copy demands a character with more energy.)

- What is the product or service for which the copy is written? (The subject of the copy often dictates a specific type of character.)

- What is the character's purpose, or role, in the script? (Protagonist, antagonist, delivering the message, part of a story script, comedic role, or that of straight-man)

- What life events or actions brought the character to this moment in time?

- What does the character want from telling the story?

Finding answers to questions like these will help you develop a visual image of your character. With a well-formed visual image, you will instinctively know what is needed to deliver the copy effectively and believably. You will know, for example, if the character needs to speak quickly or slowly, with an accent, or with an attitude.

Creating a visual image of your character and the environment he finds himself in will help to develop the necessary tension for drama. The tension here is not between characters, but rather a physical tension located somewhere in your body. It is this tension that will allow you to give life to the character in the copy.

Discovering the character in the copy may appear to be a lengthy process, but, in fact, it happens quickly once you know what to look for.

FIND THE BACK-STORY

All copy has a back-story, also known as "the moment before." A *Back-story* is simply the events that occurred immediately before the first word of the copy. The back-story is the result of the wants and needs of the character that has brought him or her to this moment in time. It is the story that provides the motivation for the words, actions and reactions to what happens in the environment of the story.

In theater, the back-story is frequently unveiled during the course of the performance. With voice-over copy, there is rarely enough time to reveal the back-story or provide much character development. A :60 radio commercial must be a self-contained snippet of time — the telling of a story with a beginning, middle and an end — and with fully developed characters from the outset.

In a dialog script, you will often be able to figure out the back-story with ease. A dialog script back-story consists of the life experiences of all the characters in the script, and more important, the relationship between those characters. The interaction between characters often reveals clues to the back-story.

It can be more of a challenge with a single-voice script. A single-voice script back-story consists of the life experience of only the speaking character. There may be few, if any, clues that reveal what brought him or her to the point of speaking the words in the copy.

If a back-story is not clear from the copy, make one up. The idea is to create a believable motivation for your character that brings him or her to the particular moment in time that is taking place in the script. The back-story will reveal your character's wants and needs at this moment, and that information will help guide you in your delivery.

Define the back-story and what the character wants in just a few words. Keep it concise, believable and real.

UNVEIL THE CONFLICT

Conflict is an essential part of dialog copy, and can also be present in a single-voice script that tells a story. Conflict rarely occurs in information-based copy in which the message is more of a sales pitch than a story. Conflict creates drama, and drama holds interest.

A dialog script without conflict will be boring and uninteresting. On the other hand, a dialog script with a well-defined conflict can be funny, emotional, heartwarming, and informative — all at the same time. Look for the primary conflict in the script. Usually, this will be some difference of opinion, a crisis, an impasse, or some other obstacle. Define this primary conflict in a few concise words.

Once you have defined the primary conflict, look for any complications that support or exaggerate it. These are often secondary or minor conflicts that serve to add meaning and importance to the primary conflict.

Follow the development of the conflict to reveal its peak moment, which is the climax — the key moment in a commercial. It will usually be found immediately prior to the resolution or nonresolution of the conflict.

During the course of developing the conflict, the advertising benefit (unique selling proposition) should be revealed. The peak moment often is the point in the copy where the advertiser's name is mentioned or the purpose of the commercial is revealed.

DISCOVER THE RESOLUTION OR NONRESOLUTION OF THE CONFLICT

In commercial copy, it is through the resolution or nonresolution of the conflict that the message is expressed. Sometimes ending a commercial with an unresolved conflict can actually create a memorable impression in the mind of the listener. An unresolved conflict leaves the end of the story up to the listener's imagination, and that can be a very effective motivation for action.

Look for details in the copy that give clues as to how the message is actually communicated. Are there a series of gags, jokes, or a play on words that leads to expression of the message? Do characters in the copy shift roles (reversals)? Is there a list of information that ends with an unusual twist? Does the story take place in an unusual location? Is there something in the story that appears to be out of context with what is taking place? Is there a personality problem or physical limitation with one or more of the characters? How are these resolved — or not?

MAKE THE COPY YOUR OWN

As you analyze a script, remember that there are no right or wrong answers to the questions you ask. Use your imagination and bring something of yourself into the copy. The idea is to create a believable character and situation for the copy you are reading. Bringing your personal experience into the character you create will aid in making him or her real to the listener.

Use what you learn from the copy and the tools at your disposal to make the copy your own. If you have a naturally dry and sarcastic style of speaking, you may be able to apply that trait to your character to make it unique. If you have a bubbly speaking style, that trait might give a unique twist to a character. Don't be afraid to experiment and play with different approaches to performing a character.

To Be More Believable

The best way to effectively communicate a scripted message is to create a believable character and performance. To be believable, your performance must include variety, tension and sincerity. It must also be easy to listen to and in a style that the audience can relate to. To be believable, you must develop a performing style that is conversational and real. The best way to be more believable is to eliminate punctuation marks.

TAKE OUT THE PUNCTUATION MARKS

Periods, exclamation points, commas, and question marks are all necessary ingredients in printed copy. Punctuation marks give us visual clues as to how we should interpret a sentence as we read, where the emphasis should be, and the attitude of a written concept.

Punctuation marks in a voice-over script also give us clues as to how we should interpret the copy. They guide us as to how we should pace our timing and delivery, the attitude of the message, and even give us information about our character and the interaction between characters. However, if the punctuation marks are taken literally and performed as written, an otherwise well-written script can be performed flat and lifeless.

Taking the punctuation marks out of the copy doesn't mean literally going through the script with white-out (although I do know of one voice-actor who actually does that!). What it does mean is performing the copy in a real, believable and conversational manner. A real-life conversation is punctuated with pauses, changes of inflection, dynamics (soft, loud), emotional attitude (excitement, sadness, and so on), vocalized sounds (uh-huh, hmmm, etc.) and many other subtleties. Voice-over copy should be delivered the same way. Let your delivery dictate the punctuation.

The only way to achieve this is to allow the scripted punctuation marks to guide you, but not to take them too literally. Sometimes, changing a coma to a hyphen, or a period to an exclamation point can make a big difference in the interpretation, improving the performance. Allow the lines of a script to flow into one another as they would if you were telling the story to another person, not reading it. Take the punctuation marks out of your performance and your performance will be on its way to being more believable.

CREATING TENSION

When making copy your own, it is important to be specific when defining a scene or character and to commit to the choices you make. Using specific terms creates a tension in your body that you can use in your voice. Without tension you will be unable to create drama, which is essential for capturing and holding the attention of the listener, and communicating the message.

To create tension in you body, begin by observing your feelings and emotions as you read the copy. Allow your senses to be open to experience whatever sensations might appear and make a mental note of where that sensation occurred in your body. As you begin to add life to your character, recall the memory of the sensation you just experienced. Focus on placing your voice at that place in your body. This technique may be somewhat difficult to master at first, but keep working at it — the result is truly amazing once you get the knack of doing it.

TIPS FOR MAKING YOUR CHARACTER BELIEVABLE

Many of the following tips apply to dialog copy, and you will see some of them again in Chapter 10. However, they can also be applied to single-voice copy, whether it is for a commercial, an animated character, a corporate sales presentation, or some other narrative.

- Take the punctuation marks out of your delivery. Keep your performance conversational. Add your personal spin to make the copy your own.

- Be careful not to overanalyze your copy. It's easy to fall into the trap of analyzing a script to death. Overanalyzing can cause you to lose spontaneity and cause your delivery to become flat and uninteresting.

- Don't become so focused on your character that you lose sight of the whole story, the drama and the relationships between characters and conflict.

- Be careful not to exaggerate your character's attitude, speech patterns, or other characteristics, unless the script specifically calls for an extreme characterization.

- Try to internalize the wants and needs of your character, both physically and emotionally. Find the place in your body where a tension develops. Hold it there and read your lines. In theater, this is called "setting the character." Don't set your character too soon. Only after running through a script several times will you be able to find the true voice for your character. Stay in the moment, listen and answer, and react authentically to the other characters.

- Speak your lines to another person, real or imagined, expecting that they will respond. Pretend you are speaking to your best friend. Keep in mind the wants and needs of your character and express those to someone, with tension in your body, expecting a response.

• Underplay, rather than overplay. Louder is not better. If in doubt, pull back, speak softer and be more natural. Remember, "less is more."

• Keep your body posture (physical attitude) in a stance consistent with the character you have decided on. Maintain this attitude throughout your performance.

• Don't read! Be conversational. Talk *to* the audience, not *at* them. Be careful not to overenunciate. Less is usually more.

• Find the rhythm in the copy. All copy has a rhythm. Find the rhythm and phrasing and be consistent throughout the copy.

• Keep it real. Speak as quickly as you would if you were talking to someone and speak as quietly as you would if you were in a real conversation. If "uhhhs," "hmmm's" or "ahhh's" seem appropriate for your character, ad-lib them into your delivery even though they might not be written into the copy. This is called *pulling lines*. It is a technique for making a scripted character more human.

• Get into the moment by ad-libbing situations or lines. Give yourself a realistic lead-in to the copy and ad-lib that lead-in before you start. Make your lead-in specific and concrete.

• Stay in the moment. Pick up cues. Interact with other performers. Don't let your lines be separated from those of the other performers. Listen to yourself the director and the other performers and respond appropriately ("listen and answer").

• Don't allow any air between your line and the other character's line. The only exception is when a pause is logical or makes sense in the context of the story.

All voice-over performances are a form of theater, and you are the actor. When you become the character in the copy, you will be believable to the audience, creating a suspension of disbelief. When the audience suspends their disbelief in what they hear, they become more open to the message being communicated. Remember, it all starts when you discover the character in the copy.

---

[1] "Understanding Consumers and Markets," *Why People Buy*, RISC, 1997 (1-2).
[2] RISC AmeriScan compass, map and other materials copyright RISC, 1997.
  used by permission of Marshall Marketing & Communications, Inc.
[3] "Understanding Consumers and Markets," *Why People Buy*, RISC, 1997 (3).
[4] *MM&C RISC AmeriScan Guidebook*, copyright RISC, 1997 (5).

8

Words That Sell

This chapter reviews many of the techniques discussed in Chapters 4, 5 and 7. Chapters 9, 10, 11 and 12 include a variety of scripts that have been aired as radio and television commercials, used for corporate presentations, or for other real-world applications. The scripts in these chapters are all authentic and will give you a good idea of the types of copy you may be asked to perform as you begin to do auditions and work sessions. Each script is reproduced as accurately as possible, including typos, awkward phrasing, grammatical mistakes and other things that might seem odd, yet are commonplace in voice-over copy.

Directing Yourself: The Director in Your Mind

As a performer, over time, you will develop instincts as to how to develop your character, deliver your lines, and create drama in your performance. These instincts are good and necessary for a professional performer. However, if they are simply left at the level of instincts, they will limit your abilities to find the nuances and subtlety of the performance — those seemingly insignificant things that make the drama powerful, or the dialog interesting, or a comedic script hysterical rather than just humorous.

All voice-over copy is written for the purpose of selling something — a product or service, information, or an emotion or feeling. However, it is not the words in and of themselves that sells, it is the *way* in which *the words are spoken* that sells. It is the details of the performance behind the words — the nuance — that allows a performer to bring a script and a character to life. And behind every performer, there is a director. Somewhere in your mind is a director. You may not have realized it, but that director is there.

Voice-over copy is theatrical truth — not real-life truth — and your internal director is the part of you that gives you silent cues to keep you on track when you forget this. As you work with copy, you will find a little voice in your head that tells you, "Yeah, that was good" or "That line needs to be done differently." Your mental director is the result of critical thinking. He or she is the part of you that keeps you on track, helps you stay in the moment and gives you focus and guidance with your performance. Think of this director as a separate person (or part of you) who is watching your performance from a distance, yet close enough to give you cues.

Over time, your internal director and your performance will become as one — a seamless blending of director and performer resulting in a truly professional dramatic artist. This is the level to strive for. This is what theater is all about. This is what you, as a voice-actor, can achieve with any type of copy you are asked to read.

The Process of Pretending

Acting is the process of pretending. An actor momentarily pretends to be someone or something other than his or her true self. Effective acting is making the process of pretending believable to the audience. To make a performance believable, the actor must understand the character in the script and must temporarily take on the appropriate personality traits and other attitudes of that character.

Effective actors will search within themselves to find something from their personal experience that can be applied to their character's situation or to the performance in general (*sense memory*). If there is nothing in the actor's past to draw on, then the actor simply makes something up! The idea is to create an emotional, mental and physical connection between the performer and the character in the script. This connection, which exists purely in the mind of the actor, helps give life to the character in the script, making the character more real and believable to the audience.

Bring a part of you to the words on the page and your performance will become more believable. Decide on what your thoughts and feelings will be as you perform your lines (subtext) in order to make the copy your own. Let's review some of the keys to successful voice-acting that have already been discussed elsewhere in this book.

LET GO OF JUDGMENTS AND INHIBITIONS

One of the major keys to success with voice-acting is to let go of any judgments, inhibitions and concerns. It is important to leave your self-critic outside. There is an important difference between being analytical about your performance and judgmental. Judgmental thinking would be:

- "The way I delivered that last copy was just horrible! I'll never be able to do these lines right."
- "I just can't get into this character!"
- "I can't do this kind of copy!"
- "I shouldn't feel embarrassed when I do copy like this."

Analytical, or critical thinking would be:

- "I didn't like the way I delivered the copy — it just didn't seem real."
- "I know I can be more effective than that last read."
- "What can I do to make my character more believable?"

Judgmental thinking usually approaches the subject from a negative point of view, stops you in your tracks and prevents you from discovering the solutions you need. Critical (analytical) thinking is constructive and helps move you toward solutions that will make your performance more believable.

UNDERSTAND THE COPY

As you study the copy, do a quick character analysis to figure out who your character is. Also determine to whom you are speaking (your listener or audience) as well as any special requirements of the scene. What is the subject of your copy? Do a script analysis as you run through the copy once or twice. Commit to your decisions and allow the words to become your own.

You need to know the following three things:

- Who is the audience?
- Who are you as the character?
- Why is the character speaking these words? (What is the character's motivation or purpose in speaking and what gives your character the authority to be speaking the words in the script?)

WORK BACKWARDS

To quickly get an idea of the copywriter's intent, the target audience, the client's message, and some solid clues about your character and the story in the copy, try looking at the last line of the script first. The end of a script is where the resolution or nonresolution of conflict occurs and is usually the point where a character's attitude or true motivation is revealed. It is also where the most important part of the client's message usually resides. By working from the bottom of the script to the top, you will be able to learn important information that you can use to quickly create a basic character and attitude. Then use other clues in the copy to more fully develop your character.

MOVE

Don't just stand in front of the microphone stiff and rigid! Relax! Keep doing relaxation exercises to develop the habit and condition your body and mind to the experience of relaxation. A relaxed mind and body will make it easier to release your inhibitions and be nonjudgmental. Use your face, arms, and upper body to "act out" the scene in the copy. Use gestures when the script has you talking to someone. Make a fist when emphasizing a strong point in the copy. Use a smile, a frown and other facial expressions to help convey the feeling or emotion in the copy. Feelings must be expressed in your body and your face in order to become real through your voice. Keep moving!

FIND THE RHYTHM TO ADD VARIETY

Find the rhythm in the copy! Don't deliver every line with the same inflection and intonation. Add some variety to the way you deliver your lines, staying in character, of course. Broaden you vocal range (changes in pitch and intonation) and your dynamic range (soft to loud). Use a soft, gentle voice to emphasize something tender or romantic or to create a feeling of warmth, intimacy or friendliness. Use a louder voice to project anger, aggression or hostility. A soft voice with tension can be an effective way to project a character's pent-up emotions.

Use your face and body to add variety and feel the rhythm of the copy. Put a smile on your face to create a feeling of fun or happiness, frown to create a mood of frustration or anger. Use breath control to support your voice as your character expresses the emotions present in the copy.

Ad lib natural human sounds like "uh," "hmm" and so on, in appropriate places as you deliver the copy. You might also leave a short pause between words or sustain certain word sounds to add variety and create realism.

ADJUST YOUR PHRASING

Try looking at voice-over copy as if it were classical music. Classical music constantly shifts from loud, fast sections to slower, softer sections. Each of these sections has its own unique tempo (pace) and rhythm according to the feeling or emotion being communicated. A voice-over performance can do exactly the same thing. Don't be afraid to slow down, speed up or even leave a second of complete silence, if you feel it is necessary to create realism and believability in the copy you are reading.

STUDY OTHER PERFORMERS

Study film and television actors. Watch how they deliver their lines and interact with other characters. Listen to the dynamics of their voices. Notice that most actors use a lot of variety and inflection — they don't speak in monotone or with limited range (unless those characteristics are part of the character). They also move and express emotion physically as well as verbally, just as they would in real life. Mimic and imitate what you see other actors do and how they speak so you can get the experience of what they are doing. Study the techniques they use and apply them to your style of performance. You will soon find the boundary of your comfort zone — the point where your stretch becomes uncomfortable. To grow as a performer, you need to find a way to work past that boundary.

TAKE THE "VOICE" OUT OF "VOICE-OVER"

Don't just read your copy. Have a conversation with the listener. Talk *to* your audience, not *at* them, always striving to motivate, persuade or move the listener to action. Remember that even if you are the only person in the booth, the *other* person is always there. Visualize your best friend, wife or husband on the other side of the microphone, and deliver the copy to them.

Do whatever you can to draw the listener into your story and expect a response. You are a storyteller! Remember:

- Use drama (emotional hooks) to attract and hold the listener's attention.
- Talk in phrases, not word by word.
- Don't read.
- Let the content of the copy determine your pace and attitude.
- Have a conversation with the listener.
- Talk out loud to yourself to find hidden treasures.

- Experiment with different attitudes, inflections and expressions of emotions.

- Take out the punctuation marks in the copy to make the copy flow more naturally and conversationally.

- Develop a mental attitude that allows you to create a feeling of reality and believability. If you believe that your character is real, your listener will.

LOOK FOR QUESTION MARKS IN THE COPY

Question marks are opportunities for dramatic punctuation. I'm not referring to the punctuation mark — ?. I'm referring to words or phrases in the copy that give you the opportunity to ask a question. If the copy specifically asks a question, you should make that clear with your performance. Question marks that do not ask questions are usually found in sentences that describe or explain something. Someplace in the sentence there will be an opportunity to answer the unasked question.

Find those spots and figure out your own answers to the questions. Your answers will be valuable to your character because they are part of the character's knowledge or history, which helps make the character real and believable. For example, here's a :30 TV script. Some of the places where question marks present opportunities for discovering information are noted in parentheses:

She's just a few days old (HOW MANY DAYS?) and you're already worried (WORRIED ABOUT WHAT?).
What kind of world will she grow up in? (COPY ASKS A SPECIFIC QUESTION – COME UP WITH AN ANSWER.)
How will she get the education she needs? (ANSWER THIS QUESTION.)
And learn the values (WHAT VALUES?) to sustain her in trying times?
She's counting on your knowledge (WHAT DO YOU KNOW?) and concern (WHAT ARE YOUR CONCERNS?).
Shouldn't you have a newscast you can count on for that same thing? (WHAT THINGS CAN YOU COUNT ON?)
KNSD News. Coverage (WHAT KIND OF COVERAGE?) you can count on.

You can take this process as far as you like, even to the point of asking questions about every word in the script. As you decide on your answers to the unasked questions, you will be creating the foundation of your character's attitude and personality. Commit to the answers you come up with and use them as tools for giving your character life.

FIND EMOTIONAL HOOKS

These are the words or phrases that carry an emotional impact. Call on your past experience to recall a memory of a similar emotion (sense memory). Notice that the memory of the emotion creates a certain tension someplace in your body. Observe the tension's position in your body and what it feels like. Hold this tension or sensation as you deliver the copy, reexperiencing the emotion or feeling. Now speak from that place in your body, fully expressing the tension. This technique helps to make your performance more believable and your character more real.

STAY IN THE MOMENT

Don't let your mind wander — stay focused. Don't be thinking about what you are having for lunch or dinner, or about how bad the traffic was when coming to the studio. Stay focused on the performance at hand. Allow yourself to experience the moment taking place in the script. Concentrate on staying in character and maintaining that role throughout the session.

MAKE EVERY TIME THE FIRST TIME

Make each and every performance seem as if it is the first time. It is very easy to get sloppy by take 27. Take 28 should sound as fresh and real as take one — only better. Unless the producer or director tells you otherwise, you should maintain the same energy and attitude for each take. Use the director's guidance as a tool to help you focus in on your best performance. Add a little spin to a word, or shift your emphasis here or there with each take, but keep your energy and attitude consistent. This becomes very important to the editor who needs to put the final project together long after you have gone. Many times, bits and pieces from several takes are assembled to arrive at the finished product. Variations in your performance energy can stand out very clearly if you are not consistent.

LISTEN AND ANSWER

Most people have a hard time listening. Listen to yourself as you perform the copy. Listen to the producer or director for instruction on how to modify your delivery. If you are doing dialog, listen to the other performers. Listen for opportunities to inject small human sounds: uh-huh, ummm, clearing your throat, breath sounds and so on, all to make dialog more real and believable. An inexperienced actor will just do his or her lines. An experienced actor will give the same lines life by adding the little details that make the conversation real.

ADD DRAMA

Even dry, boring copy can be made interesting if it is performed with drama. A dramatic performance is much more than just reading the words on the page. It involves body movement, a wide range of vocal pitch and dynamics, body tension, and an understanding of the character. The key to effective drama is the element of surprise. Lead the audience in one direction, and suddenly end up someplace else. This is also the key to effective comedy. In both types of performances, the actor must never tip his or her hand and let the audience in on what's happening too soon. Variations in vocal tone, dynamics and physical energy are what makes a voice-over performance interesting and captivating.

PRACTICE DIFFERENT ATTITUDES

Practice developing your basic acting skills by pretending different moods or attitudes at times when you are by yourself. Read from a book striving for intensity, clarity and meaning in every word. Perform the same copy or section of a book as different characters with different attitudes. Record these practice sessions and listen for the believability in your performances. To achieve drama, try changing your energy or attitude for different sections of the copy. Use your emotions to express the mood of the copy and don't hold back. To express anger, be loud and aggressive. To express tenderness or romance, be soft and gentle. Practicing in private helps you overcome your self-consciousness and gradually opens you up to being able to express powerful emotions and feelings when in a working environment.

STRETCH YOUR BOUNDARIES

Don't be concerned with how you will appear or sound to anybody! As a voice-actor, your job is to perform the copy and your character in the best manner possible. If you need to make strange faces, or wave your arms wildly to get into the character, then that is what you need to do. Whenever possible, leave your inhibitions and self-conscious attitudes outside the studio door.

Stretch beyond what feels comfortable to you, even in a recording session. It is better to stretch too far rather than not far enough. It is easier for a director to pull you back after setting a character that is too far out there than it is to stretch you further. Remember, there is no absolutely right or wrong way to perform. Each performer is unique and different techniques work better for different performers. Do whatever works best for you to make your performance real and believable.

As you stretch your abilities, you will probably feel uncomfortable at first. Remember to be nonjudgmental and to not worry about how well you are doing. Each of us has an individual concept of some point at which we feel we would be going too far, or over the edge. This is usually the line between what we would call *normalcy* (sanity) and *craziness* (insanity).

Practice taking yourself just a little bit over that line until you begin to feel uncomfortable. Then take yourself a little bit further. The more you take yourself beyond the point where you think sanity ends, the faster you will develop the ability to take on any character — and momentarily become that character.

BE WILLING TO TAKE RISKS

You must be willing to risk total failure. Intend to perform to the best of your abilities. Become the character and do whatever it takes for you to get *into* character. Remember that you are uniquely you, and that you are interesting just as you are. Also remember that the people you are working with have insecurities of their own and may actually know less about the business than you do. Know that you know what you are doing. If you never risk, you can never learn. Use each audition or session as a learning experience. Keep an attitude of always being in training.

ACT PROFESSIONAL

Play the part! Act professional and you will be treated with respect. Enter a studio with the attitude of a professional there to do a job. Be friendly, cooperative, and ready to work. Making money does not make you a professional. Acting professionally makes you money. When you act like a pro, the people hiring you will believe you are a pro and will respect you. Remember that this business is all about creating believability in the mind of the audience. When you enter a studio, your first audience will be the people who hired you. Make them believe you are good at what you do and prove it with your performance.

Become the child you once were!

Pretend!

Play!

Have fun!

Tips for Performing All Types of Copy

Remember, voice-acting is theater of the mind, and you are the actor. When you become the character in the copy, you will be believable to the audience, and a suspension of disbelief will be created. When the audience suspends their disbelief in what they hear, they become more open to the message. This all starts when you discover the character in the copy.

- Don't overanalyze your copy. Overanalyzing can cause you to lose spontaneity and cause your delivery to become flat and uninteresting. You can also become so focused on your character that you lose sight of the whole story, the drama and the relationship between the characters and the conflict.

- You need to be able to get just enough information from the copy to understand your character and know what is taking place. Understand the drama, then add your personal spin to make the copy your own. Find the USP in the copy and let everything you do lead to that goal.

- Rely on your instincts, and the director in your mind will guide your delivery to keep it on track.

- Tell the story. All scripts tell a story, even dry, technical scripts. Storytelling is always about relationships. As a voice-actor, it is your job to understand the relationships, discover the story and communicate it to the audience. To be believable, make the relationships seem real.

- Play, have fun, be natural and feel free to experiment. If you go too far, the producer or director will pull you back.

- Keep a strong mental image of your character and the story in your mind. Pretend that what you are saying or that the situation your character is in is real. Make your character believable by adding something of yourself. Let your imagination run wild. If you believe in the reality of your performance, the tension of your belief will come through in your words and the audience will believe.

Examples of Voice-Over Copy

The following four chapters contain actual voice-over scripts that have been used for television, radio and corporate projects. As you work with these scripts, keep in mind the various tips for the type of copy that you are reading. A discussion of each script is also included to help you discover the target audience, your attitude and the character in the copy.

9

Single-Voice Copy

Single-voice copy is written for a solo performer who will deliver the entire message, with the possible exception of a separate tag line. There is no interaction between characters, although there may be some implied interaction between the performer and the listener. Most radio and television commercials, public service announcements, corporate nar-ratives, telephone messages, books-on-tape and some CD-ROM projects fall into this category.

All single-voice copy is communicating information, often attempting to reach the listener on an emotional level. To communicate effectively, it is essential to grab the listener's attention, and hold it. Reading or announcing copy will not achieve either of these goals. Both reading and announcing direct the performance inward and imply that the performer is speaking to himself or herself. The target audience of a single-voice script can usually be determined pretty easily: however, sometimes it can be a challenge to define the character speaking. Well-written copy that clearly tells a story makes the character easy to define. Poorly written copy that contains only information can make this difficult.

Consider single-voice copy as a story you are telling. Find your storyteller and commit to the attitude and style choices you make. Deliver the copy from a set point of view by finding the subtext (how you think and feel) behind the words you speak and express it through your voice.

The key to effective single-voice copy is to use the basic dramatic principle of having a conversation with another person — talking to the listener who is not really there. Make your conversation natural, keep it candid, and remember to speak to only one person at a time. *Shotgunning*, trying to speak to several people at once, tends to make your delivery sound more like a speech than a conversation.

Make the other person someone you know — anyone who might be a good candidate for the message. Do not have the conversation with a pet or stuffed animal but rather give the subject of your conversation a base in reality. Make the person real in your imagination. A strong visual image will help lead to feelings and emotions in your conversation. When you have feelings and emotions, your experiences communicate through your voice.

In single-voice scripts, as in others, there can be many different written references to the performer, such as MAN:, WOMAN:, TALENT:, ANNCR: (announcer), VOICE 1:, AVO: (announce voice-over), and so on. These all refer to the performer and are often used interchangeably. Scripts also include references to music and SFX (sound effects), which are not to be read by the performer. A TV script may or may not include a separate column for video instructions. If the column is there, use the video description to your advantage to help get valuable information about the audience, your character and how you can best perform the copy.

Tips for Performing Single-Voice Copy

Remember, single-voice copy always tells a story and stories are always about relationships. The relationships can be between people or between people and other things. Stories and relationships are present even in copy that contain only information. If the story is not clearly written in the script, use your imagination to make it up. If a relationship is not clear, it might be simply a relationship between the character speaking and the audience. The following suggestions will help you create effective performances for single-voice copy.

- Analyze the copy for character, mood, attitude, conflict, rhythm, etc. (See Chapter 7, The Character in the Copy).

- Find the unique selling proposition (USP) in the copy. What is the ultimate message, image, feeling or unique quality about the product or service that the advertiser wants to communicate to the listener?

- Find the subtext for the words you are speaking. What are you thinking, and how do you feel?

- Determine who your primary audience is and why they should be listening to what you have to say.

- Determine what places your character in a position of being an authority on the subject of the script.

- Determine the creative strategy that will enable you to build dramatic tension and allow for expression of the message. Use sense-memory techniques to recall your past feelings in a similar situation. Locate where the tension is in your body and speak from that place.

- Keep your delivery conversational. Remember that the other person is always there, just not visible. Make the other person real in your imagination. Keep the attitude of moving or persuading them with your words, and have the expectation of a response. Talk to the other person, not at him or her.

- Be believable by staying in the moment, keeping spontaneity, and making the copy your own.

- Be careful not to telegraph the message or send a message of "here comes another commercial."

- Talk to a single person, real or imagined. A photograph can be used to give you focus.

Single-Voice Scripts

As you work with the following scripts, you might find it interesting to read through the script before reading the Copy Notes provided for each one. Come up with your own interpretation for attitude, pacing, character and performance, then read through the notes to see how close you came to what the producers of these projects intended.

ASICS — SPORTS CHALET

Title: Asics — Sports Chalet "Car Noises," Running Local Radio :60
Agency: VitroRobertson, San Diego
USP: "They work." Asics shoes work. Sport Chalet is "The Asics Expert."
Target audience: Adult men who run.
Style: Serious tone.
Character: ANNCR 1 is a storyteller. ANNCR 2 is tag only.
Copy Notes: Deliver as telling an unusual story. Interest is maintained by keeping the story interesting and not revealing the message until the last paragraph. Keep the delivery interesting by shifting attitudes to reflect mood changes in the copy. The climax of the copy is the last paragraph of ANNCR 1. ANNCR 1 copy length is :55. ANNCR 2 tag is :05. Even though the tag is only :05, it still needs to be delivered with meaning. The tag is very important because it repeats the product name and tells the audience where to purchase.

Practice your storytelling techniques to make this believable. If you have run a marathon, recall an interesting experience. If you have never run a marathon, recall any interesting or unusual experience and pretend it happened during a race. Notice where in your body you feel the experience and speak from that place to make your story believable.

ANNCR 1: I knew a guy who made car noises when he ran. He would make these noises not to himself, but quite audibly so that anyone running close to him could hear. The noise would vary depending upon how he felt during that particular race. When he was feeling good he would sound like a precision sports car. And on those off days when he was grumbling along, he would try to make adjustments in tone to improve his performance. As if he was a mechanic tuning an engine.

Though a bit unusual, he was an accomplished marathoner. And as he crossed finish lines it was not uncommon to hear, "Hey, there's the guy who makes car noises when he runs."

I never questioned him, because I know that for him, making car noises works. And I know that if I ever asked him why he makes car noises when he runs, he would simply downshift and leave me behind.

When you run, you have to find what works. If you can't make convincing car noises, you might just try a pair of Asics running shoes. They work.

ANNCR 2: You'll find Asics running shoes in all sizes and styles at Sports Chalet, the Asics experts.

DEBT-FREE AMERICA

Title: "Disappearing Cards," TV :30
Agency: LAK Advertising, San Diego
USP: "Stop the stress — let us help." Stress-free help to get out of debt.
Target audience: Financially troubled adults.
Style: Serious tone.
Character: Spokesperson.
Copy Notes: This is a :30 television commercial. The VISUAL side of the script describes the picture, while the AUDIO side of the script contains the copy (see page 111). You can often get a good idea of how to deliver your copy if you know what the producer is planning to do visually. Sometimes a storyboard will be attached to the script. A storyboard is much like a cartoon strip with drawings that show the intended visual flow of the commercial.

Debt-Free America — TV :30

VISUAL	AUDIO
1. ECU Credit Card. Pull back to reveal a whole tabletop full of credit cards and more get thrown on from all sides as pull back continues. SUPER: Too much debt.	1. AVO (Music Under) Do you live on your credit cards? Have you piled up way too much debt?
2. Double expose "worried" man's face over the scene. SUPER: Consolidate your bills.	2. If you worry day and night, it's time to consolidate your bills.
3. Credit cards rapidly pop off screen until they have all disappeared.	3. We can help make your problems disappear . . .
4. Morph to DFA logo. Logo cell has "Debt-Free America" at top with phone number underneath and room under that for a series of copy supers.	4. . . . at "Debt-Free America".
5. SUPER: Save thousands in interest.	5. Save thousands in interest.
6. SUPER: One low monthly payment.	6. Make one low monthly payment.
7. SUPER: No credit check.	7. No credit check.
8. SUPER: Not a loan. Not bankruptcy.	8. Not a loan. Not bankruptcy.
9. SUPER: Call for free consultation.	9. Call for a free consultation.
10. Lose super and dissolve to legal copy line: Debt consolidation services provided by a 501(c) (3) non-profit corporation.	10. 1-888-CALL-DFA
11. Hold scene.	11. Stop the stress. Let us help. 1-888-CALL-DFA

This spot is designed to have a *music bed*, or underscore, to help support the copy and set the mood of the spot. The character's attitude should be that of a compassionate person who has important information to share which will help people in trouble get out of debt. TV copy should be read in :29 or less for a :30 spot. The extra second is needed for visual transitions at the beginning and end. Even though this copy is not written as a conversation, it can still be performed in a conversational manner if you visualize who you are talking to. An alternative, but perhaps less effective, delivery style would be to use a more "hard-sell" attitude, much like pitching a product in the style of an announcer. A hard-sell delivery might conflict with the message of "stop the stress."

To make it interesting and something the listener can emotionally relate to, this type of copy requires creativity on the part of the performer. This style of writing is very common for spokesperson television copy.

RECYCLING AWARENESS

Title: "Start Recycling — Sarah," TV :30 Draft #2
Agency: KNSD-TV Direct — Community Relations
USP: "It's so easy, even a child can do it!" Educational; learn how to reuse recyclable items.
Target audience: Environmentally concerned adults; general adult audience.
Style: Storyteller.
Character: Concerned friend.
Copy Notes: The "Closing the Loop Recycling Awareness Campaign" was a series of Public Service Announcements (PSA) designed to inform the viewing audience about recycling and to motivate them to recycle. This script has two distinct parts: the first half presents the problem of little Sarah and what will happen as she grows up. The second part introduces a solution to the problem — recycling. The "problem" section is a serious story and should be delivered in a concerned tone and attitude. The "solution" section starts at the last paragraph and should be delivered with a lighter attitude. Try using a concerned expression on your face for the first part, changing to more of a smile for the solution.

Although this is a television PSA, a storyboard is not provided for the performer and there is not a video column on the script. The only information available to the performer is the copy in the script. A music underscore sets the serious mood of the message and becomes somewhat lighter for the solution.

It may be helpful to use some contractions, such as "she'll" instead of "she will" to help the flow. Also notice that there are several opportunities for pauses and emphasis, which are not indicated by punctuation marks.

Try deleting the punctuation marks and letting you instincts and the copy provide natural, conversational punctuation. Look for key phrases that can be emphasized or "billboarded," such as ". . . 17 tons of trash" and ". . . no where to throw it away." Tap into your own physical and emotional feelings to connect with the emotion in the copy (subtext). Be careful of phrases where the end of one word is the same letter as the beginning of the next word. The two "Ps" in "Loop partnership" should both be heard. It should not sound like "Loo-partnership."

BY THE TIME SARAH TURNS 12 YEARS OLD, SHE WILL HAVE PRODUCED 17 TONS OF TRASH. AND SHE'LL HAVE NO WHERE TO THROW IT AWAY. BY THEN ALL THE LANDFILLS IN SAN DIEGO WILL BE FULL.

WE ALL NEED TO START RECYCLING. IT'S SO EASY . . . EVEN A CHILD CAN DO IT.

WATCH FOR THE "CLOSING THE LOOP" RECYCLING AWARENESS CAMPAIGN AND FIND OUT HOW THE THINGS YOU USE CAN BE RE-USED. IN THE COMING MONTHS, WE'LL BE SHOWING YOU HOW.

THIS KNSD MESSAGE IS SPONSORED BY THE CLOSING THE LOOP PARTNERSHIP.

EYES OF KNSD

Title: "Photographers #2," TV :30
Agency: KNSD-TV Direct
USP: "Coverage You Can Count On." KNSD photographers see things differently
Target audience: Adults who watch TV news — all ages.
Style: Dramatic.
Character: Storyteller.
Copy Notes: This script is a TV promo designed to capture the unique storytelling talents of the KNSD news photographers. Here's an excellent opportunity to stretch your ability to communicate emotions. Each line of the script focuses on a different emotion or feeling and should have a unique delivery. Find a way to connect with the feeling of each line and express that feeling. Use your body and gestures to get into the feeling of each line. The story here will have little or no meaning if it is read "flat" with no drama or emotion behind it. However, if you express the drama of each line through your voice, you can create a powerful emotional connection with the listener.

This spot has a dramatic, fully orchestrated musical underscore and uses slow-motion images of news photographers in action as they cover major news events. Each letter of the station's call letters, KNSD, should be given equal weight. Deliver the call letters as K-N-S-D, not K-NSD.

They're the eyes . . .
That tell the story.
That see the pain.
That see the glory.
They're the eyes of KNSD news.
Award winning photojournalists.
National photographers of the year.
When you want to see . . .
to remember . . .
to understand . . .
to feel the story . . .
the eyes have it.
The eyes of KNSD news.
Coverage you can count on.

SAN DIEGO NISSAN

Title: "Big Top Sale" (A) Radio :60
Agency: LAK Advertising, San Diego
USP: "You'll find it all at San Diego Nissan."
Target audience: Adults in the market for a used car.
Style: Upbeat medium or hard-sell.
Character: Spokesperson.
Copy Notes: This is a pretty typical radio script for an auto dealership. The copy is underscored with an upbeat custom music jingle with singers proclaiming the dealership's name. The purpose of the commercial is to attract car buyers to the dealer by offering perks and bonuses to bring customers in. The "Big Top Sale" concept is just one of many approaches used by auto dealers to bring in crowds. Perks of free food and great car deals target the desired audience.

Performance of this copy must be enthusiastic and upbeat to match the energy of the music. As a spokesperson for the dealership you should express the excitement of the event through your performance. The copywriter of this spot has provided some guidelines for emphasis by putting certain words or phrases in **bold** print. Maintain enthusiasm by keeping an attitude of excitement and fun in your mind and physically putting a smile on your face.

JINGLE VOICES: "San Diego Nissan!"

ANNOUNCER: (Voice over music) (:50)

If you're looking to buy a **used** car, truck or van, **this** is the weekend to do it at San Diego Nissan! Friday, Saturday, Sunday and Memorial Day Monday, it's the annual "Big Top Sale" at San Diego Nissan!

See the huge selection of **used cars and trucks** — all priced to move! Plus a great inventory of 300 **new** Nissan models. And zero down delivers — O.A.C.

So come in for a terrific selection of **new and used cars** and trucks at San Diego Nissan's annual "Big Top Sale" Friday, Saturday, Sunday and Memorial Day Monday! Enjoy **free** hot dogs and soft drinks! **Free** prizes and souvenirs! Have fun and save cash at the "Big Top Sale"!

Look for the big **striped tent** and the **blimp** in the sky! That's where you'll find it all — at San Diego Nissan! Highway 8 at the Mission Gorge exit!

JINGLE VOICES: "San Diego Nissan, right now!"

AIRTOUCH CELLULAR

Title: "Complicated" (Version 2) Radio :60
Agency: VitroRobertson, San Diego
USP: AirTouch cellular service is "uncomplicated."
Target audience: Cell phone users.
Style: Upbeat, with an slightly sarcastic attitude.
Character: Frustrated.
Copy Notes: This is a cleverly written script that points out just some of life's many frustrations. The listener is led through a long list of complicated things without being given any clues about the subject of the commercial until the spot is almost finished. Clever writing is the start of a good commercial. But it takes an interesting performance to give it life.

To give it extra punch, make the list interesting by varying the delivery of each item in the list and occasionally pausing before the word "complicated." The change to "impossible" when referring to the 1040 Long Form adds humor because this is something most listeners can relate to and is a change in the sequence.

The overall attitude changes from slightly sarcastic to a lighter, friendlier attitude in the third paragraph. When the subject changes to cellular phones and Airtouch, the delivery softens and becomes more intimate. The last three lines can be pulled back even further to a very understanding attitude about how difficult life can be.

(Jazzy music throughout)

Hey, the theory of relativity is complicated. Annual percentage rates are complicated. The chemical composition of Velveeta is complicated.

Mahjong is complicated. Stephen Hawkins books, whoa, complicated. The 1040 Long Form — impossible. Don King's hairdo, complicated. Rain forest ecosystems are complicated. Playing the accordion is very complicated. Those 3D posters they sell at the mall are complicated. Early episodes of *Dallas* were complicated. Converting from degrees Fahrenheit to degrees Kelvin, trust me, complicated.

Cellular phones should <u>not</u> be complicated. That's why AirTouch created Anytime pricing. When you sign up on the Convenience Plan it's just 33 cents a minute. Everyday, every night, all the time. And if you sign up by Sunday, your hook-up is free.

33 cents a minute, Anytime Pricing. Uncomplicated.
Because <u>life</u> is complicated enough.
Call 1 800-AIRTOUCH.

10

Dialog Copy: Doubles and Multiples

Your understanding of the whole story and your character's part in it will directly affect how your performance is received during an audition. The casting person, producer or director is looking for performers who can make their character and the situation appear real.

Types of Dialog Copy

THE CONVERSATION

As with single-voice copy, dialog copy involves a conversation between two or more characters. The primary difference with dialog copy is that the other person you are talking to, is in the studio with you and is participating in the performance.

Unlike most single-voice copy, dialog copy usually involves a story with a specific plotline. It is important for you to understand the whole story, not just your part in it. If you limit your understanding to just your role, you may miss subtle details that are vital to effectively interacting with the other characters. You may have difficulty creating the dramatic tension that is so necessary for giving the characters life and making them real to the listener.

COMEDY

Comedy is a very popular form of dialog copy. It is not the words on the page that make a script funny, it is the intent behind the words. In part, comedy is based on the unexpected — leading the audience in one direction and then suddenly changing directions and ending up someplace else. Comedy is often based on overstating the obvious or placing a totally serious character in a ludicrous situation. Comedy can also be achieved by creating a sense of discomfort in the mind of the audience.

Don't play a comedy script for laughs, think of it as life — with a twist. If you play your lines for laughs, you won't get them. The laughs will only come when the audience is surprised.

Rhythm and timing are essential with comedy dialog copy. The interaction between characters can make or break a comedy script. Overlapping lines, or stepping on lines, usually gives a more natural, real feeling and helps set the rhythm and pace of the copy. A feeling of realism can also be achieved by adding pauses (where appropriate), and adding natural vocal sounds.

Jokes are good examples of comedy that lead in one direction and end up someplace unexpected; for example:

VOICE 1: Class, it is an interesting linguistic fact that in the English language a double negative makes a positive. However, in other languages, like Russian, a double negative still makes a negative.
There is no language in which a double positive makes a negative.

VOICE 2: (sarcastically) Yeah, Right!

It is a good idea to ask the producer or director before you take too many liberties with any copy; this is especially true with comedy copy. If the producer understands comedy, he or she will usually let you experiment with your character and how you deliver your lines. It might be a good idea to do the lines as written for at least a few takes before experimenting with ad-libs or taking your character too far out.

The most important thing about comedy is to not telegraph the punch line. Don't let your character's attitude tip off the ending. Say your lines in a natural, conversational way, appropriate to the situation, and the comedy will happen.

Tips for Performing Comedy Dialog Copy

To be effective, comedy dialog must have a sense of reality, even if the situation is ludicrous and the characters are exaggerated. The following tips and suggestions will help you perform comedy copy effectively.

• Be real. Keep your character spontaneous and natural. To help you get "in the moment" of the dialog, you can create a believable back-story or lead-in line.

- Find the comedy rhythm. This might include appropriate "beats" or pauses, which can provide the punch necessary for the peak comedic moment. Remember, dialog copy has a rhythm for each character and a rhythm for the overall dialog.

- Speak your lines to another person, real or imagined, expecting him or her to respond. Pretend you are speaking to your best friend. Keep in mind the wants and needs of your character and express those to someone, with tension in your body, expecting a response.

- Where appropriate, add natural sounds and reactions, such as "uhh," "yeah," "uh-huh," "mmm," or a groan or clear your throat. All of these sounds help give the feeling of a real, natural conversation. Ask the producer before making changes to the copy.

- *Subtext* — how you think and feel as you perform — is especially important with comedy. If your character is that of a normal person in a ludicrous situation, you need to have a subtext of normalcy. If your thoughts anticipate the punch line, it will be communicated through your performance.

- Do not telegraph the punch line. Be careful that your character's attitude doesn't give the audience more information than they need to know.

Tips for Performing Dialog Copy in General

The following tips and suggestions will help you perform more effectively in all types of dialog sessions.

- Internalize the wants and needs of your character, both physically and emotionally. Find the place in your body where a tension develops. Hold the tension there and read your lines. In theater, this is called *setting the character*. Don't set your character too soon. Only after running through a script several times will you be able to find the true voice for your character. Stay in the moment, listen and answer, and react authentically to the other characters.

- Underplay, rather than overplay. Louder is not better. If in doubt, pull back, speak softer and be more natural.

- Don't read! Be conversational. Be real. Talk *to* the audience or other performer(s), not *at* them. Be careful not to overenunciate. Less is usually more.

- Find the rhythm in the copy. All copy has a rhythm. The rhythm for a comedic script will be different than that of a more serious script. Find the rhythm and be consistent throughout the copy.

- Keep it real. Speak as quickly as you would if you were talking to someone and as quietly as you would if you were in a real conversation. If "uhhhs," "hmmms," or "ahhhs" and other reactions seem appropriate for your character, ad-lib them into your performance, even though they might not be written into the copy. This is called *pulling lines* — a technique for making your character more human.

- Get into "the moment" by ad-libbing a situation. Give yourself a realistic lead-in to the copy and ad-lib that lead-in before you start. Make your lead-in specific and concrete.

- Stay in "the moment." Pick up cues. Interact with other performers. Listen to yourself and the other performers and respond appropriately (*listen and answer*). Don't allow any air between your line and the other character's line. The only exception is when a pause is logical and makes sense in the context of the story.

Dialog and Multiple-Voice Scripts

As you work with the following scripts, you might find it interesting to read through the script before reading the Copy Notes provided for each one. Come up with your own interpretation for attitude, pacing, character and performance, then read through the notes to see how close you came to what the producers of these projects intended.

NBC 7/39 NEWS

Title: "Coffee Time with the Moms, Baby Clothes Days 1 and 2," Radio :30
Agency: NBC 7/39 Direct — Creative Services
USP: "Coverage you can count on."
Target audience: Adult women with families.
Style: Serious tone, conversational.
Characters: Mom #1 & Mom #2 are both parents with children.
Copy Notes: These are a two radio commercials for a news feature series scheduled to run on consecutive days during a "sweeps" period. *Sweeps*, or ratings, occurs four times a year and is a time when a television station's news department makes a special effort to attract viewers. Advertising rates are based on the outcome of a ratings period.

In these spots, both moms are already aware that the station is preparing something about a subject they are both interested in. The main focus of their conversation is the subject of the report and its relevance to their lifestyle.

The title gives a clue as to mood and attitude. Coffee time implies a casual conversation between the two characters. Each has an opportunity to express an opinion and share their feelings. In the spot for Day 2, both women are eager to find out what new things they will learn in part 2. Sound effects of a small restaurant and a rhythmic music track support the dialog.

Notice that these commercials have three different versions. This is common for commercials that promote a specific, topical or timely event. The script would first be performed in its entirety using the first version. Then, the lines for the other versions would be recorded so that the engineer can edit them into the final projects as needed. The process of going back to record lines again is called a *pick-up*.

COFFEE TIME WITH THE MOMS — DAY 1 - RADIO :30

MOM #1:	Aren't they adorable?
MOM #2:	. . . It's amazing . . .
MOM #1:	. . . you'd do just about anything to protect them . . .
MOM #2:	. . . like Monday's (Tomorrow's) (Tonight's) special report on NBC 7-39.
MOM #1:	When is that?
MOM #2:	At 5.
MOM #1:	It's about baby clothes . . .
MOM #2:	are they safe?
MOM #1:	I hear their investigation discovered some new laws.
MOM #2:	. . . yeah, that I didn't even know about.
MOM #1:	Doesn't that just make you mad?
MOM #2:	Yeah . . . but better to hear from them Monday (tomorrow) (tonight) so we can keep these precious ones safe.
MOM #1:	It's Monday (tomorrow) (tonight) at 5?
MOM #2:	That's right, on NBC 7-39.
MOM #1:	They're the ones that give you coverage you can ALWAYS count on . . .
MOM #2:	to keep our families safe.

COFFEE TIME WITH THE MOMS — DAY 2 - RADIO :30

MOM #1:	Did you see last night's news on NBC 7-39?
MOM #2:	Yes, thanks for the tip . . .
MOM #1:	Great information about flammable baby clothes that I didn't even know about . . .
MOM #2:	. . . what are they doing tonight?
MOM #1:	. . . something about fabric softeners . . .
MOM #2:	. . . hmmm . . .
MOM #1:	. . . and what they do to your baby's clothes.
MOM #2:	Ahh . . . but I love that fresh smell . . .
MOM #1:	But you may not like the disastrous result!
MOM #2:	When is that on?
MOM #1:	Tonight at 5.
MOM #2:	That's right, on NBC 7-39 . . .
MOM #1:	They're the only ones that give you . . .
MOM #2:	I know . . . coverage you can count on!

SOUTHERN CALIFORNIA BEEF

Title: "California Beef — The Obscene Phone Call," Radio :30
Agency: Commercial Clinic
USP: "The best steak you'll ever eat."
Target audience: Adult men and women.
Style: Serious at start, shifting to light-hearted; fast conversational.
Characters: Man is a bit of a prankster, playing a joke on his wife.
Woman takes the call seriously, not getting that the call is her husband.
Punch line is when the woman lets her secret be known.
Copy Notes: The overall pace and interaction between the two characters must be fast to get this into :30. Choose your character and *imagine* how you would handle this situation. Use your internal feelings and thoughts to help create the character and make it real. Both characters have shifts in their attitude: the man from prankster to loving husband and finally surprise; the woman from upset and angry to relieved and finally embarrassed at her last line.

MAN:	Hello, is this Mrs. Ernest Simpson, that fabulous blonde?
WOMAN:	Yes, who is this, please?
MAN:	You know, you've been missing out on something, baby - Southern California Beef. It's tender, younger, leaner, not to mention fresher.
WOMAN:	*(somewhat upset)* How did you get this number?
MAN:	Never mind that. Just look for the red, white and blue label at your favorite meat counter.
WOMAN:	*(getting angry)* Look, I've heard about these calls, and I'm going to report you to the police. Now, who is this!
MAN:	It's your husband, silly. I'll be home in ten minutes with two of the best steaks you'll ever eat. I just learned about Southern California Beef.
WOMAN:	*(relieved)* Oh, Ernie . . .
MAN:	. . . And break out a bottle of the bubbly . . . you know, we're going to celebrate.
WOMAN:	Honestly, I thought it was Sam.
MAN:	Who's Sam?
WOMAN:	*(embarrassed reaction)*

TOYOTA CARLSBAD

Title: "Birthday Gift," Radio :60
Agency: The DOCSI Corporation, dba Dick Orkin's Radio Ranch
USP: "No Pressure, No Hype."
Target audience: Adult men and women in the market for a car.
Style: Very conversational.
Characters: Mom and Dad give their son a birthday present — with a twist. Mom and Dad are both a bit eccentric in their attitudes while the son is more "normal" and reacts to his parents unique gift.
Copy Notes: Mom and Dad both think their gift is a big deal, when, in fact it is not. The humor in this spot arises from the son's expectations and reaction to Mom and Dad's sincerity in giving a gift that is not what he expects. This is an example of leading the audience in one direction and ending up someplace else to arrive at a humorous outcome.

This script includes many of the ad-libs and direction cues that were created by the original performers. Notice that Mom and Dad continue their lines as the son speaks, making the scene believable. For the comedy in this commercial to work, the conversation must be nonstop with no pauses, voices must overlap and the characters must appear real. Be careful of rhythm and timing, and be careful not to tip the punch line. There is no music, except for the jingle at the end. The running time for the dialog is :55 with a :05 announcer tag at the end.

MOM & DAD:	*(singing end of song)* Happy birthday to you . . . *(Mom & Dad enjoying themselves, light chuckle)*
SON:	Oh, thanks mom and dad . . .
MOM:	And for your gift . . .
DAD:	A little envelope . . .
SON:	Ahhh. Thanks! *(SFX: paper rustling)*
DAD:	Now before you open it, your mom and I want to say we know you need a new car, young man.
SON:	*(reaction)* Oh! You guys are the best!
DAD:	One stipulation here . . .
SON:	Mom, I'll drive you to the hairdresser anytime!
MOM:	*(Dad reacting under)* Oh no ya nut. You need to buy this car at Toyota Carlsbad.
SON:	*(Mom and Dad reacting under)* Oh, I know all about Toyota Carlsbad. They're famous for being relaxed and friendly . . .
MOM & DAD:	*(melodically)* No pressure, no hype . . .
	(SFX: Envelope being opened)
SON:	Oh boy, its . . .
MOM & DAD:	Surprise!
SON:	*(with disbelief)* . . . written directions to Toyota Carlsbad.
MOM & DAD:	MOM: The friendly, relaxed place to buy a car . . . DAD *(with smile, acknowledging)*: Yes . . .
MOM & DAD:	*(melodically)* No pressure, no hype!
DAD:	Look at his face, he's stunned. *(chuckles)*
SON & MOM:	SON *(reading)*: I-5, Cannon Road exit . . . MOM: We love you so much, honey.
SON:	S - So, this is the whole gift?
MOM & DAD:	MOM: Oh, of course not . . .

DAD:	Noooooo
SON:	No. *(relieved - laughing)*
MOM & DAD:	DAD *(sympathetically with a smile)*: **For crying out loud.** MOM: **George, open your wallet.**
SON:	*(happy)* **Oh, you guys . . .**
DAD:	Here you go.
MOM:	Surprise.
SON:	*(incredulous)* **A bus token.**
MOM:	To get you to Toyota Carlsbad. *(Jingle fades in)*
DAD:	Look at his face, I think he's going to cry . . .
MOM:	We really love you, honey . . .
DAD:	Yes we do, we really do . . . *(continuing under SON)*
MOM:	Let's all have some cake . . .
SON:	*(matter-of-factly with disbelief)* **A bus token.**
DAD:	Chocolate, my favorite . . .
JINGLE:	TOYOTA CARLSBAD
ANNCR:	Toyota Carlsbad. I-5, Cannon Road exit, Car Country, Carlsbad.

RED BULL ENERGY DRINK

Title: "Frog Prince," TV :30
Agency: VitroRobertson.
USP: "Red Bull Gives You Wings."
Target audience: Adult men and women.
Style: Humorous; fast conversational with attitude.
Characters: Princess is a female searching for her prince charming with excitement and anticipation. Frog/Prince is a male character of a frog who turns into a prince with emotional hangups.
Copy Notes: This is one of seven scripts created for a United States regional television ad campaign introducing Red Bull Energy Drink. These spots were the result of ad-libbed performances by improvisational actors creating story lines for animated commercials produced in Europe. The basic story line for this script is that of a princess finding her frog/prince

and the prince, who has a problem with commitment, flying away after drinking a can of Red Bull.

Both characters have a shift in attitude during the spot. The frog/prince initially welcomes the change from frog to prince, but is not really interested in the princess. He quickly expresses his fear of commitment and runs (flies) away. The princess is excited about finding her Prince Charming and feels saddened, frustrated and rejected when the frog/prince leaves her. (Those frog/prince types are all alike!)

FROG/PRINCE: (AS FROG) Ribbit, Ribbit.

PRINCESS: Single male frog looking for a princess, here I am!

FROG/PRINCE: Nice bangs.

PRINCESS: Oh, I really want to kiss your shiny green lips.

FROG/PRINCE: That won't be allowed, but I could use a Red Bull. It's an energy drink, and it lifts up your body and your mind. Do you have one of those?

PRINCESS: Yeah, I have some right here. Enjoy! It's yummy!

FROG/PRINCE: Ooooh. Thank you. (vocalized glug, glug sound of drinking) Heh, Heh, Heh. . .

(FROG CHANGES TO PRINCE AFTER DRINKING)

PRINCESS: Oh, my goodness. You're everything I ever dreamed of. Your red hair, your big nose.

FROG/PRINCE: (OVERLAPPING PRINCESS) Thank you. (FROG PRINCE SPROUTS WINGS — PRINCESS TRIES TO KEEP FROG/PRINCE FROM FLYING AWAY)
I. . . gotta go. Don't pull on me. Don't try and change me. Look, you know, I'm so scared of commitment I can't even be with myself!

(FROG/PRINCE FLIES AWAY)

PRINCESS: Wait — can't we just be friends? Red Bull gives you wings. Jerk!

11

Character Copy

Vocalizing Characters

Most character and animation voices are an exaggeration of specific vocal characteristics or attitudes, which enable the performer to create an appropriate vocal sound for the character. In some cases, a character voice can be difficult to sustain for long periods of time. Be careful not to overexert or injure yourself when doing character voices, especially when it is for a talking inanimate object or some other unusual character.

It can be tempting to force a vocal sound or attitude in a attempt to create a voice. A forced voice is rarely the most effective, is difficult to sustain and can actually cause physical damage to your vocal cords. The most effective character voices are those that emphasize or exaggerate the attitudes and emotions of the character you are portraying.

ANIMATION AND CHARACTER VOICES

Character and story analysis are most important with this type of copy. Many factors will affect the voice of the character, so the more information you can uncover about your character, the easier it will be to find its true voice. Since animation and character work can be in the form of single-voice or dialog copy — and the voice may have many special attributes — all the principles of good voice-acting apply even more here.

Consistency is extremely important in character voice work. When you find the character's voice, lock it into your memory and keep the proper attitude and quality of sound throughout the script, adapting your character's voice when the mood of the script changes. The important thing here is to avoid allowing the sound of your character to *drift*. To make your character believable and real to the audience, the quality of the voice must not change from the beginning of the script to the end. Consistency is especially important in animation work because sessions can be lengthy and a script can be recorded out of sequence over a period of several days.

Most animation voice-actors have a repertoire of several voices. A typical session may begin with one voice, followed by lines for a different voice later on. After lunch, they may do lines for yet another voice and then go back to record more lines for a character they did earlier in the day. This sort of schedule means character voice-actors must be extremely versatile and must be able to accurately repeat and sustain voice characterizations. These demands on character voice-actors make animation work a challenging niche to break into, and one of the most creative in voice-over.

In addition to voices and sounds for animation, character voice work can also include dialects, regional accents and even celebrity imper-sonations. Special accents and dialects require an ability to mimic a sound or attitude that is familiar to a portion of the listening audience. Usually, this mimicking is a *stylized* interpretation and doesn't necessarily have to be 100 percent accurate unless the character is represented as being authentic to a region or culture. In this case, to give the character believability, vocal accuracy is important. Most of the time, however, a slight exaggeration of certain regional vocal traits tends to give the character attitude and personality. Personal familiarization with the culture, region or dialect is also helpful.

Celebrity voice impersonations are often the most challenging because the celebrities are usually well known. The voice-actor's job is to create a voice that offers recognition of the celebrity, yet hints at being just a bit different. Celebrity impersonations are usually done in the context of a humorous commercial in which some aspect of the celebrity's personality or vocal styling is exaggerated or used as a device for communicating the message. Any commercial using a voice that represents a known person must have a disclaimer stating that the celebrity's voice is impersonated. As long as the voice is recognizable, this is a legal requirement whether or not the persons name is included in the copy.

In most cases, if a producer wants an extremely accurate celebrity voice, they will hire the celebrity. It may cost more to hire the actual person behind the voice, but the increased credibility is often worth it. Also, a disclaimer is not required if the real person is performing.

FINDING YOUR VOICE

Begin creating a character's voice by doing a thorough character analysis to discover as much as you can about him or her (or it) and the story. Based on the copy, make the decisions and commit to who you are talking to and if your character has any special accent or attitude. Finally, decide where in your body the character's voice will come from.

Visualize the voice coming from a specific location in your body and work with the copy until the voice *feels* right. Use your choices about the character's physical size and shape to help you localize the voice in your body. A voice coming from the top of your head might sound small and tiny; a voice from deep in the chest may sound big and boomy. The following list includes some physical locations and their associated vocal sounds:

top of head (tiny)	under tongue (sloppy)	nose (nasal)
behind eyes (nasal)	diaphragm (strong)	chest (boomy)
top of cheeks (bright)	loose cheeks (mushy)	throat (raspy)
front of mouth (crisp)	back of throat (breathy)	stomach (low)

Practice different voices with different attitudes. Use computer clip art, comic strips and other drawings to get ideas for character voices. Record yourself doing a variety of voices and listen to your tapes. If all of your voices sound the same, you need to work on range and characterization.

Tips for Character and Animation Copy

Character voice work can be challenging, but lots of fun. Use the following tips and suggestions to help find your character's voice.

- Understand your character and the situation. Remember that acting is reacting. In animation, you often must make up what you are reacting to.

- Discover who the audience is and understand how the audience will relate to the character.

- Maintain a consistent voice throughout the copy and be careful not to injure your voice by stretching too far to create a character. It is better to pull back a little and create a voice that can be maintained rather than push too hard for a voice you can only sustain for one or two pages.

- If a drawing, photo or picture of the character is available, use it as a tool to discover the personality of the character.

- Use your *physical-ness* to take on the physical characteristics of the character. This will help you find the right voice.

- Find the place in your body from which the voice will come.

Character and Animation Scripts

As you work with the following scripts, you might find it interesting to read through the script before reading the Copy Notes provided for each one. Come up with your own interpretation for attitude, pacing, character and performance, then read through the copy notes to see how close you came to what the producers of these projects intended. These scripts are reproduced as closely as possible to the original copy, including typos, grammatical errors and awkward phrasing.

CALIFORNIA DENTAL ASSOCIATION

Title: "Hunger Strike," :60 Radio
Agency: Hoffman/Lewis, San Francisco
USP: Preventive dental care promoted by a self-proclaimed dental advocate.
Target audience: Health-conscious adults.
Style: Serious tone; somewhat tongue-in-cheek delivery.
Character: Determined, self-proclaimed spokesperson.
Copy Notes: Copy is delivered as though a letter is being read out loud as it is typed. Matter-of-fact delivery with a serious tone to contrast the off-beat, humorous content of the letter. A sound effect of typing underscores the entire spot. No music.

This is just one of a series of radio commercials featuring Harry J. Krinsky. This character is constantly offering his suggestions for promoting preventive dental care, and takes his ideas very seriously, even though there is always an off-beat twist. This script gives you an opportunity to explore different attitudes as you look for the one that will best *sell* the message.

The humor in this copy comes from the character's attitude as he leads the audience toward an apparently serious subject. As the character starts to explain his ultimatum, the listener begins to realize that things may not be quite as expected.

AVO: Dear California Dental Association:

My name is Harry J. Krinsky and I am writing to lend a hand to your noble cause. How brave the California Dental Association is to champion preventive dental care in a world so reluctant and, I'll say it, downright frightened of going to the dentist. But, my friends, you are not alone. The whales have Greenpeace. The rainforest has that crunchy ice cream. And the California Dental Association has Harry J. Krinsky. Now, desperate times beget desperate measures. So until every man, woman and child in

California agrees to save their teeth and see their dentist at least twice a year, Harry J. Krinsky will not eat. No food, no water. Well, maybe water. And popcorn. All right, water, popcorn, peanut butter and jelly. And bread. I hungrily await the happy news of more frequent dental visits. Until then I am,

Harry J. Krinsky
Dental Advocate

JIFFY LUBE

Title: "Book of Lube/in The Beginning," Rev #2, Radio :50/:10 Tag
Agency: The Fuller Group — Writers: Julie Prendiville and Bob Peluso; Creative Director: Boni Peluso; Producer: Bob Peluso.
USP: "Southern California's Number 1 Oil Change." Jiffy Lube is more experienced and faster than the competition and guarantees its work.
Target audience: Men and women who drive.
Style: Serious tone.
Character: Conservative "preacher" delivering a sermon
Copy Notes: Here's a great opportunity to have fun creating a stereotyped character. Recall memories of sermons you have experienced and use those memories to recreate the style of a conservative preacher. This script should be delivered in a soft, very matter-of-fact style.

The style of a Southern gospel or fire-and-brimstone preacher would probably be too harsh, although it might be an interesting style to experiment with. There are lots of places here to use inflection and emphasis to punctuate the copy. There are also several opportunities to vary the pace to create visual images in the listener's imagination.

The :10 live announcer tag is intended to be read by radio station DJs as the commercial airs. The idea behind a live announcer tag is to create a local identification with the advertiser and provide localized information.

The problem with live announce tags is that most DJ's are not voice-actors, and their delivery of the live tag sometimes can be counter-productive to the overall effectiveness of the commercial. A high-quality performance of a creative script, followed by a poorly delivered live tag that sounds "read," can be a reason for the listener to change stations or be turned-off by the message.

Even though the tag is giving details and serves to wrap-up the commercial, it should still be performed in an interesting manner, not just read as words on a page. The tag should not be done in the same character or attitude as the body of the spot, but should be more in the character of a spokesperson for the advertiser. Talking to the listener throughout the tag will help keep it interesting.

MAN:

The Book of Lube. Chapter One.
In the beginning, there was a place where the car was worshipped above all. And it was called Jiffy Lube. The people rejoiced of fast, professional service and no appointments. They drove there, in well, droves to keep safe their warranties and their engines humming. For there, at Jiffy Lube, transmission fluid was as plentiful as milk and the Pennzoil flowed like honey. But then false lubes descended like locusts. Multiplying faster than evil bunnies. (Oooh) There were Rapid Lubes and You-Name-It Lubes. But the people were not fooled. For neither were those places as experienced as Jiffy Lube. Nor as fast. There was a place that gave the people a guarantee. And it was Jiffy Lube. And it was good.
ANNCR: Jiffy Lube. We wrote the book of lube.

(:10 Live Anncr.):   Southern California's daily driving conditions demand the best care for your car. Jiffy Lube provides this service to thousands of cars every day. Jiffy Lube. Southern California's number one oil change.

NBC 7/39 NEWS AT 4

Title: "Expensive Homes Day 1," TV :30
Agency: NBC 7/39 Direct — Creative Services
USP: "Coverage You Can Count On."
Target audience: Adult men and women.
Style: Upbeat.
Character: Robin Leach type — in the best "Lifestyles of the Rich and Famous" style of delivery.
Copy notes: This script is a TV promo for a ratings period news feature series on expensive homes. The obvious choice for voice talent was to either hire someone who could do a realistic impersonation of Robin Leach (host of *Lifestyles of the Rich and Famous*), or actually hire Robin Leach, himself. Since the promo was going to be produced in the style of a *Lifestyles* program (complete with similar music), the choice was made to book Mr. Leach for the session.

Having the real celebrity do the commercial gave credibility to the program and allowed the producer to include the unique nondisclaimer "Celebrity Voice NOT Impersonated." The session for this commercial was done as a phone patch, with Mr. Leach recorded on DAT at a studio in Los

Angeles while being directed by the producer via telephone from San Diego.

Note that there are three different versions for this promo. The performer would either do the complete script for one version, then *pick-up* only the lines for the alternate versions after getting a good read on the body of the copy. Or they might do the first complete line for one version, then repeat for the other versions before going on to the body of the script. The same process would be repeated for the three version mentions at the end of the script. A third option would be for the voice talent to perform the entire script for each of the three versions. The session with Mr. Leach was done in three takes using only one version, followed by pick-ups for the alternate version lines at the top and bottom.

If you are not familiar with Robin Leach, his delivery is very "in-your-face," with a quality of extreme enthusiasm. His delivery style is one of almost shouting, but not quite, with a wide vocal range and consistent dynamic range (loud volume). Mr. Leach is one of very few personalities who does only one voice — his! He has managed to capitalize on his style to create a highly recognizable voice.

One other interesting aspect about this script is the fact that his name is not mentioned. Mentioning his name in the copy would imply that Mr. Leach personally endorsed the TV station and the news program, and that personal endorsement would have been very expensive. The producer's decision to use only his easily recognized voice without mentioning his name saved the cost of an endorsement, eliminated the requirement for a disclaimer, and still achieved the desired credibility.

Monday (Tomorrow) (Today) only at 4.
Only on NBC 7-39
You'll see San Diego's most expensive homes!
And talk about rich!
Imagine this.
The country's BIGGEST residential pool!
Or a getaway high atop a mountain.
Or how about your very own racetrack!
One look at these exquisite digs will have you begging for more!
It's definitely a case of money is no object as you'll see on
"San Diego's Most Expensive Homes!"
Monday (Tomorrow) (Today) only at 4
only on NBC 7-39.
Coverage You Can Count On.
Celebrity Voice NOT Impersonated.

NBC 7/39 NEWS AT 11

Title: "Pet Problems — Day 1," Radio :30
Agency: NBC 7/39 Direct — Creative Services
USP: "Coverage You Can Count On."
Target audience: Adult men and women who love pets.
Style: Upbeat, friendly.
Character: Spokes-dog. A talking dog discusses various pet problems and tells listeners where to get the solutions.
Copy Notes: The first two lines of the script give a big clue about the character. Since the character is a dog, it becomes necessary for the voice-actor to incorporate "dog-like" qualities into the delivery. The performer who did this spot actually did little barks and growls at appropriate places in the copy. The spokes-dog could easily be either male or female, although the actual commercial used a male voice. A light, fun and bouncy musical underscore set the mood and animal sound effects of dogs barking and cat meows were interspersed throughout the spot.

Ruff.
I am Spokes-dog here.
Here to solve Rover and Muffy's problems.
    (sfx)
The chewed up slippers.
Stained carpets.
Scratched up sofas.
And the barking!
    (sfx)
Well, Tonight ONLY at 11 and ONLY on my favorite station NBC 7-39
    (ruff, ruff)
you'll see how to gain the upper paw and have PURRRFECT pets.
Pets: Most Common Problems, Most Common Solutions.

Tonight only at 11 on NBC 7-39. Coverage you can count on.
Take it from me - this stuff works!

ZOOLOGICAL SOCIETY OF SAN DIEGO

Title: "Treasure Your Trash — A Recycling Story," Puppet show.
Agency: Zoological Society of San Diego ("ZSSD") — Direct
Writer: Robin S. Senecal
USP: "Everything old is new again."
Target audience: Children of all ages.
Style: Upbeat, friendly, very conversational.
Characters: A variety of puppet characters tell the story (characters are defined within the script).
Copy Notes: The San Diego Zoo frequently produces special programs for its Children's Zoo and educational outreach. The script that follows is for a recycling-themed puppet show to be performed in the Zoo's amphitheater.

With projects such as this, it is not uncommon for the writer to include special references or "inside" jokes. The writer of this script is a Children's Zoo Senior Keeper and one of the characters she created is "Madam Anna Lida — the psychic recycler." The inside part about this is that the first character to appear is a worm, who sets up the story, and *annelid* is the technical term for a worm — and worms play a major role in ecological recycling. Another subtle reference is the character "Phyllis, the Dill pickle jar," playing on the similarity to the name of the comedienne Phyllis Diller.

Each of the characters in this story has a unique personality and interacts with the other characters. Although this script was written as a puppet show, these could just as easily be animated cartoon characters. A few of the characters have solo singing parts, and all characters sing chorus for two songs. The entire 11-minute program was preproduced with all voices, music and sound effects. This made performing the program much easier, because different people might be required to play any of the roles at any time.

(Spring music and the sound of tweeting birds. A small worm appears in front of the curtain.)

WIGGY: It's a beautiful day, isn't it? The sun is shining, the birds are singing . . . and the trash man is making his rounds. Every year we generate about 208 million tons of trash and garbage. Just think, that's the approximate weight of 35 million elephants!! Or 135 million rhinos!! Don't worry, I checked it out! Or — anyway, most of this waste goes into landfills, but we're running out of room. What can we do? We can recycle. Now, most of you already recycle your aluminum cans, but what about the rest of the trash? Keep watching and you'll find out. Uh, oh, here comes Hank the garbage man — I'd better skedaddle! *(He disappears.)*

SCENE 1 — *The scene begins with the sound of trash can lids rattling, then a large garbage truck engine engages and revs. Continue with the motor sound of a truck moving and shifting gears. The puppets appear on cue in front of the curtain. They bounce up and down a bit to simulate the movement of the truck. After a few moments, a whispered voice is heard . . .*

RUSTY *(the Tin Can)*: Benny . . . . . Benny, are you here? It's me Rusty!

BENNY *(the Banana Peel — with somewhat of a "tough-guy" inflection)*: Yeah, Rusty, I'm here. What about the rest of the guys?

PHYLLIS *(the Dill Pickle Jar — with a high voice and a heavy Brooklyn accent)*: It's me, Phyllis. I'm here but wouldn't you know it, I broke a nail! Where's Mac?

MAC *(the Junk Mail - with a snooty, condescending accent)*: I have never been so ill treated in my life! The indignity of it all! Well, I'm here, wherever "here" is. It's just too impossible to tell because it's dark and stuffy and *(he takes a few sniffs)*, it smells a bit like sulpher.

PHYLLIS: I always knew youse guys was a bunch of rotten eggs!! *(she gives a few loud laughs, then everyone laughs.)*

RUSTY: All right guys, all right, this is serious. We've got to figure out where we are.

BENNY: Or where we're going, since we seem to be moving.

MAC: *(excitedly)*: This is is at last! Oh, I just knew it would be happening soon! This must be a special delivery mail truck and I will soon be hand carried, as is befitting my importance, to the mailbox of a fabulous mansion!

(Everyone looks around at each other)

RUSTY: Should we tell him? *(There is a pause)*

EVERYONE *(in unison as they shake their heads)*: Naaaaaaaaahhhhhhh!

*(Sound of **brakes screeching and engine shuts off**. All is quiet.)*

PHYLLIS: Hey, we've stopped!

*(A few seconds of **silence**.)*

RUSTY *(a bit nervously)*: It's too quiet.

MAC *(beginning to panic)*: I don't like this at ALL! I have a very nasty feeling about thiiiiiiiiiiis!

*(The sound of a **hydraulic jack** begins. At that moment, there is the sound of a **dump truck bed moving** and lots of noise as **trash is dumped** onto the ground.)*

EVERYONE: AAAAAAAAHHHHHHHHHHHHHHH!!!!!!!! *(The puppets move wildly is if they're falling and disappear downward.)*

(The curtain opens)

SCENE 2 — *At the city dump. There is a large sign that says simply, "CITY DUMP." In the background, you can see mounds of trash. The puppets reappear shaking their heads and moaning and complaining in various ways.*

PHYLLIS (*looking around*): What a dump!

BENNY (*incredulously*): Look at that sign, guys; we ARE at the dump. I can't believe it, we've ended up at the city dump with the useless trash and garbage.

PHYLLIS (*very dejected*): Wow, the dump. I guess I thought I had more class. I always hoped I'd be recycled into something wonderful and exciting instead of winding up wallowing at the dump.

RUSTY: Recycled!? Come on, Phyllis, look at us. It's not like we're aluminum cans or 2 liter plastic bottles. Everyone recycles those and even gets MONEY back. I'm a can of pork and beans, you're a dill pickle jar and Benny — Benny's not even a banana — only the peel. We're just the riff-raff!

MAC: (*sputtering with indignation*): Riff-raff . . . . . . RIFF-RAFF!! **I** am not riff-raff! I'll have you know I am a very important document!

PHYLLIS: You? You're just junk mail.

MAC (*now highly insulted and gesticulating wildly*): Junk mail??!! Did you say JUNK MAIL???? I'll have you know I am an extremely valuable piece of U.S. mail. Just read; go on, read me!!!

EVERYONE (*reading in unison*): "MYRTLE FLUGENMEYER, YOU ARE OUR NEXT TEN MILLION DOLLAR WINNER." (*everyone looks at each other*)

RUSTY: Should we tell him? (*There is a pause*)

EVERYONE (*in unison as they shake their heads*): Naaaaaaaahhhhhhhh!!

BENNY: So, what are we gonna do now?

PHYLLIS: Do? What can we do besides lie around at the dump 'til the end of our days?

(*Sound of birds tweeting and strains of spring music fill the air. A little worm appears.*)

WIGGY (*looking up at everyone and trying to get their attention*): Excuse me, excuse me . . . but maybe I can help.

RUSTY (*looking around*): What was that?

WIGGY (*standing upright with a **stretching sound** *): Down here!!

MAC (*with disdain*): It's a WORM!

WIGGY: That's right, Wig L. Worm at your service. All my friends call me Wiggy. I couldn't help hearing your troubles, but I think I can help.

PHYLLIS (*looking down*): Well, honey, that's very sweet of you but you're awfully small and things do look pretty hopeless.

WIGGY: Well, lots of small creatures accomplish very big things. And as for your situation looking hopeless, someone famous once said, "It ain't over 'till it's over!" I think you should go see my auntie, Madam Anna Lida. She's the psychic recycler. She can look into her crystal ball and tell you what your future can be. You may not be aluminum cans but I'll just bet it's possible for <u>you</u> to be recycled, too!

BENNY: Well, what have we got to lose?

WIGGY: That's the spirit! Just remember my auntie's motto, "Everything old is new again."

(*As the curtains close behind the puppets, the song "Everything Old Is New Again" begins to play. **REMOVE THE CITY DUMP SCENE** The puppets sing and dance to the music as they travel to the recycling parlor.*)

WIGGY (*singing*):   Your troubles cause anguish
                  If at the city dump you have to languish.
                  You should see my auntie then,
                  'Cause everything old is new again.

                  Things are not as bad as they seem,
                  To be recycled is your fondest dream.
                  At Madam Anna's, I will give you a clue,
                  You can become something useful and new!

ALL (*singing*):   Don't throw your trash away!
                  You may need it for another day.
                  Recycling will begin
                  And everything old will be new again.

(*Music stops and Wiggy disappears as the curtains open on the new scene.*)

SCENE 3 — Madam Anna Lida's parlor

(*Everyone looks around and "Oohs and Aah's over the splendor.*)

RUSTY: This must be the place.

PHYLLIS: Oh, my, isn't this fancy! Such class!

(*Madam Anna Lida appears to the shimmery sound of tinkling bells.*)

MADAM: Welcome, welcome to all. I am Madam Anna Lida, the psychic recycler. My nephew tells me you are unhappy with where life has taken you.

MAC: Humph! You can say <u>that</u> again!

MADAM: You feel there is more you can become. There is hope. Perhaps Madam can help; many new processes allow trash to become treasure.

(*The table with crystal ball appears in a waft of smoke.*)

MADAM: Gather around; we will gaze into the crystal ball to see what your recycled future holds. (*Everyone gathers around. Shimmery sound as Madam as Madam gazes into the ball.*) Rusty the tin can, as I gaze deep into the crystal ball I see beneath the tin coating is a heart of steel; I see strength and support; I see a high flying future for you! You may now enter the recycler.

RUSTY: Hey, that sounds pretty good! See ya around guys! (*Rusty exits the stage. There is a **noisemaker sound, a "whee" whistle, a bell, and a puff of smoke**.*)

MADAM (***shimmery sound***): Benny banana peel, your future is dark (*Benny moans*), but do not despair. Out of the darkness I also see you will bring new growth and beauty to the world.

(*Benny exits and again the **sound of the recycler** is heard. Benny reappears in a puff of smoke as a bag of mulch.*)

BENNY: Wow! Look at me! I'm not garbage anymore, I'm a bag of mulch!

PHYLLIS: That's wonderful! You'll help all the plants and flowers grow and blossom! I'm so excited, I'll go next!

MAC: After me, after me! Madam, what do you see in the crystal ball?

MADAM (***shimmery sound***): Mac, the junk mail, I see a long journey. From this journey you will emerge as some of the most important and sought-after paper in the world. I can see that you will really clean up.

MAC (*very happy and excited*): Yes, Yes, most important! I always knew it! Where is that recycler! Out of my way! (*Mac pushes past everyone to the recycler. **Recycler sounds** and Mac emerges in a puff of smoke as a roll of toilet paper. No one says anything but Mac is excited.*) Look at me everyone! I am the most important paper in the world! I will be sought after! I will clean up! This is wonderful!

BENNY: Should we tell him? (*There is a pause.*)

EVERYONE: Naaaaaaahhhhhh!

PHYLLIS: At last it's my turn. Madam Anna, please look into the crystal ball and tell me my future.

MADAM (***shimmery sound***): Phyllis, the dill pickle jar, I see beauty and grace; I see high class living. Life for you will truly be a bowl of cherries.

PHYLLIS: Did ya hear that? I'm gonna be high class! (*She rushes offstage. **Sound of recycler** and she appears in a puff of smoke as a jar of maraschino cherries.*)

BENNY: Phyllis, is that really you? You're graceful; you're beautiful! Why, you're a jar of maraschino cherries!

PHYLLIS (*Her voice is different, similar to Eva Gabor*): Yes, Benny, it is I. Dahling, this is so marvelous, don't you think? I am SO happy. If only my friends could see me now!

(*Song — "If My Friends Could See Me Now" introduction begins to play.*)

PHYLLIS: (*singing*):   If they could see me now,
A work of art in glass.
A maraschino cherry jar
Has lots of class!

BENNY (*singing*):   To help the flowers grow
Is my specialty.

MAC (*singing*):   I'm most important now,
I have dignity!

ALL (*singing*):   All I can say is WOW!
With joy we're gonna jump.
We thought we'd end our days
Down at the city dump!

We've been recycled, HOLY COW!
They'd never believe it
If my friends could see me now!

(**Music continues** but only instrumental. A potted plant appears.)

BENNY: Look guys, a potted plant. Let's see what a little mulch will do. (*He disappears behind the plant and it immediately blossoms.*)

EVERYONE: Wow!

MAC: Say, whatever happened to Rusty?

(*Sound of a **jet engine** as plane flies overhead trailing a banner that says "PLEASE RECYCLE".*)

PHYLLIS: There he is! Talk about high flying, he's part of a classy jet airplane!

(**Music continues** for a few moments. The puppets dance, confetti is tossed and **tweeting birds** are heard as Wiggy appears in front of the curtain.)

WIGGY: So, you see, in recycling everything old is new again. And we're getting better. We now recycle over one-fourth of our solid waste. But we can do even more. Next time you're ready to throw something into the trash can, think of Rusty and Phyllis and Benny and Mac, and keep recycling!! See ya!

(*Music plays to big finish*)

12

Corporate and
Narrative Copy

Sales presentations, marketing videos, in-house training tapes, point-of-purchase videos, film documentaries and many other types of projects all fall into the category of corporate and narrative. Frequently, these scripts are written for the eye and not the ear. That simply means they are written to be read and not spoken.

Writers of corporate and narrative copy are often not experienced writers, or usually write copy for print. There are exceptions to this, but overall you can expect copy in this category to be pretty dry. Corporate and narrative copy is often full of statistics, complex names or phrases and terminology specific to a business or industry. These can be a challenge for even an experienced voice-over performer.

As you perform a corporate or narrative script, you are still performing a character telling a story, just as for any other type of copy. You should know who your character is, who you are talking to, and what you are talking about. You also need to find a way to create an image of knowledge and authority for your character. What is it about your character that gives him the authority to be speaking the words? Is your character the owner of the company, a satisfied customer, the company's top sales person, or a driver for one of the delivery trucks? To create an image of credibility, figure out an appropriate role for your character and commit to your choice.

A corporate or narrative script for a video project might have several on-camera performers. These are often professional actors, but may include employees of the business. There also may be several voice-over performers for different sections of the script. Many scripts in this category are written for a single voice-over performer, but there may be two or more performers alternating lines or doing different sections. There may also be some dialog sections of the script. The complexity of a corporate script will vary greatly depending on the intended purpose and the company's budget.

It is sometimes more challenging to deliver a script of this nature in a conversational manner, but it is possible. Facts, numbers, unusual terms and complex names all contribute to a presentation more like a lecture than a conversation. However, the information is important, and the audience must be able to relate to the presentation as well as clearly understand what they hear. If the presentation of the information (your performance) is interesting and entertaining, the effectiveness of the communication will be much better.

Tips for Performing Corporate and Narrative Copy

The following tips and suggestions will help you with corporate and narrative copy.

- Talk *to* the audience on their level, not *at* them, even though the script might be full of facts, statistics and unusual names or phrases.

- Take your time delivering the copy. Unlike radio or TV copy, which must be done within a specific time, there is rarely any time limitation for corporate and narrative copy.

- Be clear on the facts and pronunciation of complex words. These are important to the client and need to be correct and accurate.

- Slow your delivery or pace in sections where there is important information, speak more quickly in other parts of the script.

- If you are alternating lines with another performer, and the script is not written for dialog, be careful to not overlap or step on the other performer's lines. Keep your delivery more open for this type of script, unless the producer specifically requests that you tighten your delivery.

Corporate and Narrative Scripts

As you work with the following scripts, you might find it interesting to read through the script before reading the Copy Notes provided for each one. Come up with your own interpretation for attitude, pacing, character and performance, then read through the notes to see how close you came to what the producers of these projects intended. The following scripts are reproduced as accurately as possible, including typos, grammatical errors and awkward phrasing.

COULTER CORPORATION

Title: "Introducing AcT," Multimedia Presentation for General Medical National Sales Meeting, version 1.

Agency: Hansell 'Maginations

USP: "The first family of hematology analyzers — imagine the possibilities."

Target audience: Medical industry sales representatives and buyers.

Style: Part one is game show announcer style; part two is authoritative spokesperson.

Characters: ANNCR starts with a "show-biz" master of ceremonies style and shifts into a game show host. Male and female characters are game show contestants.

Copy Notes: This multiscreen multimedia presentation was designed to be presented numerous times during the course of a single day. The preproduced portion had interaction with live actors who had done some of the introductory voice-over (not included here) as well as the game show contestant voices. At the end of the produced video, the program moved to live action for the final two minutes. The entire production was underscored with music and game show sound effects where appropriate.

The message is designed for a very specific audience in the medical industry and contains a few long sentences with a few technical terms. The first sentence is a good test of your breath control and enunciation. Try reading the line out loud at a constant volume and energy level. If you run out of air, you probably need to work on breath control and increasing your breathing capacity.

Two sections of this six-minute program are excerpted here. The first section is an example of a multiple-voice corporate script in which there is no interaction between characters. For the second part of the script, the announcer continues the message of Coulter's superiority with a monologue in a more authoritative and businesslike style, shifting out of his game show host voice. It is important to maintain an attitude of knowledge and authority, even during the game show segment, in order to establish credibility with the audience.

SHOW BEGINS — *MUSIC is bold and dynamic, loud and attention-getting.*

ANNCR: And now, Coulter (*pronounced Coal-ter*), the same company that brought you the ONYX high volume analyzer and MD series of medium volume analyzers, introduces the first inexpensive, low volume hematology analyzer.

For the fourth time in the last 5 years, Coulter, the world leader in hematology analysis, introduces its newest analyzer, designed for the alternate care market . . .

The AcT (ACK tee)

MUSIC is exciting and dynamic, building to climax.

Coulter brings you a complete family of hematology analyzers with a product to fit every customer's needs.

MUSIC TRANSITIONS TO GAME SHOW STYLE

ANNCR: (*game show host voice*) For years, you have heard doctors say they would be interested in performing laboratory tests. Except they: Don't have the space

GAME SHOW MALE: Even Shaquille O'Neal's shoe is bigger.

ANNCR: Can't afford the expense.

GAME SHOW FEMALE: Under $259 — Are you out of your mind?

ANNCR: Don't have enough volume.

GAME SHOW MALE: It takes just one-a-day.

(*part two*) * * * * * *

ANNCR: The most frequently ordered laboratory test is the CBC or complete blood count consisting of a Red cell count, White cell count and Platelet count. Now your doctors can have the convenience of this valuable diagnostic tool at their fingertips.

The AcT 8 offers an 8 parameter CBC. The AcT 10 has the added option of a lymphocyte count, at no additional charge.

The AcT is designed to take less than two feet of counter space. Unlike any other hematology instrument, the AcT reagent packs take up no additional space because they are placed directly inside the instrument.

QUALCOMM CORPORATE BUSINESS COMMUNICATIONS

Title: "GSM Network Over CDMA Air Interface Site, Newbury, UK." Video script, Draft 11 — Revised FINAL Draft
Agency: In-house.
USP: N/A

Target audience: Corporate executives and engineering department.
Style: Informative.
Character: Narrator is very matter-of-fact, reporting with *NO* marketing feel.
Copy Notes: The purpose of this in-house video was to document the successful outcome of tests for a new wireless telephone system configuration. The copy is typical of corporate presentations. It is very dry and contains a considerable number of acronyms and terms that are unique to the business and are meaningful only to the intended audience. When working with copy of this sort, the voice-actor must find a way to speak with authority, projecting an understanding of what is being said — and keep the material interesting. As the speaker of the words, it is implied that you are an expert on the subject, and you must create a character who clearly projects that image.

Even if you have absolutely no idea what the subject is about, you must have a mind-set and attitude that you know everything there is to know about it. If your mind-set and attitude are anything less, any confusion or lack of understanding of the subject, or of what you are saying, will come through in your voice. Your insecurity will be sensed by the audience, affecting their ability to accept and assimilate the information being presented. It is easy to fall into a trap of delivering this type of copy in a monotone, but that must be avoided at all cost. Acronyms and inside terms can be pronounced either as words or by their individual letters, depending on the term and direction from the producer.

For this script, all acronyms are spelled out by their letters. The actual script for this project runs 23 pages and included detailed information about the video portion of the project. The following excerpt is taken from pages 1 through 6.

For the past year, QUALCOMM's engineering teams have been working on CDMA integration with GSM networks. A system trial to prove the integration feasibility was performed in 1997 in Newbury, England.

The main objective of the trial, was to demonstrate a CDMA radio access, on a GSM-MAP network over the standard A interface. There were no changes to the A interface, the GSM-MSC, HLR, or other GSM network equipment.

The trial verified all of the air interface benefits of CDMA in the GSM-CDMA configuration. It also demonstrated GSM network features including call waiting, call hold, conference calling, SMS, and GSM authentication. We hope you enjoy this program, and are as excited about the test results as we are.

As wireless communication becomes increasingly popular world-wide ... operators and equipment suppliers continue to investigate new technologies and new services to offer customers.

In 1997, QUALCOMM . . . the developer and leader in CDMA technology . . . in a joint effort with Vodafone — a leading GSM operator and service provider . . . tested a CDMA air-interface to a GSM network over the standard GSM A interface . . . in Newbury, England west of London.

The architecture configuration used in the GSM-CDMA trial system was implemented without any service interruptions to the GSM commercial system . . . This diagram shows the functional system architecture of the GSM-CDMA trial. (*1 beat pause*) The GSM-CDMA subsystems can be implemented without reconfiguring the entire system or existing GSM equipment. Standard QUALCOMM subscriber units were modified to operate with the GSM-CDMA system.

BTSs, RFFEs, and standard antennas were deployed on four pre-existing Vodafone cell sites . . . Canal House, Welford, Hermitage and Shaw.

All BTSs are standard, unmodified, 3 sector IS-95 CDMA commercial equipment at 1900 Megahertz. The Base Station Controller (BSC) . . . is located in Canal House, Hambridge Road in the MTX room. The BSC is the heart of the GSM-CDMA trial system. It allows a CDMA interface with a GSM-MAP network . . . withOUT modifications to the GSM network . . . while supporting GSM services and security features — including authentication.

Let's review each of the BSC components of the GSM-CDMA system in more detail.

QUALCOMM's QCP-1900 CDMA subscriber units were modified to include SIM card functionality, to allow full GSM subscriber services over the IS-95 CDMA air interface. The hardware configuration for the phone includes a standard CDMA handset with the addition of a SIM Interface Board - (SIB). The software for the phone simply removes the CDMA call management, mobility management, and user interface . . . and replaces them with equivalent GSM software and SIM control software.

The interworking function integrates the GSM software with the CDMA level 2 IS-95 software. This provides GSM signaling over an IS-95 air interface.

13

Your Demo Tape

Your demo tape is your best first opportunity to present your talents and abilities to talent agents, producers and other talent buyers. Many times, you will be booked for an audition or for a session simply based on something the producer hears in your demo. The purpose of a demo tape is to get you work!

Your Professional Calling Card

In the world of voice-acting, your demo tape is your calling card. It is your portfolio. It is your audio résumé. It is your letter of introduction. It is the single most important thing you *must* have if you are to compete in the world of voice-over.

Since your demo tape may directly result in bookings, it is extremely important that you be able to match the level of your demo performance when under the pressure of a session. It is quite easy for a studio to create a highly produced, yet misrepresentative, demo that gives the impression of an extremely talented and polished performer. If the performer's actual abilities are less that what is depicted on the demo, the shortcomings will be quickly revealed during a session.

I know of one voice-actor who was booked through an agent based solely on the demo tape. The tape sounded great and had logos of major television networks and other advertisers on its cover. The impression was that this performer had done a lot of work and was highly skilled.

The performance was recorded during an ISDN session in San Diego with the performer in a New York studio. A few minutes into the session, it became apparent that the voice-actor could not take direction and would not be able to perform to the caliber of the demo. The producer gracefully ended the session and a different voice-actor was hired to complete the session the following day. The producer refused to pay the talent agency's commission because she felt the talent agency had misrepresented the voice-actor's abilities. The original performer was never told that the session was unsatisfactory and actually sent a nice thank-you note to the producer. The performer did get paid, but the recording was never used.

It turned out that the agent had never worked directly with the performer, and had been promoting the person based solely on a highly produced demo. A few days later, it was learned that the performer was actually attempting to memorize the copy due to a problem with dyslexia that made it difficult to perform the lines as written.

The talent agent later apologized to the producer and mentioned that this performer had done some excellent self-marketing and presented a very professional image during the agent's interview. The only problem was that the performer had created a demo that clearly exceeded his actual abilities.

Let me say it again: You *must* be able to perform to the level of your demo when booked for a real session.

VERSATILITY IS YOUR SELLING TOOL

A good demo presents the performer in a wide range of styles, including a variety of examples showing different emotions, attitudes, characters and voices. Good actors can do dozens of different voices and characters because they are able to find a place in their body from which to center the character and place the voice. It is the range and variety of styles that keep a demo interesting and hold the listener's attention.

Every performer has a unique style, range and ability. It is these qualities that make each performer different. You need to capitalize on your strong points and present them in the best possible manner in your demo. The range of attitudes, emotions and characters you can express during a voice-over performance is your own vocal versatility. Your strongest, most dynamic and most marketable voice is called your *money voice*. This is the voice that will get you the work and may eventually become your trademark. Your other voices are icing on the cake but are necessary to clearly show your range and versatility.

Demo Tape Basics

The analog audio cassette continues to be the format of preference for voice-over demos although larger talent agencies will compile their talent demos into a CD format, usually creating separate CDs or sections for male and female talent. Many voice-actors will have separate demos that reflect their talents in several areas of voice work — commercial, narration, character, animation, and so on. These may be combined into a single demo, but more frequently each side of a tape is specialized: side 1 — commercial (singles, multiples and character), side 2 — narration. In the world of voice-acting, some major players market their various demos on a single CD. For someone who is just starting out, a CD is not practical, partly because of its high production cost, but mostly because a performer new to the business just doesn't have the credibility to support a CD demo.

DEMO DOS AND DON'TS

Plan the content of your demo carefully to include copy you can perform well and that is appropriate for the type of market you want to reach. A demo of commercial copy is not appropriate for a producer of corporate projects. And a demo of character and animation voices is not appropriate for a commercial producer.

Producers often listen to a demo tape with their finger poised on the eject button, ready to toss the tape in the trash. This is somewhat due to time constraints, but is largely due to the fact that dozens of poorly produced demos cross the desks of producers every day. Remember that producers make their decisions about a voice within the first 15 to 20 seconds of listening to a demo. If you are going to make it past that crucial first 15 seconds, your demo performance must be well-presented and highly skilled.

A good demo keeps the producer listening: It has entertainment value with a new surprise, emotional hook, acting technique, vocal variation or character twist happening about every 5 to 15 seconds. A good demo does not give the listener an opportunity to turn the tape off.

If you are just starting out, your demo should be focused on the type of voice work you do best. Here are some Dos and Don'ts for your first demo:

- Do include a wide range of variety in style and character. Keep the listener guessing as to what will happen next.

- Do keep each "clip" to only a single, concise statement or few brief sentences. You only have a brief time to catch and hold the listener's attention.

- Do focus on what you currently do best, then revise and prepare new demos as your talent grows and you acquire copies of projects you have worked on.

- Do keep your demo short. If the producer listening to your tape is going to make his or her decision in 15 seconds or less, you would be wise to have your strongest material in that first 15 seconds.

- Do start with just one or two very specific demos.

- Don't do a demo until you are ready. Make sure you have done your homework and have mastered voice-acting skills.

- Don't try to include material from too many different facets of voice work because this only detracts from the effectiveness of your demo.

- Don't think you can put a demo tape together at home and expect it to sound professional. A poor quality tape — in either performance or audio quality — is a waste of time and money.

You will be far better off with a solid 1-minute and 45 seconds of fast-moving entertaining material than with a slow-moving 2 minutes of uninteresting material lacking variety and range. As you gain a reputation and become more versatile, you can justify a longer demo. A number of voice-actors have produced CD demos that include anywhere from 5 to 8 short demos in specific categories. The length of the CDs vary from about 11 minutes to almost 20 minutes, but each category averages just over 2 minutes. Each short demo is well produced, moves quickly and features a different aspect of these performer's talents. The format of multiple demos on a single CD makes it easy for a producer to quickly find and listen to only the particular style he or she is interested in. However, the cost of producing and marketing a CD demo can easily reach several thousand dollars.

COMMERCIAL DEMOS

There are no hard-and-fast rules for producing a demo tape, but there are certain production techniques that consistently grab and hold listeners' attention. Commercial demo tapes are generally produced on a bell curve with the performer's *money voice* (the voice that sounds best and gets the voice-actor booked most often) at the beginning and end. In between are a variety of performance attitudes and styles that reflect the performer's range and abilities. Having the same voice at the beginning and end provides a reference point for the listener and gives him or her an opportunity to categorize the performer's vocal age and personality type.

A good tape will begin at a certain pace and pick up speed and intensity as it travels its course. At certain spots the pace should slow again to give the listener a chance to catch his or her breath, and then pick up once again. A demo tape needs to end on an uplifting, fun and positive note to leave the listener with a good feeling.

Commercial demos are among the most common, simply because radio and television commercials provide a large number of opportunities for voice-over work.

CHARACTER AND ANIMATION DEMOS

Character and animation demo tapes are often structured a bit differently and may include a number of character voices juxtaposed in an incongruous manner, or having a scripted conversation, to hold the listener's attention. For example, one character might have the line: "Our mattress makes all the difference." This might be followed by a totally different character voice saying: ". . . because we do amazing things with rocks and stones."

This form of character demo is called a *concept tape*. A clever scenario is introduced to provide a story or reason for the various characters to converse with one another. As the story continues, there will be changes in attitudes, pacing and character development. Concept tapes are challenging to write and must be thought out very carefully. When done well, concept demos can be quite effective and memorable. If done poorly, they will be "filed," never to be listened to again. Concept demos fall into one of two categories: extremely good and unbelievably stupid!

The most common method of producing a character demo is to place vocal excerpts randomly to demonstrate the widest possible versatility of vocal talents. A demo of this sort usually has a bell-curve structure similar to a commercial demo with changes of pacing and "wackiness" as it progresses.

CORPORATE AND NARRATIVE DEMOS

Corporate and industrial demos tend to contain copy that is somewhat longer than the copy in a commercial demo. The longer length of copy allows the producer time to more accurately assess your reading and delivery skills. It also gives them an opportunity to hear how you handle complex words, concepts and sentences. As with the other types of demo tapes, your money voice and strongest material should lead the demo, followed by a variety of styles, range and versatility. Narrative demos offer a good opportunity to use various microphone techniques, a range of delivery speeds and storytelling techniques to good advantage.

Ideally, demo tapes should be compiled from actual projects you have worked on. However, for the person just starting out, this is not possible. You will need to create your own copy and design a demo that will catch the listener's attention and hold it. Even working professionals sometimes need to make up copy to create a demo that really puts their voice in the spotlight. This can be a challenging task, but it can pay off big. The rest of this chapter and the next chapter will cover everything you need to know about demo tapes, from finding the copy to getting your demo recorded. You will also learn how to create your marketing campaign and get your demo into the hands of agents, producers and other talent-buyers.

Don't Do a Demo Until You Are Ready

Producing a demo before being ready is one of the biggest mistakes many people make when they are eager to get started in the voice-acting business. Producing your demo too soon may result in difficulty finding an agent who will represent you. Not to mention the fact that the presentation and performance quality is likely to be much less than is needed to be successful in this business. Producing your demo too soon is simply a waste of time and money, and potentially can affect your credibility as a performer later on. Remember the story of the dyslexic performer who had a wonderful demo, but who was unable to perform under the stress of a session.

Before you even think about having your demo tape done, make sure you have acquired the skills and good performing habits necessary to compete in this challenging business. Remember that there are a lot of other people trying to do the same thing as you. Anything you can do to improve your abilities and make your performing style just a bit unique will be to your advantage. Study your craft, learn acting skills and develop a plan to market yourself *before* you do your demo. Take classes — lots of classes!

Your demo tape should be professionally produced by someone who knows what they are doing. Don't think you can put a tape together at home and expect it to sound professional. Even if you have a home project studio, a sophisticated computer system, or have a friend who has a home studio, you still need the assistance of a good director. It is extremely difficult for one person to deal with both the engineering and performing aspects of producing a demo tape at the same time. You need to be focused on your performance and not dealing with any equipment.

You need a director who can listen to your performance objectively, help you stay focused and help get you in touch with the character in the copy. Performing effectively without a director, or by simply directing yourself, is very challenging. Although many professional voice-actors believe they don't need a director, all voice-actors do. In fact, they need a director to bring out their best work. Most working professionals will tell you that they perform much better when they have a good director who can guide them through their performance.

When you go to the studio to produce your demo, you should consider the session to be just like a real commercial recording session. You need to be able to get a good read, or performance, in three or four takes. If you consistently need more than six or seven takes to get the right delivery, you may not be ready to do your demo.

Become an expert at communicating with drama and emotion before you have your demo produced. Here are some of the things you need to keep in mind:

- **Study acting.** Acting is the key to an effective performance. Learn how to act and learn how to use your voice and body to express drama and emotional tension.

- **Do your exercises.** Set up a daily regimen for doing your voice exercises. Get into the habit of keeping your voice in top condition. Your voice is the "tool" of your trade — take care of it.

- **Take classes and workshops.** Have an attitude of always learning. You will learn something new from each class and workshop you take or repeat. The voice-over business is constantly adapting and new trends become popular each year. You need to be ready to adapt as new trends develop.

- **Read other books about voice-over.** Every author on this subject presents his or her material in a slightly different manner. You may also learn new techniques or get some fresh ideas from reading a variety of books on the subject.

- **Practice your skills and techniques.** When you are working on a piece of copy, rehearse your performance with an attitude of continually perfecting it. Have a solid understanding of the techniques you are using and polish your performance in rehearsal.

Producing Your Demo

Remember, doing your homework before going to the studio to produce your demo will save you time and money. Rehearse your copy with a stopwatch, and know how you want to deliver each script. Do a complete script analysis for each script. Make notes on your scripts about the character, attitude, and emotional hooks, as well as ideas for music style and sound effects if appropriate. Consider mic placement for each script. Mark off what you believe to be the strongest :10 to :15 of each script and consider a possible sequence for the demo. Be flexible enough to understand that this will probably change.

Ideally, you should find a director who can assist you with the production of your demo. Hiring a director will allow you to focus on your performance so you will not have to worry about the technical details of the session.

Above all, when you are in the studio recording your demo, have fun and enjoy the experience! Through the process of producing your demo, you will learn a lot about the production process and what really goes on behind the scenes in a recording studio.

HOW LONG SHOULD MY DEMO BE?

Your demo tape should be approximately 2 to 2½ minutes in length. This doesn't sound very long, but remember that the person listening to your tape usually decides if your voice performance is right for them within the first 15 to 20 seconds.

You should include about 15 to 20 short excerpts demonstrating your range and talents. The length of each clip will depend on its content, but on average should be between 6 and 15 seconds. The length of clips for narrative demos should be a bit longer (15 to 20 seconds) to provide a better presentation of long-form copy. The engineer or producer you hire to put your demo together should be able to sequence the clips into a logical order that will hold the listener's attention and offer plenty of variety.

The clips in your demo do not need to mention any product names, but should demonstrate your ability to communicate emotionally with a variety of styles and attitudes. There are actually two schools of thought on this. Some agents and producers believe that including product names lends credibility to the performer (especially if the spot is one that the performer actually worked on) and that they give a good opportunity for the producer to hear how the performer "sells" the client, or puts a spin on the product name. Other producers feel that the most important aspect of a demo is the performer's talent and ability to communicate effectively on an emotional level, and that product names can actually become distracting.

It would probably be a good idea to include a few product names in your first demo just so you can demonstrate how you can sell the client or product. If you have not done any real sessions, and you are producing your first demo, make up the product names. As you acquire copies of projects you have worked on, you should include several product names from actual spots in your updated demos. When using product or service names, be careful that you do not misrepresent yourself by implying, either on the tape or its packaging, that spots on your demo actually aired if, in fact, they have not.

WHERE DO I GET THE COPY FOR MY DEMO?

There are several approaches to obtaining copy for a demo. Some demo studios provide the copy and handle all the production. This is fine if you don't mind taking the chance of other people in your market having the same copy on their demos. The only real advantage of having the studio provide the copy is that your demo session becomes more like a real recording session; that is, you won't have the opportunity to see the copy in advance. The downside is that your session may take considerably longer because you will be working the copy cold and relatively unrehearsed. You might also feel rushed when you are "on the clock" to get through all the copy necessary, which might affect the quality of your performance.

However, the major problem with the studio providing the copy is that you can easily end up using copy that is not right for your performing style. The purpose of your demo is to present your talent in the best possible manner. Performing copy that is not right for you can only work against you, no matter how well the demo is produced.

A much better approach to finding copy for your first demo is to listen to radio and TV commercials and browse through magazines. By listening to commercials on radio and TV, you can find copy that matches your style and abilities. Record the commercial breaks on audio cassette or on your VCR. As you find commercials you think might be suitable for you, transcribe them, putting each script on a separate piece of paper. Transcribe the entire commercial even though you may end up using only a small portion if that script makes it into the demo. Having the entire script in front of you will help you discover the emotional content of the commercial and the target audience.

Also, when browsing through magazines, look for ads that include a lot of copy. Technical, news, travel and women's magazines frequently have ads that can be easily adapted for voice-over. Most print ads are written for the eye, designed to be read, and include a lot of text that may not be appropriate for voice-over. Look for ads that target specific audiences: men, women, young, older adults and so on. Look for products or services that will allow you to perform the copy in a variety of styles: serious, humorous, hard-sell, soft-sell, dynamic, emotional and so on. Look for key phrases and sentences that have emotional content — these will be your keys to an effective performance. Since print copy is written to be read silently, you may need to rewrite the copy somewhat so that it can be used for voice-over. You don't need to completely rewrite a print ad, just take the strongest sections and rework them so that they make sense as a voice performance.

Another possibility for obtaining copy is to call advertising agencies in your area. Advertising agencies have files of old scripts and might be willing to let you use some of them for your demo. If you take this approach, try to get a variety of scripts from several ad agencies so that you will have an assortment of writing styles and attitudes. You might also try contacting radio and TV stations or recording studios in your area; try to get connected with a producer who might have some old scripts you can use. Recording studios usually throw out scripts when a session is finished, but they might be able to give you a lead to a producer or ad agency that would be willing to give you some old scripts.

Obtain as much copy as you can and narrow the scripts down to about 30 to 40 different ads from radio, TV, and magazines. Also find several brief passages from technical journals, magazine articles or other suitable corporate or narrative copy. Make sure the copy you gather includes a variety of styles that will reveal your full range of capabilities: slow, fast, dynamic, emotional, character and so on.

Be prepared to perform the entire script at your demo session. The reason for this is that you may actually end up with an extremely effective delivery on a segment of the script that you may not have expected. If you only rehearse portions of your scripts, you might overlook an opportunity for a perfect transitional element in your demo, or an especially emotional performance. Your director or engineer can help you do your best performance for each script and you may end up actually only recording a small portion of the copy. However, you should be ready to perform each script in its entirety.

Make sure you have at least three clean copies of each script when you go to the studio for your session. You will need one copy for yourself, one for the engineer and the third for your director. Your notes and thoughts on delivery should be on a separate copy.

WHAT ABOUT DIALOG, MUSIC AND SOUND EFFECTS?

In some cases you might be inclined to include a dialog spot on a demo. For your first demo, this may not be a good idea. The purpose of a demo is to feature *your* voice-acting performance. Including other voice-over performers should be done judiciously. If you include a dialog spot, make sure that yours is the featured performance and that the other voice is of the opposite gender. This may seem obvious, but you'd be surprised at the number of demos there are that have two voices that are hard to tell apart. Also be certain that the other performer knows how to act and work dialog copy. Of course, if you are talented at performing a variety of character voices, you might want to include a dialog spot in which you perform all the voices.

As you prepare your demo copy, make notes on your scripts if you have an idea about music or sound effects, but don't worry about finding them. The engineer will handle that at your session. What you need to focus on is finding copy you can perform effectively. You have the luxury of being able to prepare for your performance. Take advantage of it! You will not have this luxury in a real-life studio session.

Do an appropriate script and character analysis for each piece of copy, making notes on the scripts. Practice your performance for each script just enough to become familiar with it. Be careful not to get yourself locked into any specific attitude or character. Keep in mind that your session engineer might direct you into a performance completely different from what you had decided on. If that happens, you need to be able to adapt to the engineer's direction. If you can't, or if you find yourself getting stuck in the same delivery style for each take, then you are not ready to have your demo produced.

HOW MUCH WILL MY DEMO COST?

The cost of producing a voice-acting demo tape varies from market to market and, to a certain extent, depends on your performing abilities. For recording studios, time is money, and the faster you can record a high-quality performance (fewer takes), the sooner your demo will be completed and the less it will cost.

Expect to pay anywhere from $500 to $1,000, or more, for the production of your voice demo. Although actual session fees vary, and may be somehwat lower or higher, the following shows how the cost for a typical demo session might break down:

PRODUCTION ELEMENTS	TIME AND FEES	SUBTOTALS
Studio time (voice recording)	2 hours @ $100/hour	$200.00
Postproduction (editing, music)	2 hours @ $100/hour	200.00
Track sequencing and/or dubbing	1 hour @ $100/hour	100.00
Music licenses (for music used)	1 blanket license	200.00
Outside producer/director	1 flat fee	200.00
Materials (cassette, DAT), including tax		50.00
	Total Demo Cost	$950.00

This example assumes a certain level of competency in the performer. The actual time it takes to record your copy may vary considerably, fees may vary and not all of these items may be required, thus affecting the price.

The cost of studio time varies greatly from city to city and depends on the complexity of your session. Some studios charge a fee for the music used in your demo while other studios will provide the music at no charge. In most states, the cost of studio time and music license fees are exempt from sales tax, but the materials and recording media are not. Check with your studio to find out what portions of the session or materials will have sales tax applied.

WHAT DO I NEED TO KNOW ABOUT STUDIOS?

As you prepare for your demo tape, you will be wearing the hat of a producer. In that role, you will have already prepared your copy and directed yourself in your performance during practice and rehearsals. Some of your other duties as producer will be to make all the arrangements for studio time, printing, tape duplication and distribution of your final tape.

Most larger cities have at least several recording studios and radio stations. In this age of easily accessible high technology, even many small towns have studios capable of recording a high-quality demo tape. You will find commercial recording studios advertised in the telephone book. However, there may also be many excellent home-based project studios in your community that are not advertised anywhere. Even though recording services and studios may be plentiful in your area, this does not mean that all studios are able to produce an effective demo tape.

The majority of commercial recording studios are designed to handle music sessions. The engineers at these studios are usually very competent at recording music, but may not know much about producing commercials or directing voice-over talent. Home-based project studios are most often designed to handle the recording needs of musicians and composers, but may not be suitable for, or capable of, recording quality voice-over work. Larger recording studios and production houses and even some radio stations are expanding their production capabilities to include a much wider range of services, including voice recording and commercial production.

When you book a recording studio to do your demo, you may be assigned an engineer who is not interested in demo production. If you are doing the demo on your own, you need to be prepared for this. As the producer of your demo, you need to be ready to guide your engineer through the process and have a good idea of what you want in your demo, including the selection of music and sound effects, and the final sequencing of clips.

After you have selected your scripts and rehearsed them — and are confident that your performing skills are up to par, its time to start calling the studios in your area to schedule your session.

HOW DO I BOOK A STUDIO?

The following pages contain some questions to ask as you call around looking for a studio to hire to produce your demo, as well as some important basic information about recording studios.

- **Does the studio record radio and TV commercials, or primarily music?** If the studio is primarily a music studio, they may not be capable of handling your needs for a voice-over demo. Look for a studio that is experienced in producing commercials.

- **Does the studio have an engineer who knows how to direct voice-over talent?** Unless you have hired a director, you *will need* an engineer who can direct you as you perform your copy. Many studios have engineers who know how to record the human voice, but don't know the first thing about directing talent for an effective voice-over performance. When you enter the studio, you need to take off your producer hat and become the performer. Even if you hire a director, you need to find a studio that has an engineer who knows how to produce and direct for voice-over.

- **Does the studio have any experience producing voice-over demos?**
  You may have this question answered when you find out if the studio
  has an engineer who knows how to work with voice-over talent.
  However, even if a studio does a lot of radio commercials, it does not
  mean that they also produce voice-over demos. Unlike a :60 radio
  commercial that is a continuos script, your 2 ½-minute demo will
  consist of anywhere from 15 to 20 very short clips. The sequencing of
  these clips will play an important role in how the tape is perceived by
  the final listener. If the studio has produced demos in the past, ask to
  hear what they have done for others or for the names of other voice
  performers for whom they have produced demos.

- **Does the studio have session time that will coincide with your
  availability?** If you can't book the studio at a time when you are
  available, you need to find another studio. Many recording studios
  offer evening or weekend studio time, but may charge an extra fee for
  those sessions. You may be able to get a reduced fee for late-night
  sessions, but you may not be able to get an engineer experienced with
  voice-over.

- **What is the studio's hourly rate for voice recording?** Many studios
  have a sliding scale of prices depending on the requirements of the
  project. Other studios book at a flat rate, regardless of the session.
  Shop the studios in your area to find the best price for your demo
  production. Also, find out if there are any price changes between the
  voice recording session and the production session. Find a studio that
  will give you a flat hourly rate for your entire project. Some studios
  will give a block discount for sessions booking a large amount of time.
  A demo session probably won't fit this category, but it couldn't hurt to
  ask.

- **Does the studio use analog or digital equipment?** Some studios may
  have a higher rate for digital production and a lower rate for analog —
  or vice-versa. The difference between digital and analog production in
  a recording studio is primarily in the area of editing and
  postproduction. Analog quality in a recording studio is extremely high
  and should not be a consideration for your demo recording; however,
  analog production may take some additional time since it usually
  involves multitrack recording. Digital workstations can reduce the
  production and editing time considerably because the audio is
  recorded and edited within a computer. Analog recordings use reel-to-
  reel tape recorded at 15 ips (inches per second) and cut and-splice
  editing or multitrack production, both of which can be very time-
  consuming. Today, most studios have some form of digital recording
  equipment and analog tape decks are becoming less popular every
  year. However, analog audio cassettes are still the preferred format for
  demos and are likely to be with us for many years to come.

- **Does the studio have access to music and sound effects libraries?**
Your demo will need music and possibly sound effects to underscore
your performance. Many recording studios do not have any CDs of
music that can be used in a demo, even though their primary business
may be recording music. Find a production studio that has one or more
music libraries that can be used to underscore your spots. A music
library is a collection of music created by a company that produces
CDs of music specifically designed for use in commercials, TV and
film production. As you were preparing for your session, you made
some notes on music and sound effect ideas. Discuss your ideas with
your engineer at the beginning of your session.

    It is not a good idea to use music from your personal music
collection for your demo. Even though your demo is meant for limited
distribution and will not be for public sale, the possibility of copyright
infringement for unauthorized use of the music does exist. Also, the
use of familiar or popular music may create a distraction if it is not
used wisely. If you have a specific sound in mind for some of your
demo tracks, you might want to take in some examples from your
personal collection, but keep in mind that they probably should not be
used in the final demo. If you do take in your own music, make sure it
is all instrumental and appropriate for the copy.

- **Does the studio have any additional charges for music or sound
effects used?** Some studios charge a fee for any music used in your
demo, while other studios include the music as part of a package
price. If there is a music use fee charged by the studio, make sure it is
a *blanket license* rather than a *laser-drop* license. A blanket license
cover all music used in a project and is considerably less expensive
than a number of single laser drop licenses. Usually, there is no
charge for sound effects. If you provide your own music, there will
be no charge, but you take the risk of any problems that might arise
from its use.

- **What other fees will the studio charge for materials, including
sales tax?** What does the studio charge for cassettes, digital audio
tape (DAT) and any other materials used in the production of your
demo? Does the studio have any additional charges for archiving
(backing up) your demo project? What portions of the demo
production will have sales tax applied? All of these items will affect
the total cost of your demo.

- **How much time does the studio estimate it will take to produce
your demo?** You should plan on at least six to eight hours for the
completion of your demo, although you may be able to have it
completed in much less time. The studio's experience in producing
demos will be a factor here, as well as your performing abilities. If

the studio has experience producing demos, ask for an estimate of production time and an average cost breakdown.

- **What will you leave the studio with when your demo is completed?** In most cases, you can expect to leave the studio with at least two high-quality cassette copies and a DAT of your demo. Keep one cassette and the DAT in a safe place. You will need them later for duplication. Use the second cassette as a backup or to make some interim copies if you have a dubbing cassette deck, but don't plan to send these copies out to agents or clients because the quality most likely will not be up to professional standards.

  You should request a DAT of your completed demo. You may or may not have the proper equipment to play this tape, but get one anyway. Keep the DAT as your master copy of the demo. Some cassette duplicators can use the DAT instead of a cassette for duplicating your demo. You may also find the DAT useful for maintaining high quality on future demos. Most studios have a DAT recorder and can make a direct digital recording of your DAT when you need to update or change your demo. Use a separate DAT tape to store projects you work on that might be included in future demos.

- **What kind of cassette tape should be used?** Even though your demo is primarily voice, make sure that any cassettes you take with you are on high bias (CrO^2), music-quality tape rather than normal bias tape. The difference in tape quality may not be apparent to you when listening to your cassette, but it will become apparent later, after duplication. Normal bias tape (voice-quality) has a substantially greater amount of noise, or hiss, than high bias (music-quality) tape. Metal tape is not recommended for a demo master because there is little difference between high bias and metal tape for a voice demo. Also, most cassette duplicators prefer high bias tape.

- **What is this thing called Dolby®?** Another point about the cassette master is to have the tape clearly labeled as to whether it was recorded with Dolby ON or OFF, and if it is Dolby B or C. The Dolby noise-reduction process affects the high frequencies (hiss) inherent in analog tape by boosting the higher frequencies of the source audio during recording. (Dolby is not a factor with digital recordings.) When a processed tape is played back with Dolby ON, the previously boosted high frequencies are reduced to a normal volume. Since tape hiss is inherent in the tape and is not a part of the recording, when the overall high frequencies are reduced during playback, the hiss volume is decreased proportionally, effectively eliminating hiss and resulting in a very clean sounding recording.

If a tape recorded *without* Dolby is played back with Dolby ON, the unprocessed recording will have its high frequencies reduced, resulting in a "muddy" or "muffled" sound lacking crispness and clarity. On the other hand, if a Dolby processed tape is played pack with Dolby OFF, the previously boosted high frequencies will *not* be reduced resulting in a somewhat "brighter" or "crisper" edge to the sound. Ideally, a processed tape should be played back with Dolby ON, and an unprocessed tape with Dolby OFF. However, if there is any question as to how the tape will eventually be played back, my recommendation is to record with Dolby ON. This will only give the recording a brighter sound which is generally better than a muddy, hard-to-understand sound, if the tape is played in the wrong mode.

- **What about putting my demo on a CD?** Some studios may give you the option of having your demo recorded directly onto a CD. This is called a *one-off* CD, and although it may be nice to have, it really isn't necessary and may be just an additional expense. The usual format for demos delivered to agents and their clients is audio cassette. If your demo master is on CD, the cassette duplication company usually transfers the recording on the CD to a cassette before duplication anyway. If you do get a one-off CD, handle it carefully. This type of CD is not quite as durable as commercially manufactured CDs and is more susceptible to scratching.

- **How will your demo be backed up?** Some studios offer a choice of backup options such as DAT, minidisk, ZIP drive, Syquest, JAZ or some other digital format. A backup is different from the master of your session. The *master* is the final version of your demo in a form that will later be presented to an agent. A *backup* is a copy of all the elements of the project, not necessarily in any particular order or structure. A digital backup only applies when your session is produced on a digital audio workstation. Even though the backup will contain everything from your session, often including out-takes, it will most likely be in a format that cannot be used anywhere except the recording studio where your demo was produced.

  DAT is probably the most universal media for a backup, but regardless of which format you choose, or that the studio has available, you should have your demo project backed up. The backup is usually kept by the studio; however, they should be able to make you a backup for your own files as well, should you feel you need one. Just be aware that the backup format and data may not be usable by another studio unless they are using the same equipment that was used in the production of your demo. In addition, there may be an additional charge for downloading the backup into the studio's audio workstation when you upgrade your demo.

Your Demo Recording Session

If you have practiced and mastered your voice-acting skills and are prepared and ready to work, your demo session can be a lot of fun, and an educational experience. If, on the other hand, you go to your demo session unprepared or without having mastered the necessary skills, your session can be very uncomfortable.

Because you are the producer as well as the performer, you are the one person responsible for making sure your demo is well produced and that it will be a useful tool for marketing your talents. This means you will have the opportunity to supervise the entire process of your demo production. You won't often have this chance when you are doing real-world sessions. Keep in mind, though, that when you are in front of the mic, you need to be focused on your performance, and not on other aspects of your demo. This is where hiring a director or having an engineer who knows how to direct becomes important. Things, such as track sequencing, music, sound effects, cassette duplication, packaging and distribution, can all be left for later.

ARRIVE ON TIME AND PREPARED

In recording studios, time is money. If a session is scheduled to start at 10:00 AM and you don't arrive until 10:10, that's at least ten minutes of wasted time and money — probably more, because it takes a certain amount of time for the engineer to prepare the studio. Recording studios will usually bill you for their time whether or not you are there at the scheduled time. The lesson here is to *be on time* for your session! If you live your life in a constant mode of running late, you might want to set your clocks ahead, or do whatever is necessary to make sure you arrive at your session on time, or preferably a bit early. Arriving late for real-world sessions will get you a bad reputation in a hurry, and will cause you to lose work. Arriving late for your demo session will put your performance under unnecessary stress, costing you valuable time and money.

The same goes for being prepared. In real-world sessions, there is little more you need to do than to show up at the studio at the appointed time, ready to perform. However, for your demo session, you are also the producer, and you must be prepared with rehearsed copy and ideas to discuss with the engineer handling your session. If you hire someone to produce or direct your demo you need to make sure that the two of you take the time to rehearse your copy to find the strongest material and that you both have a good idea of what you want to achieve from your demo.

Here are some other tips to make your demo session a productive and pleasurable experience:

- Arrive at your session a bit early.
- Eat a light meal or snack before your session.
- Arrive in good voice, fully warmed-up and ready to perform.
- Have a bottle of water with you.
- Do not wait until arriving at the session to rehearse your scripts.
- Make a note of which scripts you think are your strongest.
- Plan in advance for a possible sequence of scripts.
- Plan ahead for music and sound effects.
- Be ready to accept new scripts that the engineer might have available.

WORKING WITH YOUR ENGINEER/PRODUCER

Aside from your director, if you hire one, your engineer/producer will be one of the most important people you work with during the production of your demo. Your director may or may not be the engineer. In any case, it is important that you and your engineer work together as a team on your project. Remain flexible and open to your engineer's suggestions. If you are careful in booking the studio, you will probably have an engineer who knows much more about voice-over work than you do. You can learn a lot from a good engineer and he or she may even become a good contact for work later on.

KEEPING YOUR DEMO CURRENT

Your demo tape will probably be useful for about six months to a year. As you begin doing paid sessions, you will want to get copies of your work and update your demo occasionally. Most voice-actors update their tape with fresh material about once a year. Your agent may request an updated demo or a cut-down (shortened) version for inclusion on their house demo CD. Each time you update or change your demo, you will need to book a new session.

Plan ahead by budgeting for the studio time and have a good idea of the tracks you want to include. Send a current demo to people you have worked for. A new demo is a good opportunity to stay in touch with past clients and to inquire about upcoming projects that might benefit from your talent.

14

Your Demo Is Done,
Now What?

You've spent a good deal of time studying your craft, and you have made an investment in producing a high-quality, marketable demo tape. Essentially, you have set yourself up in business. As you begin making contacts for voice work, you will be speaking to, and meeting professionals who may have been in this business for many years. These people have seen it all, and have little time to waste on an amateur trying to break into the business. Your first impression needs to be memorable and professional.

Present Yourself as a Professional

From here on, you need to maintain the level of professionalism you have worked so hard to establish with your demo. Presenting yourself as a professional is important when you submit your demo to agents and talent buyers. A professional attitude and visual appearance, with your printed materials and personal contacts, shows that you mean business, and take your career seriously.

YOUR PROFESSIONAL IMAGE AND GRAPHICS LOOK

One of the best ways to create a professional image is to have a coordinated look in print or even a logo. You might use a special graphic design, a clever application of some computer clip art, or simply a unique font style. Whatever you do, it needs to be clean, clearly legible and professionally presented.

Creating a graphic identity is not always an easy thing to do, and it is something you might not want to tackle yourself. Fortunately, there are quite a few talented graphic design artists in the business who you can hire to assist you. Even if you hire someone to design your graphic image, you still need to provide some input. You might even want your graphic designer to hear your demo to get a better idea of what you do. Graphic designers can get their inspiration from just about anything, so be as thorough as possible when presenting your ideas.

Your graphic look should reflect your individual personality and be consistent in all printed materials. Your visual image is an important part of your marketing campaign.

Many voice-actors incorporate a USP, or unique selling proposition, into their graphic design. A USP is what sets you apart from everyone else. It is intended to make a statement about what makes you special, different, or better. A USP can be anything from a single word to a short phrase. Some well-known USPs from major advertisers include: "The real thing" (Coca Cola), "The king of beers" (Budweiser), "Generation Next" (Pepsi), and "America's truck stop" (Dodge). Although not necessary for successful advertising, a USP can be an important part of a marketing campaign.

Here are just a few USP possibilities taken from current voice-over demo tapes:

- *"Vocal Magic"* (Catheryn Zaro)
- *"I am not an announcer"* (Rick Calvert)
- *"Brand new spots you've heard a thousand times"* (Mike Roth)
- *"The voice with a smile"* (Paula Hasler)
- *"Let me do the talking"* (Jennifer Barrick)
- *"Your talking head"* (Dawn Comer)
- *"Voices"* (Casey Hayes)
- *"Voice Workout"* (Bobbi Frant)
- *"Variations"* (R. W. Elliott)
- *"Straight up or with a twist . . ."* (Jim Staylor)
- *"Communicator"* (Don Ranson)

If you have an interesting name that can be adapted to a graphic image, that may be something you can use creatively. Michelle Ruff uses a caricature graphic of a dog in front of a city skyline as her graphic logo. Of course, the drawing of the dog has a text balloon that says "Ruff." Possibilities are limited only by your imagination. Be creative and let your imagination run wild. Come up with as many ideas as you can and narrow them down to a few that work for you. Pick the best one and use it everywhere. If you use a USP, it should be included in every piece of print material.

SETTING UP SHOP

You will probably want to set up some sort of office space in your home, or at the very least keep some records on your computer. Of course, your office can be put together over a period of time, and you may already have much of it in place.

The purpose of setting up a formal office area is so that you can really keep yourself in a mind-set of handling your talent as a business. The record keeping and organizational aspects of a business become increasingly important as you begin doing sessions and generating income. If or when you join a union, you will want to keep track of your session work, and your union paperwork. There are also certain tax advantages to setting up a formal business and you would be wise to consult a tax advisor or accountant on this matter.

Some of the items you might want to consider for your office include the following:

- **An answering machine, voice-mail box or service** — This is essential for taking calls when you are not otherwise available. Be sure to check for new messages frequently, especially when you get an agent.

- **A pager or cell phone** — Although these are not as critical as an answering machine or voice-mail box, a pager and cell phone can become useful tools when you are on the road. If you use a pager, please remember to have it on vibrate, or turned off, when you are in the booth.

- **Business cards, letterhead and envelopes** — You will be making many contacts as you develop your voice-acting business. As a professional, you should consider each contact as potential work. Your first impression often leaves a lasting memory. Professionally prepared and printed business cards and stationery are essential to creating a professional image.

  A business card is an absolute necessity as a voice-actor. As part of your personal networking, you will want to let everyone you meet know what you do. Your business card is the first and best introduction to you and your talent, followed closely by your demo tape. Always carry a supply of business cards with you and hand them out every chance you get.

  The two most important things on your business card are your name and a telephone number where you can be reached. The most common problem with business cards is that the telephone number is too small to read easily. The second most common problem is too much information on the card.

The purpose of a business card is to be a reminder of who you are and how you can be contacted. Include only the most important information about yourself on your card. If you are using a USP, that should be on the card as well. Keep the design clean and simple for best results (see Figure 14-1).

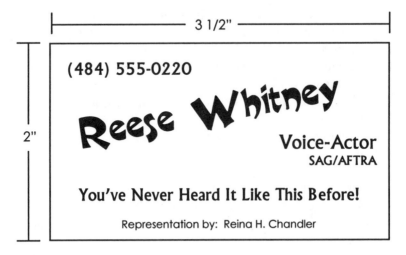

Figure 14-1: Business card dimensions with sample layout.

- **Thank-you notes** — A frequently overlooked, yet very important, business practice is the thank-you note. A brief note of thanks is often all it takes to leave a good feeling with a producer or client. These little notes can easily be prepared in advance, help generate positive memories of your work and provide a gentle reminder that you are available.

- **Newsletters and Postcards** — Some voice performers send out a brief newsletter on a regular basis to clients and producers. Newsletters can take the form of anything from a simple postcard to a brief letter (mailed in an envelope or simply folded and stapled). Content usually includes a brief description of recent projects and clients and any other interesting information. Of course, your graphic identity should be a part of the newsletter. The purpose of the newsletter or postcard is to keep your name in front of the talent buyer. Keep your copy short, concise, interesting and to the point. Too much information will result in the mailing being thrown away without even being read.

Printed Materials

There are several items you will want to consider having professionally printed, including business cards, envelopes, and stationery. For best results, take your layout to an experienced printer. However, if you are on an extremely tight budget and posses the necessary computer skills, you can use a laser printer or high-quality, color ink-jet printer to create some of your own print materials.

Consult with a printing service about paper stock and ink colors. These people are in the business of making printed materials look good and may be able to offer some valuable suggestions. If you do your own printing, a variety of colors for index or cover stock (for J-card cassette inserts) can be purchased at specialized paper outlets or office supply stores. There are also many types of paper stock for letterhead, postcards and business cards. You can even purchase sheets of preformatted business cards, blank J-Cards and cassette labels ready to be loaded into your printer.

PHOTOS

One of the nice things about voice-acting is that your physical appearance is far less important than your ability to act. Unless you also intend to market yourself for on-camera work, it is generally not a good idea to include a photo of yourself in your promotion materials. After all, you are selling yourself as a voice that will help your clients communicate their message.

No matter how good your demo might be, a photograph is going to give the talent buyer a face to go with that voice. It is not uncommon for a performer to be pigeon-holed or stereotyped because of the visual image from a photo included in the demo package. Many agents and producers will associate a face to a name before they associate a voice to a name. Although not intentional, this can be a real disservice for the voice actor. You are generally better off keeping your image clean and simple without photos, and let your voice do the selling.

Of course, there are exceptions to not using photos in your promotion. If you are marketing your talents as a model, an on-camera performer, or if you also do live theater, a photo is a must. As a multifaceted performer, a photo can actually work to your benefit because it will tend to associate your versatility with your name in the mind of the talent buyer.

If you decide to use a photo as part of your packaging, it should be a black and white portrait head shot. Hire a professional photographer to take the picture and make sure the photo reflects your money-voice personality. Your photo is an important part of your image and must be of high quality.

THE J-CARD

A *J-Card* is the insert inside a hard-shell cassette box (see Figure 14-2). It is the first thing a person sees when they pick up your demo tape. For a voice-actor, there are only three things that need to be on a J-Card: your name, your agent's name, and a phone number (your agent's and/or your own). You can also identify what is on each side, and any union affiliation.

Figure 14-2: J-Card dimensions with sample layout.

You might choose to include more detailed information about the content of the tape on the inside of the J-Card. Some voice-actors have an imprint only on the cassette, but then it becomes impossible to refer to the performer's information when the tape is playing.

The J-Card for your demo should reflect your individuality and unique personality. It should be eye-catching and enticing. It should say to the recipient. " . . . there's something interesting inside that you should listen to." Don't feel limited to a standard type style on white paper. Colored paper, an interesting font, a catchy USP and a creative layout can all help your demo stand out from the crowd and get listened to.

Your name should be in two places: on the front panel and on the spine. When you do your layout, make sure your name on the spine is facing toward the short flap. Figure 14-2 shows the proper dimensions for a J-Card and a typical layout. The dotted lines indicate folds for the J-Card to properly fit a hard-shell cassette box.

Printing costs vary widely depending on your city and your artwork, but you can plan on spending approximately $150 to $200 for 1,000 J-Cards with black ink. Color increases the cost quite a bit. If you decide to use color for your J-Cards, you might want to consider having them professionally printed — even if you have a high-quality color printer connected to your computer. Remember, you want to present a professional image of yourself, and your own color printer cannot compare to the quality of a professional print shop.

THE CASSETTE LABEL

Just as your cassette box needs a J-Card to identify your demo, so does the cassette need a label to identify the tape. There are two options for labeling cassettes: (1) imprinting the label information on the cassette itself, and (2) printing a paper label that is attached to the cassette.

Imprinting is done by a machine that prints the label information directly to the cassette shell. It is done as part of the cassette duplication process. Cassette imprinting has a professional look, but you will be limited to only a few possible ink colors, and only one color can be used. Imprinting is usually less expensive than paper labels because of lower

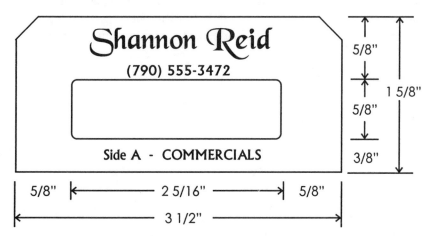

Figure 14-3: Cassette label dimensions with sample layout.

manufacturing costs, less labor and no additional materials, except for some ink. Another disadvantage of cassette imprinting is that the imprint area is a bit smaller than that of a paper label.

Paper labels are most popular for demo tape labeling probably because they are more versatile (see Figure 14-3). Paper labels can use multiple colors and color bleeds to create a very eye-catching tape. With a little creativity, the cassette label and J-Card can be color-coordinated with a matching layout. This makes for a professional look that can attract the attention of someone searching for an interesting demo to listen to.

Getting Your Demo Out There: Duplication and Distribution

You will need to have your demo tape duplicated and there are a few different ways to approach this. Duplicating tapes yourself is not a good idea. It's a time-consuming process, and will most likely not result in high-quality copies. You really want your demo to be of the highest quality possible, so the best approach is to have copies made by a cassette duplication company. Look in your Yellow Pages under Recording Services — Sound and Video.

There are two basic types of cassette duplication: high-speed and real-time. High-speed duplication may save you a few dollars, but the lower quality may not be worth it. Real-time duplication on high-bias tape is recommended for the highest quality.

You will probably need about 50 copies of your demo to start with, for distribution to the people you contact. When you get an agent, he or she will let you know how many copies the agency needs to keep on hand, and you will want to keep at least 25 extras for your own use. The cassette duplicator can help you with different types of labels, or imprinting, and may even be able to handle J-Card printing as well.

15

Getting Paid to Play

Acting for voice-over may be one of the best-kept secrets around. You get to be serious, funny and sometimes downright silly and your voice may be heard by thousands. Working hours can be relatively short, and you get paid for it! In short, you get paid to play!

Well, to be perfectly honest, voice-acting can be very challenging at times. There will be moments when you wish you were somewhere else. You will encounter producers and/or directors who do not seem to know what they are doing. You will be faced with cramming :40 of copy into :30 — and the producer will expect it to sound natural and believable. That's show-biz!

Fortunately, the uncomfortable moments are relatively rare, and the majority of voice-over work is enjoyable and often downright fun. If you really enjoy what you do, and become good at it, even challenging sessions can seem like play, although it may appear to be hard work to everyone else. To a large extent, your level of success as a voice-actor will depend on your attitude and how you approach your work.

Many successful voice-actors do much more than just perform. It is not uncommon to find voice-actors wearing many hats — ad-agency rep, copywriter, producer and performer. As you master voice-acting skills, you may find yourself developing other talents as well. This diversification can provide income from several sources.

Making Money Doing Voice-Over Work

There are only two ways to get paid for voice-over performing: union jobs and nonunion, freelance jobs. If you are just starting out, it is a good idea to do as much nonunion work as possible before joining the union. It's sort of like "on-the-job training." You'll have the time and opportunities to get the experience you need and accumulate some tapes of your work.

If you pursue voice-over work as a career, you may, eventually join a union, especially if you live in a large market. However, it is not necessary to join a union to become successful. There are many independent voice-over performers in major markets who are earning substantial incomes, even though they are not members of any union. The choice of whether or not to join a union is one that only you can make.

THE UNIONS

This section is not intended to either promote or discourage union membership. However, this is an important decision for anyone pursuing the *art of voice-acting*. If you are just beginning to venture into the world of voice-acting, a basic knowledge of the unions is all you need. As you gain experience and do more session work, you may want to consider union membership. Much of the information in this section can be found in the information packet available from your local AFTRA or SAG office[1].

There are two unions that handle voice-over performers: AFTRA (American Federation of Television and Radio Artists) and SAG (Screen Actors Guild). The job of both unions is to ensure proper working conditions, to make sure you are paid a reasonable fee for your work, and to help you get paid in a timely manner and receive health and retirement benefits.

These two performing unions came into being in the early days of film, radio and, later, television. Unscrupulous producers were notorious for not paying performers a decent wage — some not even paying them at all. So, the unions were set up to make sure performers got paid and were treated fairly.

As the unions grew, it was decided that it was unfair for a person just working once or twice a year to have to join the union and pay dues every six months. The result was the Taft-Hartley act. This law gives you (the actor) an opportunity to work under the jurisdiction of the union for 30-consecutive days without having to join AFTRA. You then become "Taft-Hartley'd" and must join the union if you do another union job. What this means is that if you do a lot of freelance work, you can still do a union job without having to join the union or pay union dues. The trick is that the next union job you do, you must join the union, whether it is three days or three years after your first union job. Immediately after the 30-day grace period you have the option to join or not join the union.

One of the advantages of being in the union is that you are more likely to be paid a higher fee, or scale, than if you did the same job as a freelancer — although, in some situations, you can actually negotiate a higher fee as a freelancer. Union *scale* is the fee set by the union for a specific type of work. By the time you reach the level of skill to have been hired for a union job, you will most likely be ready to join the union.

AFTRA is an *open union*. Anyone can join by simply paying the initiation fee and current dues. SAG works a little differently in that you must be hired for a union job in order to join the union, and you must join the union when you are hired for a union job. It used to be that you had to somehow get a union job to join SAG. However, today you can join SAG if you are a paid-up member of AFTRA or another affiliated union for one year, and have worked at least one job as a principal performer during that time in that union's jurisdiction.

AFTRA and SAG cover different types of performing artists and do not duplicate the types of performances covered. Certain types of voice-over work are covered by AFTRA (radio, television and sound recordings), while other performances are covered by SAG (film and multimedia). For example, if you were hired to work voice-over for a CD-ROM interactive program, you probably would be working a SAG job (although some interactive work is covered by AFTRA). A radio commercial or corporate video would be covered by AFTRA. There are some gray areas, but if you are a member, the union office will help sort out the details. Although separate unions, AFTRA and SAG work closely together and even share office space in many cities.

Both unions have a one-time initiation fee to join and semi-annual dues. Joining AFTRA and SAG requires payment in full of the initiation fee and current dues. The initiation fee and dues charged by AFTRA and SAG vary from city to city, based on market size, and are adjusted regularly. Call the AFTRA or SAG office in your area for current fees. New member information packets, which will answer most of your questions about the unions, can be purchased for a nominal fee. You can also ask the union what the current scale is for the type of work you are doing (commercials, industrial, and so on). The staff at the AFTRA and SAG offices are union members and will be happy to answer your questions.

One function of the unions is to protect your rights as a performer. A recording of your performance can be used for many different projects, and unless you are a union member, there is little you can do to protect yourself. A voice-over performance for a radio commercial can also be used in a TV spot or for an industrial video. Each of these different types of projects is covered under some 400 different AFTRA and SAG agreements and have different pay scales. Radio and TV commercials are paid based on the market in which they air and how long they will be aired. Industrial videos and CD-ROMs are handled in other ways. Without the union you are potentially at the mercy of the person hiring you, and your voice may end up being used for projects you never agreed to.

A union member working in a nonunion production, cannot be protected if the producer refuses to pay, pays late, makes unauthorized use of the performance or in any other way takes advantage of the performer. Any legal action taken by the performer is at the performer's expense, and the union may actually discipline the member with fines, censure, suspension or even expulsion.

As a member of AFTRA, you are free to audition for any job, including nonunion jobs. If you are hired for a nonunion job and the employer is not a signatory, the union may contact the producer and have him or her sign a signatory agreement before hiring you. If you are a union member, and are not sure about your employer's status with the union, call the union office in your area.

One way for a union member to work a nonunion job is a waiver called a *One Production Only* (O.P.O.) *Limited Letter of Adherence*. This waiver is good for one job only, and the work you do on that job is considered union work. The advantage is that the nonunion producer agrees to the terms of the union agreement, but does not have to become a union signatory. The O.P.O. contract must be signed before any sessions.

There are producers who, for one reason or another, will not work with union performers. Money is usually not the reason. It may be unrealistic demands from an agent, company policy to work only with nonunion talent, or simply a dislike of the paperwork. To get around the paperwork and other issues, some agents and production companies will work as a union signatory effectively separating a nonunion producer from the union. This is a win-win situation — because the producer does not have to deal directly with the union, the quality of the talent remains high and union performers have the opportunity to work for a greater variety of clients at a fair level of compensation. Some voice-over performers operate their own independent production companies as signatories and essentially hire themselves. It is also possible for you, as a union member, to handle the paperwork, thus making it more attractive for a producer to hire you.

It is generally a good idea to put off joining AFTRA until you have mastered the skills necessary to compete with seasoned union talent. Producers expect a higher level of performance quality and versatility from union performers and it takes time and experience to master those skills. Joining AFTRA too soon not only may be an unwise financial expense, but could have the potential for adversely affecting your voice-acting career.

Here are some reasons to consider union membership when you feel you are ready, or when you begin getting calls for union work:

- Union membership is considered an indicator of professionalism and quality. Producers know they will get what they want in 2 or 3 takes instead of 20.

- Your performance is protected. Union signatories pay residual fees for use of your work beyond the originally contracted period of time. The usual life span of a radio or television commercial is 13 weeks.

- You will also be paid for any time over one hour on first and second auditions, and paid a fee for any additional callbacks.

WORKING FREELANCE

Nonunion, freelance work is an excellent way to get started in the business, and there are lots of advertisers and producers who use nonunion performers. As a nonunion performer, you negotiate your own fee, or take what is offered — the fee will be a one-time-only buy-out payment. There are no residuals for nonunion work. The going rate for freelance voice work can be anywhere from $50 to $250 or more depending on the project, the market, your skill level and what you can negotiate. For nonunion work, or work booked without representation, the negotiated terms are between you and the producer.

If a nonunion producer should ask your fee, and you are not sure what to say, the safest thing to do is to quote the current minimum union scale for the type of project you are being asked to do. You can always negotiate a lower fee. If you have an agent, the correct thing to do is to ask the client to contact your agent.

As a freelance voice-over performer, you need to protect yourself from unscrupulous producers (yes, they are still out there). The best way to protect yourself is to use a simple agreement known as a *deal memo*. The format for this can be as simple as a brief letter or an invoice, to something more formal, such as a contract for services. Keep it as simple as possible. A complicated, legal-sounding document might scare off a potentially valuable employer.

A written agreement is your only proof in the event you need to take legal action to collect any money owed to you, or if your performance is used in a manner that you did not agree to. It's a common practice and should be used whenever possible.

Usually, you will want to arrange for payment at the end of a freelance session. If you agree to payment by mail, you should create a simple invoice for your services, or modify your deal memo to reflect the arrangement. When you agree to payment by mail, you might want to have the producer sign your copy of the invoice or deal memo *before* you start the session.

Getting the paperwork out of the way before the work begins is a good way to make sure that the terms of your performance are understood by all parties and that the producer doesn't try to change the agreement after you have done the work. If you are booked early enough, you might want to fax a copy of the agreement to the producer in advance. But you should still plan on having two copies with you when you arrive for the session — the producer is probably not going to bring his copy. Leave one copy for the producer and make sure you have a signed copy before you leave the studio.

The following is an example of a simple deal memo letter. This deal memo includes all the necessary information to confirm the agreement, yet it is presented in a nonthreatening and informal manner.

Mr. Producer
The Big Store
1234 Fifth Ave.
This City, TS   12345

Dear Mr. Producer:

    Thank you for booking me to be the voice for The Big Store's new radio commercials. As we discussed on the phone today, I will be doing (4) radio commercials (including tags) for $150 per spot as a buy-out for radio only. If you later decide to use my voice for television spots or other purposes, please call me to arrange for a new session. You have also agreed to provide me with a DAT recording of the final commercials. I'll call you next week to arrange to pick it up.
    I will arrive at Great Sound Recording Studios, 7356 Hillard Ave. on Tuesday the 5th for a 10:00 AM session.
    For your records, my Social Security Number is 123-45-6789. Please make your check in the amount of $600.00 payable to My Name so I can pick it up after the session.

I look forward to working with you on the 5th.

Sincerely,

    Some larger companies, such as major radio and TV stations, will not accept or sign a performer's deal memo or contract. These, and other reputable businesses, usually have their own procedures for ensuring payment. You will be asked to provide your social security number and sign their document before you can be paid. If you are not offered a copy, you should request one for your own records in case payment is delayed. You usually will not be paid immediately after your session, but will receive a check in the mail within four to six weeks. If you have representation, this detail will be handled by your agent. However, if you are working freelance, some producers and large companies can take advantage of a 30-day payment agreement by basing the payment terms on 30 working days rather than 30 calendar days. This can result in your payment arriving long after you expected it. If you have not received your payment by the agreed upon time, it is up to you to call your client and gently remind them.
    Another common problem with working freelance is that you can do a session today and be called back for changes tomorrow, but unless you are redoing the entire spot, the producer may expect you to do the second session for free. Callbacks for changes are common — the callback might be for something as simple as changing a single word or correcting a date to something more elaborate such as redoing a paragraph or two.
    When you are called back to fix a problem, the callback session is technically a new recording session. As a union performer, the producer

must pay you an additional fee to return to the studio. As a freelance voice-actor, it is up to you to negotiate your fee for the second session. This can present an awkward situation, especially if you want to keep a good working relationship with the client. Unless the problem was your fault, you should be paid for the follow-up session. The producer must be made to understand that you are a professional and that your time is valuable. You are taking time away from other activities to help fix their problem and you are entitled to fair compensation. A good producer knows this and the issue of additional compensation is something they will bring up.

Try to find out what needs to be fixed before you begin talking about how much you should be paid to do the new session. If you are redoing most of the copy, you might want to ask for a fee equal to what you charged the first time. If the fix is simple, you might ask for one-half the original session fee. If you are exceptionally generous, and expect to get a lot of work from the client, you might offer to do the new session for free. If you do negotiate a fee for the follow-up session, make sure you get it in writing in the form of an invoice, a deal memo or a copy of their paperwork.

UNION COMPENSATION

By joining AFTRA and working union jobs, you will be assured of reasonable compensation for your talents and protection from unscrupulous producers and advertisers. Your union-approved agent will normally handle the negotiations for your work and will sometimes negotiate a fee above scale. Regardless of what you are paid, the agent will only receive 10%, and that amount is usually over and above your fee. With AFTRA the "plus-10" (plus 10%) is automatic. With SAG it must be negotiated, or the 10% agent commission will be taken out of your fee. A performer just starting in the business may make less than scale, but the agent's commission will still be added on top of the performer's fee. The signatory also contributes to the union's Health and Retirement (AFTRA) and Pension Welfare Fund (SAG). For many voice-over performers, the health and retirement benefits are the primary advantage of being an AFTRA or SAG member.

Residuals were implemented to guarantee that performers are paid for their work as commercials are broadcast. Each airing is considered a separate performance. Commercials produced by an AFTRA or SAG signatory have a life span of 13 weeks. After the original run, if the advertiser reuses the commercial, the performer's fees, agent commission and union contributions must be paid again. This happens for every period in which the commercial is used. In radio, residuals begin on the date of the first airing. In television, residuals begin on the date of the recording session, or the "use" date.

If an advertiser is not sure whether the company wants to reuse an existing radio or television commercial, a *holding fee* can be paid. This fee, which is the equivalent of the residual fee, will keep your talents exclusive to that advertiser, and is paid for as long as the spot is held. Once the commercial is reused, residual payments are made just as for the original run. If the advertiser decides the spot has lived its life, your residuals end. At that point, you are free to work for a competing advertiser.

Union recording sessions are divided into several fee categories and specific types of work within each category. For radio and television work, the performer's pay varies depending on the type of work and the market size where the product will be aired. The following is a description of the basic AFTRA performance fee categories. Although some of the details may change from time to time, this will give you an idea of the broad range of work available in the world of voice-acting. Fees are not included here because they will vary from market to market and are constantly being adjusted.

- **Session Fee.** The session fee applies to all types of union voice-over work and will vary depending on the type of work you are doing. A session fee is paid for each commercial you record. For radio and TV commercials, an equal amount is paid for each 13-week renewal cycle while in *use* (being rebroadcast) or if the spot is on *hold* (not aired).

  Session fees for dubbing, ADR and looping are based on a performance of five lines or more, and residuals are paid based on each airing of the TV program (network, syndication, cable or foreign).

  Animation voice work is paid for individual programs or segments over ten minutes in length. Up to three voices may be used per program under one session fee. An additional session fee applies for each additional group of three voices, plus an additional 10% is paid for the third voice in each group of three voices performed.

  For off-camera multimedia, CD-ROM, CDI and 3DO, a session fee is paid for up to three voices during a 4-hour day for any single interactive platform. Additional voices are paid on a sliding scale and there is a one hour/one voice session fee and an 8-hour day for seven or more voices. Voices used on-line or as a lift to another program are paid 100% of the original session fee.

  Industrial, educational and other nonbroadcast narrative session fees are based on the time spent in the studio. A day rate applies for sessions that go beyond one day.

- **Wild Spot Fee.** This fee is paid for unlimited use of a spot in as many cities, for any number of airings, and on as many stations as the client desires. The Wild Spot *use rate* is paid based on the number and size of the cities where the spot is airing, usually for a 13-week *use*.

- **Tags.** A *tag* is defined by AFTRA as an incomplete thought or sentence, which signifies a change of name, date or time. A tag can occur in the body of a radio or television commercial, but is usually found at the end. For radio, each tag is paid a separate fee. For television, tags are paid based on a sliding scale whenever two or more tags are recorded.

- **Demos.** These are "copy tests" for nonair use. An advertiser might produce a demo for a commercial to be used in market research or for testing an advertising concept. If a demo is upgraded for use on radio or television, the appropriate *use fee* applies. Demos are paid a fee somewhat less than a regular session fee.

- **Use Fee.** This fee begins when a commercial airs. Voice-over performers for national television spots earn an additional fee every time the commercial airs. A standard of 13 weeks is considered a normal *time-buy* that dictates residual payments. For radio commercials, the cycle begins on the first airdate of the commercial. For television, the cycle begins on the date of the recording session, or use date.

PRODUCT IDENTIFICATION

Radio and television commercials are unique in that they both create an association between the performer and the product. This association is used to tremendous advantage by television advertisers when they use a celebrity spokesperson to promote their product. The viewing audience associates the performer with the product, and the advertiser gains a tremendous amount of credibility.

Product identification can, however, result in some serious conflicts, usually for spots airing in the same market. If one of your spots is a national commercial, it may affect what you can do locally. For example, if you performed the voice-over on a national television commercial for a major furniture store, you may not be able to do voice-over work for a local radio commercial for a competing furniture store. You will need make sure both spots are not airing in the same market, even though one is for radio and the other is for TV. Conflicts are not a common problem, but they do occur from time to time and usually with union talent. As usual, if you have any questions, the best thing to do is to call your union office.

LIMITED RELEASE PRODUCTIONS

Many projects are never broadcast, such as in-house sales presentations, training tapes, programs intended for commercial sale and point-of-purchase playback. For most of these projects, performers are paid a one-time-only session fee, with no residuals, known as a *buy-out*. These projects usually have no identification of the performer with the product or service in the mind of the audience, and therefore present little possibility of creating any conflict. Buy-out fees are usually based on the type of project and its affect on the performer's marketability in other areas.

Casting Agencies, Talent Agencies
Personal Managers and Advertising Agencies

The jobs of casting agents, talent agents and personal managers are often misunderstood by people not in the business or just starting out. They all have different functions in the world of voice-over as discussed in the following sections.

THE CASTING AGENCY OR CASTING DIRECTOR

A casting agency is hired by an advertiser or production company to cast the talent for a particular project. They may also provide scriptwriting and some producing services, such as directing talent. They may even have a small studio where some of the production is done. Casting agent fees normally are charged directly to the client and are in addition to any fees paid for the talent they cast.

Most voice casting agencies have a pool of talent that covers all the various character styles they use. Talent from this pool is used for all projects they work on and they will rarely add a new voice to their pool unless there is an opening or special need. The talent in their pool may be represented by several talent agents.

THE TALENT AGENCY

The talent agent is the direct representative for the performer. Talent agencies are licensed by the state and must include the words "Talent Agent" or "Talent Agency" in any print advertising, along with their address and license number. The talent agent works with advertising agencies, producers, and casting directors to obtain work for the performers they represent.

A talent agent receives a commission of 10% based on the scale they negotiate for their performer. For AFTRA work the commission is above and beyond the performer's fee (scale plus 10%). In some cases, the commission may be taken out of the talent fee, especially for freelance work obtained by an agent. For talent agencies to book union talent, they must be franchised by the local AFTRA and SAG unions. Contact the union office in your area for a list of franchised talent agents.

Unfortunately, this is not a perfect world, and there are many unscrupulous agents who will attempt to relieve you of your money. If anyone asks you for money up front to represent you or get you an audition, he or she is trying a scam. Period! The same is true for 1-900 numbers that charge a fee for information on auditions and casting. Most of the information is available elsewhere, either for free or a minimal charge. The best thing to do is find a reputable agent and stay in touch with him or her.

THE PERSONAL MANAGER

A personal manager is hired to manage a performer's career. The personal manager attempts to get the talent agent to send the performer out on auditions, and encourages the agent to go for a higher talent fee. Managers usually work on a commission of up to 20% of the performer's fee, which is taken out before payment to the performer. Some managers may work on a retainer. Either way, a manager can be expensive, especially if you are not getting work. Personal managers are fairly rare in the world of voice-over.

HOW ADVERTISING AGENCIES WORK

Advertising agencies work for the companies doing the advertising, coordinating every aspect of an advertising or marketing campaign. They write the scripts, arrange for auditions, arrange for the production, supervise the sessions, handle distribution of tapes to radio and TV stations, purchase air time, and pay all the fees involved in a project.

Ad agencies are reimbursed by their clients (advertisers) for production costs and talent fees. They book airtime at the station's posted rate and receive an agency discount (usually about 15%). They bill their client the station rate and get their commission from the station as a discount. If the advertising agency is an AFTRA or SAG signatory, they will also handle the union fees according to their signatory agreement. Since the ad agency books all airtime, they also handle residual payments, passing these fees on to their clients.

Most advertising agencies work through production companies that subcontract everything needed for the production of a project. Sometimes the production company is actually a radio or TV station that handles the production. In some cases a casting agent might be brought in to handle casting, writing and production. Some larger ad agencies, with in-house facilities, may work directly with talent agents for casting performers.

Ad agencies can be a good source of work. Your agent should know which agencies use voice-over and will send out your demo tapes accordingly. You can also contact ad agencies directly, especially if you are nonunion. Phone ad agencies and let them know who you are and what you do. You will find many ad agencies work only in print or use only union talent. When you call, ask to speak to the person who books voice-over talent.

The ad agency assigns an account executive (AE) or on-staff agency producer (AP) to handle the account. Sometimes both an AE and AP are involved, but it is usually the AP who knows more about the production than the AE. The AE is more involved with arranging the schedules for airtime purchases. The AP is the person who is generally in charge of selecting talent. The AE is less involved, but often approves the AP's talent choices.

Either the AE or AP may be present during auditions and is almost always present at the session. If the ad agency is producing the spot, they will want to make sure everything goes as planned. If the spot is being produced by a casting agency, someone from that company may also be at the session. Casting agencies are more common for television on-camera productions than for voice-over, but a casting agency rep may be present at an audition or session if their agency is handling the production. And, of course, advertisers are very likely to be at the audition and session to provide their input.

Finding and Working with an Agent

You will probably get your first few voice-over jobs through friends, networking or some other contact you make yourself. As you begin working, your skills will improve and your talents will become more valuable. When you reach the point where you are confident with your abilities and want to get more work, it's time to find an agent. Remember, most working pros have an agent. To present yourself with a professional image, you should too. But how do you go about finding one?

The first thing to understand is that your agent works for you! Some performers just starting out think it's the other way around. Many agents are very selective about who they represent, and even may give the false impression that the performer is working for them. It is their job to get you work by sending you out on auditions and connecting you with producers who will hire you. Once on the audition, it becomes your job to perform to the best of your abilities. Your agent only gets paid when you do. Your agent will also send your tape to casting directors, advertising agencies and production companies. Once a job is booked, the agent negotiates your fee.

As you begin your search, you will find that no two agents are alike. Some handle the paperwork for the union, while others want the client or performer to handle the paperwork. Talent agents in a large market, like Los Angeles, run their businesses totally different from a talent agent in a smaller market in the Midwest. As with much of the voice-over business, there are no hard-and-fast rules. The most important thing is that you are comfortable with your agent, and that your agent is comfortable with you.

SEARCHING FOR AN AGENT

One way to find an agent in your area is to contact your local AFTRA office. Even if you are not a union member, they will be able to provide you with a list of all franchised agents in your area. Many agents work exclusively with union talent, although some work with both union and nonunion talent.

You can also start your search for an agent by looking in the Yellow Pages of your local phone book under "Talent Agencies." Yet another way to find an agent is to go to a theatrical bookstore. In Los Angeles, an excellent theatrical bookstore is Samuel French, Inc. (7623 West Sunset Bl., Hollywood, CA, (213) 876-0570). Check the reference section for a book titled *The Agency Guide*. This book includes a brief description of every franchised agent in the Los Angeles area, how long they have been in business, the types of talent they represent, who to contact at the agency, and a wealth of other information. Samuel French also carries preprinted address labels for the Los Angeles talent agencies, which can save you time later on.

While on your search for an agent, you can also call recording studios, TV stations and production companies in your area. Ask for the production manager. Let this person know you are available for voice-over work, and that you are looking for an agent. Ask for the names of the talent agencies he or she works with. Let them know your union status. If the company is a union shop (an AFTRA or SAG signatory) and you are nonunion, it will not be able to hire you, but may be able to give you some good leads. Don't forget to let companies you contact know that you have a demo you can send to them. Follow up all phone contacts with a thank you letter.

Many talent agents specialize in certain types of performers, such as modeling, on-camera, voice-over, music recording, theatrical and so on. You can call the agent's office to find out if they represent voice-over talent and if they are accepting new performers. Keep this initial call brief and to the point, but be sure to get the name of someone to send your demo to if the agency expresses any interest.

Proper phone etiquette is important when calling an agent. Agents are busy people and will appreciate your call more if you are prepared and know what you want. Here's an example of an ineffective call to an agent:

AGENT: Hello, Marvelous Talent Agency.
ACTOR: Hi, uh, is there somebody there I could talk to about doing voice-over?
AGENT: Who's calling?

ACTOR: Oh, yeah. My name is David Dumdum, and I'd like to talk to someone about doing voice-overs.

AGENT: This is a talent agency. We don't do voice-overs, we represent talent.

ACTOR: That's what I mean, I want to talk to somebody about representing me.

This kind of call not only takes a long time to get anywhere, but the so-called actor is not at all clear about what he wants to discuss. Even if this performer had a decent demo tape, the chances of getting representation are poor simply because of a nonbusinesslike presentation. Here's a much better way to approach a call:

AGENT: Hello, Marvelous Talent Agency.

ACTOR: Hi, this is Steven Swell. I'd like to know if your agency represents voice-over talent.

AGENT: Yes we do.

ACTOR: Great! I'd like to speak to someone about the possibility of representation. Are you taking on any new performers?

AGENT: We are always interested in looking at new performers. If you'd like to send us a copy of your demo tape and a résumé, we'll give it a listen and one of our agents will give you a call in a few days.

ACTOR: That's terrific. I'll get a copy to you in today's mail. Who should I send it to?

This performer gets to the point of his call quickly and effectively. He is polite, businesslike and keeps an upbeat, professional attitude throughout the call. Even though he didn't connect with an agent on this call, he did get a name and there is now a clear process for getting his demo into the agency.

Narrow down the prospective agents in your area. You can immediately eliminate those who represent only models, print or on-camera talent. The Los Angeles area has more than 250 franchised agents, so in a larger market, you must be very specific in targeting potential agents before sending out your demo and résumé. Smaller markets can have zero to several talent agents, depending on the market size. Representation by a small talent agency in a small market can be an excellent way to break into the business of voice-over.

Prepare a brief and to-the-point cover letter that will accompany your demo. This is not the place to give your life history — keep it to no more than three short paragraphs. This is a business letter intended to introduce you to the agency. Simply state that you are a voice-over performer and that you are interested in discussing the possibilities of representation by the agency.

Each letter you send out should be an original, and should be addressed to the person whose name you learned during your research. The address on the envelope should be either typed or printed by a computer. If you have any other experience that is relevant, you should also prepare a résumé and include it in the package. Most agents require a demo tape and a résumé from any talent they are considering. Here's an example of a good cover letter:

Dear Mr. Agent:

Thank you for your interest in my demo. As I mentioned on the phone, I am a voice-actor seeking representation. I have been booking myself as a freelance performer for the past year or so and have had several successful commercials on the air.

My background, training and additional information are on the enclosed résumé. A copy of my current demo tape is also enclosed.

I believe I can be a valuable asset to your agency. I look forward to hearing from you so that we can arrange for a meeting to further discuss representation by your agency.

Sincerely,

This letter is short, to the point, gives some important basic information and suggests the performer's potential value to the agency. The letter concludes by requesting action from the agency to arrange an interview.

If you call to see if your tape was received, it will often do you no good, and may even irritate some agencies. It will also do you no good to call to get a reaction to your tape, and don't expect to get your demo tape back. Talent agents know you send out demos to other agencies in the area. If they hear something they like, agents will call you. If you are good, the agents will call quickly, simply because they don't want to miss out on representing a good performer by not getting back to you in time.

Don't get discouraged if you are declined for representation. It only means that either the talent agent has a full roster of talent, or that he or she simply feels you may not be ready. Don't expect or ask for a critique of your tape. If an agent is kind enough to critique it for you, use that information to learn how to improve your skills and create a better demo. You might even think about taking some more classes.

Sooner or later you will find a talent agent who is interested in talking to you. The agent's interest does not mean you have representation. It only means that he or she is interested in learning more about you and your talent.

INTERVIEWING AN AGENT

When you get a positive response, you will be asked to set up an appointment to meet with the agent. This can be quite exciting. What will you wear? How should you act? What will you say?

Handle this interview just as you would an interview for a new job. Dress nicely, and present yourself in a businesslike manner. Be careful to wear clothes that do not make noise. You may be asked to read a script as part of the interview. Enter the office with confidence. Play the part of the successful performer. Create your character for the interview just as you would for a script, and act as if you are a seasoned pro and already represented. Your chances of signing with an agent will be much better if your first impression is one of a skilled and professional performer.

Interview all your prospective agents as thoroughly as possible. Don't be afraid to ask questions at any time. What types of work have they booked in the last month? What is the average scale they get for their performers? What is their commission? Is their commission added to the performer's fee, or taken out? How many voice-over performers do they represent? How long have they been in business? You can even ask whom they represent and for a list of some performers you can contact.

During your meetings with agents, you may talk about everything except your voice-over work. They will want you to be comfortable so that they can get a sense of you as a person, and you will want to get to know them a bit. You need to decide if you like them and have confidence that the agency will be able to get you work.

Take your time. Don't rush to sign up with the first agent who offers to represent you. Also, if any agent gives you the impression that you are working for him or her, you might want to consider eliminating that person from your list. The agent works for you — not the other way around.

When you sign up with a talent agency, normally you will sign a contract for one year. Some agencies request a multi-year agreement, but this can cause problems if your agent doesn't promote you, and you don't get work. It is generally a good idea to renegotiate with your talent agent every year.

A large agency may have many people in the office and represent a large talent pool. A small agency may have only one or two people handling the entire business. It is easy to become a small fish in a big pond if you sign with a large agency. On the other hand, most large talent agencies sign only voice-over performers with years of experience and a solid track record. Your first agent most likely will work for a smaller agency that can give you more attention and help guide your career.

WORKING WITH YOUR AGENT

Once signed, you should keep your agent up to date on your work. Let him or her know how an audition or session went, and keep the agent current with an updated demo as needed. Calling your talent agent once a week should be adequate, unless he or she requests you call more or less frequently. Your agent can also be a very good indicator of the areas you are weak in, and may recommend classes and training if necessary. The key to working with an agent is to stay in touch and ask for advice.

When someone approaches you for work, refer the company or person to your agent, especially if you are a union member. As a professional performer, your job is to perform. Your agent's job is to represent you and negotiate for the highest fee. Although it is generally wise to let your agent handle the negotiations, there may be some situations where it might be best for you to handle the money-talk yourself. If you have a good relationship with your agent, and the situation warrants, you might just save the job.

I know one voice-actor who auditioned for a CD-ROM game and noticed that the other voice-actors who said they had an agent were being passed over for callbacks. After noticing this, he called his agent to discuss the situation. Their mutual decision was that the voice-actor would avoid any mention of representation until after he was booked. He handled the negotiations himself and actually managed to get a higher fee than most of the other voice-actors booked for the project. Even if you are an accomplished negotiator, your agent is your representative. Generally, it is not a good idea to take things into your own hands until you have talked things over with your agent.

As their career grows, it is common for performers to change agents several times. A word of warning, though: Changing agents can be traumatic. You are likely to have a case of the "guilts" when leaving an agent, especially if the person has done a lot to help promote you and develop your career. When this time comes, it is important to remember the reasons why you must change agents. You may have reached a level of skill that is beyond your agent's ability to market effectively, or you may simply be moving to a new part of the country. On the other hand, you might be changing agents because your current agent is simply not getting you the kind of jobs you need.

Promoting and Marketing Yourself

Getting voice-over work is a numbers game: The more contacts you have, the more you will work. The more work you do, the better known you will become. The better known you become, the more people who want to hire you, and you get more work. It's not quite that simple, but you get the idea.

Again, the voice-over business is a numbers game. Having an agent working for you is definitely to your advantage; however, that does not mean you can relax and just wait for the work to come in. It is important for you to network constantly and let your talents be known. Networking with other voice-over performers keeps you up on current trends, and, if you are nonunion, you may get a better idea of the fees other performers are earning. Always keep a few demos and business cards with you and be ready to pitch yourself when the opportunity arises. Remember, always present yourself professionally. It's a subtlety, but maintaining an attitude of professionalism communicates credibility and integrity.

Your agent, if you have one, will be pitching you to ad agencies and other producers in your area. Before embarking on an all-out promotion campaign for yourself, discuss your ideas with your agency. The agent may be able to recommend specific places for you to contact, or ask that you let the agency handle all your promotion. If you agree to let the agent do all the work, set a time limit of perhaps a few months to see how many auditions you are booked for. Working with your agent is the best way to have an organized and consistent promotion campaign for your voice-over talents.

If you do not have an agent, and are not planning to get one in the immediate future, you are on your own. If you expect to get any auditions or any work, you must devise your own promotion and marketing campaign and do all the legwork. This can be a time-consuming process, but you can make it go a bit easier if you take it in stages. As you create your promotion campaign, remember why you are doing it, and keep polishing your acting techniques.

There are many good books on marketing and advertising from which you can gain a tremendous amount of information. You can also learn a great deal by taking an adult education or college extension advertising and marketing course. Not only will you learn some good ways to promote yourself, but you will also learn some of what goes into creating the copy that you work with as a voice-over performer.

When you promote and market yourself, you are your own agent and ad agency. These simply become additional aspects of your business and you must become familiar with them if you are to be successful. There are three basic parts to the promotion of your voice-over work: the demo tape, making contacts and follow-up.

YOUR DEMO TAPE

This is your résumé and your product (at least at this point in time). Your demo is what your potential employers (your customers) will use to judge your talent as it applies to their projects. Chapter 13, Your Demo Tape, covers this subject in detail.

MAKING CONTACTS

You will need to spend a fair amount of time on the phone, contacting potential talent buyers. Before making any calls, you must be prepared, and know what you want to discuss. Be specific about the type or types of voice-over work you are promoting. If you are trying to get into animation voice-over, you don't want to call ad agencies.

When making your calls, be ready to provide the names of any producers you have worked for and some of the projects you have done. Have some prepared notes to look at so that you don't forget anything important during your call. Needless to say, your stationery should be printed, and your demo tape should be produced and ready to mail out before you begin making calls.

Remember, you need to talk to someone who is directly responsible for hiring voice-over performers for commercials, sales presentations, and in-house video projects. If you do not have a contact name already, tell the receptionist the purpose of your call, and she will most likely direct you to the person you need to speak to, or refer you to someone who might know to whom you should speak. If you can't get connected right away, get a name to ask for when you call back.

Keep your conversation short and to the point. Let your contact know who you are and briefly describe the purpose of your call. Find out if the company uses voice-over performers for any of their advertising, promotional or marketing needs, and if they use in-house talent, union talent or freelancers. You probably will find some companies that have not even considered hiring an outside professional for their voice-over needs. Undoubtedly, you will also find many that are not even interested. Remember, this is a numbers game, so don't let yourself get discouraged.

For those that use voice-over talent, offer to send a copy of your demo. Follow up by mailing your demo with a letter of introduction. It is amazing how many people never follow up a lead by sending out their promo kit. You will not get any work if you don't follow up.

FOLLOW-UP

You will need the following basic items for follow-up:

- A cover letter on professional-looking letterhead
- Business cards
- Labels or envelopes capable of holding your print materials and demo
- A voice-over résumé detailing any session work you have done
- Your demo tape

If you have a computer, a word processing program and a high-quality laser or ink-jet printer, you can design a simple form letter that can be adapted to your needs. If not, most quick-print companies can provide inexpensive letterhead and business cards. Don't use an old dot matrix printer — the quality just does not look professional by today's standards. First impressions are important, and the more professional you look in print, and sound on the phone, the more your prospect is likely to consider you for work.

You will need a formal letter of introduction. In fact, you may find that you need a few different versions, depending on whether you are following up from a phone call, or if the follow-up is from a personal meeting.

Keep your letter to no more than three or four short paragraphs in a formal business style. Personalize the heading as you would for any business letter. Thank the person you spoke to for his or her interest, and for the time spent talking to you. Remind them of who you are and what you do. Let the company know how you can help them and how they can contact you. Also, mention in the letter that you are enclosing your demo. The following is an example of a typical follow-up letter:

Mr. Charles Client
5007 Santa Monica Bl.
New Town, CA 80750

Dear Mr. Client:

Thank you for taking the time to speak with me yesterday, and for your interest in my voice-over work.

As I mentioned during our conversation, I am available to help your company as a voice-over performer for in-house training tapes, marketing presentations and radio or television commercial advertising. I am enclosing a list of some recent projects I have done, which have been used successfully for in-house productions and on-air commercials. I am also enclosing a copy of my demo, which runs approximately two minutes. This will give you a good idea of the types of voice-over work I do that can be of benefit to you.

Should you be in need of my services, please feel free to call me anytime at the phone number above. I look forward to working with you soon.

Sincerely,

If you like, you might include a copy of your voice-over résumé, provided you have some experience. If you have an agent, include the agent's name and phone number in the letter. In larger markets your agent's number should be the only contact reference. In smaller markets you may want to include your own number as well as your agent's. (NOTE: Your agent's name and phone number should be on your demo, but mention it in the letter as well.)

Two things you *do not* need to mention in your follow-up letter are your union status and fees. Your union status should have been established during your phone call, if that was an issue. Your fees are something to be negotiated either by your agent, or by you, at the time you are booked. If it comes up in a conversation, just tell the person that your agent handles that, or that you cannot quote a rate until you know what you will do. If they insist, quote the current AFTRA scale for the type of work they are asking about. At least that way you will be quoting a rate that will be close to any union talent interviewed later on. If you are booking yourself as nonunion, freelance talent, you might want to let your contact know that your fees are negotiable.

After sending your follow-up letter and demo, wait about a week, then call your contact again to confirm that the package was received. This helps to maintain your professional image and serves to keep your name on their mind. Don't ask if the person has listened to your tape. That's not the purpose of your call. If they bring it up, fine, but you should not mention it.

Before completing your follow-up call, ask if there are any projects coming up in the near future that might take advantage of your talents. If so, and if the company is considering other voice-over talent, be sure to make yourself available for an audition. Phrase your conversation in such a way that it seems like you are offering to help them. This puts you in a position of offering something of greater value to your potential employer, rather than just being someone asking for work.

Once you have established a list of possible employers, you will want to stay in touch with them. Consider sending out a brief note or postcard every six months or so and on holidays. The purpose here is to keep your name in front of the people who book talent. You can even include a list of recent projects, and enclose a reply card, or offer to send a current demo.

Perhaps the only rule for follow-up is to be consistent and persistent. Maintain a professional image and keep your name in front of your prospects, and you will get more work. Here are some ideas for follow-up reminders:

- Thank you card (after session, meeting or conversation)
- Holiday and seasonal cards
- Birthday's and anniversaries (if you know them)
- Current projects you have done
- Generic reminder postcard
- Semi-annual one-page newsletter updating your activities
- Special announcement about upcoming projects

REACHING THE PEOPLE WHO BOOK TALENT

Many large companies have in-house production units, while others hire outside production houses and work with agents. There usually will be someone who is in charge of coordinating promotion and advertising that may require the use of voice-over performers.

One problem in reaching people who use voice-over talent is figuring out which companies are likely to need your services. Here are some possibilities:

- **Watch local TV and listen to the radio.** Look for local advertisers who are doing commercials with voice-over talent.

- **Call advertisers and ask who coordinates their radio and TV advertising.** Radio stations frequently use station staff for local commercials, and will not charge their advertisers any talent fees. You need to convince these advertisers why they should pay you to do voice-over work when the radio station does it for free. When talking directly to radio advertisers, you need to put yourself in a class above the radio DJ. Some advertisers like the radio station tie-in by using station talent. Other advertisers may simply prefer to spend as little as possible on advertising. You *can* get work from these people, but it will be an education process to get them to understand the value of using you instead of doing it themselves or using a DJ for their commercials. You may find that they have other uses for voice-over talent for which you would be far more qualified than a DJ.

- **Contact the local chamber of commerce.** Get a list of the largest companies in your area. Many of them will use voice-over performers and some will do in-house production.

- **Check the local newspapers.** Call advertisers that you think might be likely prospects.

- **Use resource directories.** Many cities have a resource directory or a service bureau that can provide you with specific information about businesses in the area. Or, your chamber of commerce may be able to provide this information.

When you contact a nonbroadcast business that has a production unit, start by asking to talk to the creative, promotion or marketing department. You should talk to a producer, director or writer. Don't ask for advertising or sales, or you may be connected to a sales rep. If you ask for the production department, you may end up talking to someone in charge of an assembly line.

Television stations can be a good source for bookings. They use voice-over for all sorts of projects, many of which are never aired. At a TV station, the production department handles most audio and video production. Some TV stations may even have separate production units for commercials, station promotion, and sales and marketing projects. Start by asking to talk to the production manager, an executive producer or someone in creative services. You may end up talking to someone in the promotion department, because a promotion producer frequently uses more voice-over talent than anyone else at the station.

Recording studios usually will not be a good source for work, simply because most recording studios specialize in music recording. Usually, those that produce a lot of commercials work with performers hired by an ad agency or client. Some studios do a limited amount of producing and writing, and may book their voice-over talent from a pool of performers they work with regularly. In most cities, there are at least one or two studios that specialize in producing radio commercials. Use good judgment when sending your demo to recording studios. You might be wasting your time, but then, you never know from where your next job might appear.

Of course, contacting advertising agencies directly is another good way to reach the person who books talent. At an ad agency, the person you want to reach is the in-house producer. Some ad agencies may have several in-house producers, and some agencies have account executives who work double duty as producers. If there is any doubt, ask to speak to the person who books or approves voice-over talent.

There are no hard-and-fast rules here. As you call around, you just need to try to find the correct contact person. Once you connect, use the basic marketing techniques described in this chapter to promote yourself.

KEEPING RECORDS

As an independent businessperson, whether you have an agent or are working independently, you need to keep complete and accurate records of income and business-related expenses. This is not just for your tax records, but also so you have a way of tracking your career as a professional voice-over performer. Consult a tax advisor as to the best way to set up your recordkeeping or refer to some of the many books on the subject.

You will want to keep records of clients you have worked for, what you did for them, and when you did it. When you get called by a producer you worked for last year, you can avoid undercharging by checking your files to see what your fee was last time. You can also use these records for future promotion and reminder mailings. A simple scheduling book can serve the purpose nicely, or you can even set up a database on your computer. Personal money management computer programs are another excellent way to keep records. Most range in the price from $30 to $75.

Under the current (1998) tax code, just about any expense you have that directly relates to your business can be deducted as a business expense. Even if you work another full-time job, you can still deduct expenses that directly relate to your voice-over business. Depending on your situation, you may want to obtain a business license in your city, and eventually may want to incorporate. Setting up a legitimate business entity may have certain tax advantages. A tax advisor can help you with these decisions.

The following are some of the things you should keep records of:

- **Income** — Keep separate account categories for income from all sources, and anything deducted from a paycheck: income received, income taxes deducted, social security taxes deducted, medicare taxes deducted, state disability taxes deducted, union fees deducted, and any other deductions from a paycheck.

- **Expenses** — The costs of doing business.
    Demo production: Keep track of payments for studio time, costs and materials, duplication, printing, letterhead, business cards, mailing envelopes, postcards, résumés, J-Cards and cassette labels.
    Telephone: Keep track of phone calls made to prospects or your agent, especially any long-distance charges. You might consider a separate phone line to use exclusively for your business. If you have a cell phone or pager, these costs are deductible as well.
    Transportation: Keep a log book in your car and note the mileage for   all travel to and from auditions and sessions. Include parking fees.
    Other business expenses: Keep track of postage, office supplies, office equipment, computer equipment and other supplies. Note that the IRS tends to view computers as personal equipment, rather than business equipment, unless the use is well documented.
    Classes, workshops and books: Classes and books may be deductible as expenses for continued education and training in your chosen field.
    In-home office: Deducting a portion of your mortgage or rent, and utilities for an in-home office, although legal, may trigger an audit by the IRS. Consult a tax advisor before taking this deduction.

You may want to set up a separate checking account for your voice-over business. This can help to keep all the financial aspects of your business in one place. The bottom line is that, as a professional voice-actor, you are in business for yourself whether you work another job or not. As a business-person it is important that you keep accurate records of your business-related income and expenses.

---

[1] AFTRA-SAG Information Packet, 1997.

16

Auditions

Auditions may seem frustrating and nerve-wracking, but they are an essential part of the voice-over business. Without auditions, it would be very difficult for performers to get exposure to producers and ad agency talent buyers.

If you are a union performer, there are specific rules regarding compensation for auditions and callbacks. I know of some high-priced voice performers who demand $1,000 for an unsupervised and undirected audition. This is an extreme case, but it makes the point that if you are very good and in demand, you will be paid what you are worth.

The Audition Process

The audition process is the most efficient way a producer or advertiser has of choosing the best performer for a project. The process actually begins when the copy for a project is first written. Quite often a script is written with a particular attitude in mind, and sometimes even with a specific performer in mind.

Once a script is written, copies are sent out to talent agents and casting directors. Specific performers or character types may be requested for an audition, but usually the talent agent and casting director select performers from their talent pool that they feel will work best for the project being submitted. If a specific voice-actor is requested, the talent agent will attempt to book that performer.

You, the *talent*, are then called and scheduled for an audition. If you are just starting out, chances are you will get the call from one of your contacts, through classes, recommendations, friends, networking or sending out your demo. You may receive the call several days in advance, the day before, or even the day of an audition.

The audition could be held anywhere. Some ad agencies have a recording booth for handling voice auditions. Sometimes auditions are held at a recording studio, the client's office, a radio or TV station, or even at a hotel conference room.

You will be given a time and location for your audition, but usually you will not be asked when you are available, although you often can arrange a mutually agreeable time. Auditions are generally scheduled over one or two days, every 10 to 20 minutes and, depending on the scope of the project, there may be dozens of performers being auditioned for the same roles. You may or may not be told something about the project, and rarely will you receive the copy ahead of time. Only if you absolutely cannot make the scheduled appointment should you call the casting agent to let him or her know. The agent may, or may not, be able to reschedule you.

Preparing for Your Audition

You most likely will feel a rush of excitement when you get the call for an audition. That excitement could quickly turn to panic if you let it. Don't let yourself get caught up in the excitement. Focus on the job before you and keep breathing. Approach the audition with a professional commitment to do your best.

WHERE DID THOSE BUTTERFLIES COME FROM?

As soon as you get the call for an audition, you will probably begin to feel butterflies in your stomach. This is a good time for you to practice some relaxation exercises. You need to prepare yourself mentally and physically for the audition. Just the fact that you were called to audition is a good sign, so keep a positive mental attitude. After all, you have been invited to be there.

THE DAY HAS ARRIVED

On the day of the audition, loosen up with some stretches and voice exercises. Dress comfortably, yet professionally. Be careful not to wear clothing or jewelry that will make noise when you are on-mic. If your audition is close to a meal, eat lightly and avoid foods that you know cause problems with your performance.

Plan to arrive at you audition about 15 to 20 minutes before your scheduled time. Make sure you leave enough time to allow for any traffic problems and for parking. If you are not on time, you may arrive too late to read for your part, especially for multiple-voice auditions. When in your car, continue with some warm-up exercises and listen to music that will put you in a positive frame of mind. Sing *loud* to songs on the radio to loosen up your voice and relax your inhibitions.

Always bring several sharpened pencils for making copy notes and changes and a bottle of water. A briefcase containing your supplies, business cards and several copies of your demo tape can add that extra touch of professionalism to your image. Don't plan on giving tapes or business cards to the people you are auditioning for, unless they request them — they already know who you are. These are for other people you might meet whom you did not expect to be there.

Act as if you know what you are doing, even if this is your first audition. Watch others, follow their lead, and keep a positive attitude.

KEEP TRACK OF THINGS

Under 1998 tax laws, any expenses you incur that directly relate to earning income are deductible, including travel expenses to and from auditions and parking fees, whether or not you get the job. It's a good idea to keep a journal with you so that you can itemize your expenses. You also may want to keep a record of auditions you are sent on, who the casting people are, where the audition was held, and how you felt about it. You might include names, addresses and phone numbers to add to your follow-up mailing list.

What to Expect, and What's Expected of You

When you arrive at the audition, you may find several other performers already there. Also, you may find that several auditions are being conducted at the same time, with different copy for a variety of projects. Find the correct audition and pick up your copy. If the audition is for a large account, someone may be "checking-in" the scheduled performers. In most cases, there will simply be a sign-in sheet at the door and a pile of scripts. Once signed in, you are considered available to audition and may be called at any time. If you are early and want to take some time to study the copy, wait a few minutes before signing in.

You can expect to see the copy for the first time only after you have arrived at the audition. If the audition is for a long project, such as a CD-ROM game, you might receive copy a day or so ahead so that you can familiarize yourself with it, but this is pretty uncommon. On some occasions, for reasons only the producer can understand, you will have to wait until you are *in* the booth before you know what you are doing. I've even heard of auditions where there is no formal script and the performers are simply asked to improvise on lines or props provided by the producer. Fortunately, this is rare, but it does happen.

BE PREPARED TO WAIT

Even if the audition starts on schedule, chances are that within a short time, the producers will be running late. Have something to read or do while you wait for your turn at the mic. Stay relaxed and calm, and keep breathing. This is a good opportunity to get to know some of the other performers who are there. Remember, networking can be a valuable tool — it's often not what you know, but who you know that gets you work. Even though these people may be your direct competition, you may make a connection for future jobs that would have otherwise passed you by.

If the copy is for a dialog spot, you may find another performer willing to *run lines*, or practice the copy with you. This can be an advantage for both of you, even if you do not do the audition together. However, be aware that many performers prefer to keep to themselves before an audition and sometimes interaction with the competition can be distracting.

EXPECT TO BE NERVOUS

When you first enter a studio, you will probably be nervous. This is only natural, but it is something you need to control. You must be able to convert your nervous energy into productive energy for your performance. Focus on your acting rather than on the words in the script. Allow a loving and long — deep down through your body breath to center yourself and focus your vocal awareness. Chapter 6, Taking Care of Your Voice, explains how to do this.

You know you are nervous and so do the casting people. Don't waste time trying to suppress or conceal your nervousness. Breathe through it and focus on converting the nervous energy into positive energy.

EXPECT TO BE TREATED LIKE JUST ANOTHER VOICE

At most auditions, the people there really want you to be the right person for the job. However, if the audition is for a major account in a major city, expect the possibility of being treated rudely by people who just don't care and are trying to rush as many performers through the audition as possible in a limited amount of time. If anything other than this happens, consider yourself lucky.

PREPARE YOURSELF

Once you get your copy, use your waiting time to study it for your character, key words, target audience, and for anything that is unclear — especially words you don't understand or don't know how to pronounce. Try to get a feel for what they are looking for — What attitude? What sort of delivery? Most of the time, your choices will be clear. Sometimes, there will be a character description on the copy, or some notes as to what the producers are after. Note the important words to emphasize, the advertiser and product name, what to punch, where to pull back. Mark your copy in advance so that you will know what you need to do to achieve the delivery you want. Read the copy out loud and time yourself. Don't rehearse the copy silently by merely reading and saying the words in your mind. In order to get an accurate timing and delivery, you must vocalize the copy. Make sure you know how you will deliver the copy in the allotted time.

Be careful not to overanalyze. Read the copy enough times to become familiar with it and know what you are doing, then put it aside. Overanalyzing can cause you to lose your spontaneity. Decide on the initial choices for your performance, and commit to them. But be prepared to give several different variations. Also, be prepared for the director to ask for something completely opposite of what you came up with.

Auditions for a TV spot usually have a storyboard available. This may be attached to the script, or posted on a wall. It may be legible or it may be a poor copy. A *storyboard* is a series of drawings, similar to a cartoon strip, that describes the visual elements of a TV commercial or film that correspond to the copy. If there is a storyboard for your audition, study it thoroughly. Instead of a storyboard, many TV-commercial scripts have a description of the visuals on the left side of the page with the voice-over copy on the right side. The storyboard or visual description is the best tool you have to gain an understanding of a video or film project. If you only focus on the words in the script, you will be overlooking valuable information that could give you the inspiration you need to create the performance that gets you the job.

MAKE A GOOD FIRST IMPRESSION

Greet the producer or host, introduce yourself, shake hands, be spontaneous, be sincere and be friendly. If you are auditioning near the end of a long day, the people in the room may not be in the best of moods. You still need to be friendly and professional as long as you are in that room. Remember, first impressions are important. Your first impression of them might not be very good, but you need to make sure that their first impression of you is as good as possible. Your personality and willingness to meet their needs will go a long way.

Answer any questions the producer, agency rep or engineer ask of you. They will show you where the mic is and let you know when they are ready for you to begin. Do not touch any equipment — especially the mic. Let the engineer or someone from the audition staff handle the equipment, unless you are specifically asked to make an adjustment.

There will probably be a music stand near the microphone. Put your copy here. If there is no stand, you will have to hold the copy, which may restrict your performance if you need to move your arms or body. If headphones are available, put them on — this may be the only way you will hear cues and direction from the control room. In some cases, you may be asked to read along with a scratch track for timing purposes and you will need the headphones to hear it.

A *scratch track* is a preliminary version of the commercial that is usually produced as a guide for video editing or as a sample for the client. Sometimes, you might be lucky enough to actually have a music track to work against. This can be very helpful, because music is often used to help set the mood for a commercial and can provide clues about the target audience. If you don't have anything to work against, you might ask the producer or director to give you an idea of the rhythm and pacing for the project.

Before you start, the engineer or producer, will ask you for a "level". This is so the proper record volume can be set on the equipment. When giving a level, read your copy exactly the way you plan to when you perform the audition. Many people make the mistake of just saying their name or counting 1, 2, 3, . . ., or speaking in a softer voice than when they read for the audition. It is important to give the engineer an accurate level, or your recording may be distorted. Use this as an opportunity to rehearse your performance.

MAKE THE COPY YOUR OWN

Your best bet for getting a job from an audition is to discover the character in the copy and allow that character to be revealed through your performance. Play with the words that are written! Have fun with it! Put your personal spin on the copy! Do not change words, but rather add your own unique twist to the delivery. Use the skills of voice-acting you have mastered to make the copy your own. If they want something else, they will tell you.

Making the copy your own is an acquired acting skill. It may take you a while to find your unique personality traits, but the search will be worthwhile. Chapter 7, The Character in the Copy, discusses this aspect of voice-over work.

DO YOUR BEST

You will have only a few moments to do your best performance. Remember, you are auditioning as a professional, and those holding the audition are expecting a certain level of competency. When asked to begin, start by slating your name, then perform as you have planned. To *slate your name*, clearly give both your first and last name, your agent's name and the name of the project you are auditioning for. The following is a typical audition slate:

> "Hi, my name is Bobbie Wilson. My agent is Cameron Ross and I'm reading for Toasty Magic Squares."

After your slate, wait a few beats, then begin your performance.

You may, or may not, receive direction or coaching from the casting person. If you are given direction, it may be completely different from your interpretation of the copy. You may be asked to give several different reads, and you need to be flexible enough to give the producer what he or she wants, regardless of whether you think it is the right way. You may, or may not, be able to ask questions. It depends entirely on the producer.

Don't let yourself get distracted by the people in the room. There may be anywhere from two or three up to several people in attendance. Focus on your performance and don't worry about the people in the control room.

Many auditions are simply intended to narrow down possible voices and the performance is secondary. The copy used in some auditions may not even be close to the final version, while other auditions work with final copy. Either way, you are expected to perform to the best of your abilities. Do your best interpretation first, and let the producer ask for changes after that. It may be that your interpretation gives the producer an idea he or she had not thought of earlier, which could turn out to be the detail that gets you the job.

Some producers may be open to suggestions or a different interpretation, while others are totally set in their ways. Offering your thoughts and opinions is usually not a good idea at an audition, but it is something you can do if it feels appropriate. If the producer is not open to it, he or she will tell you. These are not shy people.

The casting person will let you know when they have what they want. Two or three reads of the copy may be all the opportunity you have to do your best work. They may, or may not, play back your audition before you leave. If you do get a playback, this is a good opportunity for you to study your performance. Do not ask if you can do another take unless you honestly believe you can do a much better performance, or unless the producer asks if you can do something different. When you are done, thank them, then leave. Your audition is over. If you like, take the script with you, unless you are asked to return it.

After the Audition

After an audition, and if this is something you have already discussed with your agent, you can call and let him or her know how it went. Most of the time, though, you will simply wait for a call from your agent. If you do not hear anything within 72 hours, you can safely assume that you did not get the job. As a general rule, agents only call if you get the booking or are requested for a callback.

While you are waiting for that call from your agent, don't allow yourself to become worried about whether or not you will get the job. Write your followup letter and continue doing what you usually do. Remember that voice-acting is a numbers game, and that if you don't get this job, there is another opportunity coming up just down the road.

WHEN THE ACTORS ARE GONE

At the end of the day, the audition staff takes all the tapes and returns to their office. There, they listen to the tapes and narrow down the candidates. They may choose the voice they want right away, or they may decide to do a second audition — called a *callback* — to further narrow the candidates. The audition producer will contact the appropriate talent agents to book talent for a session or callback, or will call independent performers directly. Voice-over audition callbacks are fairly rare, but when they occur, they are usually for a major regional or national account.

If you are scheduled for a callback, you may find there is less pressure and the attitude of the people involved may have changed a bit. At a callback, the producer may say that they really liked what you did on take 3 of the first audition. Chances are, unless they have a tape to play for you, or unless you have an exceptionally good memory, you will not remember what you did on take 3, or any of the takes for that matter. When this happens, all you can do is go for your best interpretation of the copy (which probably changed since the original audition), and use any direction from the producer to guide you.

The simple fact that you are called back for a second audition shows that there is something about your performance that the producer likes. Try to find out what it was that got you the callback. Do whatever you can to stay on the producer's good side and make friends. If for some reason you do not get this job, the producer may remember you next week or next month when another voice-over performer is needed for another project.

After the callback, the audition staff once again takes their collection of tapes (much smaller this time), and returns to their office. This cycle may be repeated several times until the producer or client is satisfied that the right voice is chosen.

BE GOOD TO YOURSELF

You've done a good job! You have survived your audition. Now you deserve a treat. Take yourself out to lunch, buy that hot new CD you've been wanting or simply do something nice for yourself. It doesn't really matter what you do — just do something special.

When you left the audition, you probably came up with dozens of things you could have done differently. You might even feel like going to your car, winding up the windows and screaming real loud. Second-guessing yourself is self-defeating and counterproductive. Instead of beating yourself up with negatives, do something positive and be good to yourself.

Demos

Not all auditions are held for the purpose of casting a final project. In some cases, you will be auditioning for a demo. *Demos* are produced by ad agencies as potential commercials that they use to sell an idea to their client. The commercial may never actually be produced for on-air use. Often, the entire concept of an advertising campaign is changed between the time a demo is produced and production of the final spot.

You may be told that the audition is for a demo at the time you are there, or at some time after your audition. Either way, the recording from your audition normally will not be the recording used for the demo. If it is to be used for the demo, you will be compensated for your time at the audition.

AFTRA has a separate rate for demo sessions, which is different from their commercial scale. Demos are usually paid for on a one-time-only fee basis. However, a demo can be upgraded to a commercial if the client decides to use it. In this case, your fee would also be upgraded to the commercial rate. Independent voice-actors need to negotiate their own fee for a demo, or let their agent handle it.

Audition Dos, Don'ts and Common Courtesies

Here are some tips for making your audition an enjoyable and productive experience:

- Do arrange your schedule so that you can attend the audition
- Do arrive early — at least 15 to 20 minutes before your audition time
- Do call to let the casting agent know if you absolutely can't make the audition

- Do be prepared to do your best
- Do be spontaneous, sincere, friendly and willing to adapt
- Do redirect your nervous energy into constructive performance energy — keep breathing and focus on performing, not on the words in the script
- Do stay relaxed and confident of your abilities — remember, you were invited to be there
- Do act as if you know what you are doing — don't let on if this is your first audition
- Do make the copy your own — add your personality and individual "spin" to the copy
- Do keep track of your expenses — the IRS requires detailed records
- Do thank the casting agent or producer when you leave
- Do leave a current demo tape — ask the casting person first if it would be appropriate for you to leave a current demo
- Do make a note of names and addresses and add them to your mailing list for holiday cards, reminders and follow-up
- Do leave quickly and quietly — when your job is done, make a professional exit
- Do treat yourself to something special — it's a gift from you to you for a job well done — whether you get the job or not
- Do your best — remember that the casting person wants you to succeed and wants you to be the person they are looking for
- Don't touch any equipment — (anything on the copy stand is OK); let the engineer make adjustments to the microphone
- Don't ever argue with the casting people about their direction or doing the performance the way they want
- Don't be afraid to let them know if you make a mistake — you can start over
- Don't ask the casting agent when they will know who is hired — they won't be able to tell you anyway
- Don't ask if you can call later — they will call you or your agent if they want you for the job or a callback
- Don't ask for a advice or critique of your work — this is not the time or place
- Don't ask if you can audition again — this is your only chance

The Voice-Over Checklist

Jim Staylor is a full-time voice-actor who has performed internationally as both voice-over and on-camera talent for hundreds of commercials, corporate projects, CD-ROM and video games. His voice-over checklist (see Figure 16-1) covers all the basics from preparing for the session to what to do afterwards.

Voice-Over Checklist

What to do before . . .
- ✓ Confirm date and time.
- ✓ Verify location and directions.
- ✓ Check for schedule conflicts.
- ✓ Bathe and dress comfortably.
- ✓ Mark script (pauses and emphasis).

What to avoid . . .
- Alcohol
- Caffeine
- Stress
- Yelling
- Dairy products
- Cold drinks
- Big meals
- Cologne and/or perfume

What to bring . . .
- ❑ Marked script
- ❑ Pencil and eraser
- ❑ Highlighter
- ❑ White-out
- ❑ Drinking water
- ❑ Lozenges or cough drops
- ❑ Talent voucher form
- ❑ Demo tapes and business cards

Warm-up . . .
- Hum up and sown throughout a range of pitch scales.
- Repeat "huh-huh-huh" in short blasts from diaphragm.
- Repeat "red leather, yellow leather, blue leather, yellow leather."
- Practice favorite tongue-twisters.

What to do during . . .
- Be confident — fake it, if necessary.
- Request breaks when needed.
- Have headphone volume adjusted.
- Ask questions if direction is needed.

What to do after . . .
- ❑ Thank everyone involved.
- ❑ Complete talent voucher form.
- ❑ Return voucher to agency.
- ❑ Forget it — don't second-guess.
- ❑ Follow-up with postcards.

Staylor-Made Communications © 1996

Figure 16-1: The Staylor-Made Voice-Over Checklist. Reprinted by permission.

A laminated pocket-size version of the checklist can be obtained by contacting Jim Staylor, Staylor-Made Communications, 12065 World Trade Drive, Suite 2, San Diego, CA 92128; e-mail: info@staylor-made.com; web site: www.staylor-made.com.

17

You're Hired!
The Session

The recording session is where your voice is recorded and all the pieces of the puzzle are put together to create a final commercial or soundtrack. Besides your voice, the project may include music, sound effects, other voices, recordings of interviews or other "sound bites," and digitally processed audio. It is the job of the recording engineer to assemble these various puzzle pieces to form the *picture* originally created in the mind of the producer or writer. It can be a challenging process.

From Concept to Creative Process

Much of the creative process involves a lot of technology and a high level of creativity from the engineer. As a voice-over performer, there is only a small portion of the recording process that involves you. To give you a better idea of how your performance fits within the whole process, the entire sequence of a project will be explained in this chapter. But first, let's review the creative process and some things you should know about studio etiquette.

THE IDEA

It all begins with an idea! That idea is put into words on a script, which may go through many revisions and changes. At some point during the script's development, thoughts turn to casting the roles in the script. In some cases, a role may be written with a specific performer in mind, but this is usually the exception to the rule. To cast the various roles, the producers listen to demo tapes and hold auditions. The audition process (Chapter 16) narrows the playing field to select the most appropriate voice talent for the project at hand. If your voice is right for the part, and your demo tape or audition was heard by the right person, you could be hired for a role.

IT'S YOU THEY WANT

When you are booked for a studio session, it is because the producer has chosen your voice over all the others that were auditioned. There is something about *you* that the producer believes is right for his or her project. It could be the way you interpret the copy; it could be a quality in your voice; it could be anything. You are the chosen one! You've got the job! Congratulations!

You probably got the call from your agent, or from the client directly if you are working as an independent performer. Either way, you need to make sure you know what your *call time* is for the recording session. You also need to know where your session will be done. If you don't know where the recording studio, radio station, TV station or ad agency is, get directions.

TIME IS MONEY

Be absolutely certain you arrive *before* your scheduled session time. It is much better to be early and have to wait a few minutes than for you to be late and hold up the session. Recording studios book by the hour, and they are not cheap. Basic voice-over session time can be in the range of $100 an hour or more, depending on the studio. You do not want to be the person responsible for costing the client more money than necessary.

Producing commercials, or any type of audio soundtrack, can be an expensive proposition. So that you are aware of what a producer is dealing with, here are some of the many costs involved in a typical radio or TV commercial:

- Voice-over talent fee (union scale plus residuals)
- Union health, welfare and pension fees (added on top of the talent fee and agent commission)
- Talent agent commission (10% of talent fee for each performer)
- Casting director fees (if one is hired for the project)
- Writing fees (if an outside copywriter is employed)
- Producing fees (if an outside producer is employed)
- Recording studio time (at an hourly rate — the studio rate could change from the voice-over session to music session and postproduction)

- Cost of recording materials (media and tape stock)
- Music licensing fees (charges for licensing the performance of music used)
- Original music fees (composer, musicians and related union fees)
- Other union charges (meal penalties, overtime, etc.)
- Cartage fees (costs related to transporting musical instruments)
- Duplication fees (cost of making copies of the finished product)
- Distribution fees (cost of distributing copies to radio and TV stations or other end users of the project)
- Airtime (cost of time on the radio or TV station to run the commercial)
- Other fees related to the project

These charges add up quickly and are usually paid by the advertiser. Obviously the advertiser wants to keep expenses to a minimum. Clients are very unhappy when a performer shows up late with an attitude of not caring about how he or she affected the session. Or worse, not caring about giving the best performance.

Time is also of the essence when you are in the studio. Things can happen very fast once you are on mic and recording begins. You need to be able to deliver your best performance within a few takes. If the producer or director gives you instructions, you need to understand them quickly and adapt your delivery as needed.

If you are working a dialog script with a performer you have never met before, you both need to be able to give a performance that creates the illusion that your separate characters are spontaneous and natural. This is where your character analysis and acting skills really come into play.

WORKING WITH PRODUCERS, DIRECTORS, WRITERS AND CLIENTS

A voice-actor friend of mine once described a producer/director as "headphones with an attitude." Regardless of the producer's attitude, you need to be able to perform effectively. You must be able to adapt your character and delivery to give the producer what he or she asks for. And you need to be able to do this quickly with an attitude of cooperation.

It is common for a producer, after doing many takes, to decide to go back to the kind of read you did at the beginning. You need to be able to do it. It is also common for a producer to focus on getting exactly the right inflection for a single word in the copy. You might do 15 or 20 takes on just one sentence, then a producer will change his mind and you will have to start all over.

Every producer has a unique technique for directing talent. You must not let a producer frustrate you. Occasionally, you will work for a producer or writer who is incredibly demanding, or simply does not know what he or she wants. When working for this type of person, just do your best and when you are done, leave quietly and politely. When you are alone in your car, driving down the freeway with the windows rolled up, you can scream as loud as you like.

There are some producers who operate on a principle of never accepting anything the first time — no matter how good it might be. Your first take might be wonderful — hitting all the key words, getting just the right inflection. However, the producer may have you do another 10 takes, looking for something better. When all is said and done, that first good take may be the one used in the final project.

WHO ARE THOSE PEOPLE?

Some sessions may be crowded with many people deeply involved with the project you are working on. Of course, the studio engineer will be present, and there will usually be someone who is the obvious producer/director. But the client or storeowner may also be there, as well as his wife, their best friend, the agency rep from their ad agency, the person who wrote the copy, and maybe even an account executive from a radio or TV station. All these people have an opinion about what you are doing, and may want to offer suggestions about what you can do to improve your performance. It's a nice thought, but too many directors will make you crazy.

You may actually find yourself getting direction from more than one person. One of the obvious problems with this is that some of the direction from one person may directly conflict with a direction from another. As a performer, you must choose one person in the control room to whom you will listen for direction and coaching. Most of the time this should be the producer handling the session. However, if it is obvious that the producer cannot control the session, you might choose someone else, if you feel the person is a better director.

Once you have made your choice, you must stick with that person for the duration of the session. Changing directors in mid-session will only make your performance more difficult. You don't need to come right out and make a statement as to who you want to direct the session. Simply focus your attention on the person you picked and direct your questions and thoughts to only that person, mentioning him or her by name when necessary.

When someone else presses the talkback button and gives you some direction, you need to bring control back to the person you chose. Allow the interruption to happen, then refer to your chosen director for confirmation or further comment. After this happens a few times, the would-be director will usually get the hint and let the person in charge handle the session. Future comments will then be routed to you via your chosen producer or director — as they should be.

SESSION DELAYS

Studio time is a valuable commodity. The producer will want your best performance as quickly as possible. In reality, it may take a while to get it. A voice-over session for a :60 radio commercial can take as little as 5 minutes to as much as an hour or longer. A long session for a seemingly simple spot can be the result of one or more of the following factors:

- There may be several voices speaking (dialog or multiple-voice copy), and it may take some time to get the characters right.
- Microphone placement may need to be adjusted or the microphone may need to be changed.
- The copy may require major changes or rewrites during the course of the session.
- A session being done to a video playback may require numerous takes to get the timing right.
- There may be technical problems with the equipment.
- The voice tracks may need to be inserted into a rough spot for client approval before the performers can be released.
- The session may be a *phone patch* (client is not in the studio, but is listening on a telephone hooked up to the recording console), and he or she may request changes that need to be relayed through the producer or engineer.
- The producer, director or client may not know what he or she really wants.
- There may be several would-be directors trying to offer their ideas, creating unnecessary delays.
- The voice-over performer may lack experience, and may not be able to give the producer the desired reading without extensive directing.
- An earlier session may have run overtime, causing all subsequent sessions to start late.

Regardless of how long you are in the studio, you are an employee of the ad agency, producer or client. Present yourself professionally and remain calm. Above all, do your best to enjoy the experience. Keep breathing, stay relaxed and keep a positive attitude.

Types of Voice-Over Sessions

There are many different types of voice-over projects for which you could be hired. The process in the studio will be basically the same for each, but you should still know the differences between them. For simplification, the various types of sessions are discussed here in terms of a radio or TV commercial.

DEMOS

Demos were discussed briefly in Chapter 16 as they applied to auditions. If you are booked to do a demo session, you can expect to be working on a project that has not yet been sold to the client. It will be a demonstration of what the ad agency is recommending. The client may or may not like it. The ad agency may or may not get the account. A demo is a commercial on spec (speculation).

Mel Blanc, one of the great animation character voices of the 1950's and 1960's, once gave the following definition of working on spec:

"Working on spec is doing something now for free, on the promise you will be paid more than you are worth later on. Spec is also a small piece of dirt!" (From *Visual Radio*, 1972, So. California Broadcasters Association)

Advertising agencies, television stations and radio stations often do projects on spec when they are attempting to get an advertiser's business. The potential profit from a successful advertising campaign far outweighs the cost of producing a spec (or demo) commercial — provided the agency lands the account.

Demos will not air (unless they are upgraded by the client), and are paid at a lower scale than regular commercials. In some cases, the demo serves as an audition tape for the ad agency. They may have several different voice-over performers booked to do the demo session. It is not technically an audition, since completed spots will be produced. Instead, demos are intended to give the advertiser a choice of performers for the final commercial. If the demo is simply upgraded, your agent will be contacted and you will be paid an additional fee. If a separate session is booked, you will be contacted, scheduled, and paid an additional fee.

SCRATCH TRACKS

A scratch track is similar to a demo in the sense that it is the preliminary form of a commercial. The major difference is that a scratch track is used as a reference for a commercial that is already in the process of being produced. Scratch tracks are most often used for TV commercials and are produced to give the editor an accurate audio track to edit to. They are often produced with nonprofessional talent doing the voice, but the music, sound effects, and other elements of the spot are most likely in their final placement.

As a voice-over performer, you may be providing the original voice for a scratch track that is being built, or you may be providing the final voice that replaces an earlier recorded voice used on an already-assembled scratch track. Either way, your job will be to perform as accurately as possible to the existing timing for the scratch track. To do this, the engineer will usually play the scratch track back to you as you read your lines.

If the scratch track is on multitrack tape or a digital workstation, the engineer may playback the spot without the scratch voice-over. You will hear the music and effects cues for your timing, but you won't have to compete with the original voice-over. If you are doing the scratch voice, there may only be some elements of the final spot in place, so some of your timing might be guesswork on your part. If you are doing the final voice, the engineer will replace the original voice with your performance when the final audio track is completed.

In a video editing session, the producer may decide that portions of the audio need to be moved or *slid*. This might require a new track to be edited. It might be possible for the audio engineer to reedit the spot using your original recording, or you may need to be called back in for a regular session. Just as for a demo session, your performance for a scratch track may be good enough for use in the final spot. You or your agent will know if the scratch track session is for a demo or a final commercial, and you will be paid accordingly. Of course, if you are doing the job freelance, your fee is whatever you are able to negotiate with the client.

REGULAR SESSION

This is a session for production of a final commercial. Many engineers refer to *regular sessions,* to differentiate them from demos, tags, scratch tracks and so on.

The only difference between this type of session and all the others is that it is for a complete commercial. You may do several reads of the copy in its entirety, or you may do the spot in pieces. Either way, when your voice tracks are recorded, the engineer will use the best parts of your performance to build the finished commercial.

DUBBING OR LOOPING SESSIONS

The term *looping* comes from the early days of film when a section of film was literally made into a loop and played back continuously. With each pass of the film, the performer duplicates his or her performance for a clean recording.

For some sessions, you may be reading your lines as you watch a video or film playback. The purpose of having the video playback is to enable you to hit very specific positions within the copy. The video will also give you a good idea of the attitude you should have as you deliver your lines.

A *dubbing session* is one at which you are replacing an existing audio track (similar to a scratch track session). For example, you might be hired to do the English version of a commercial that originated in France.

One form of a looping session is when you are replacing the voice of an on-camera performer. Looping sessions are also known in the business as *ADR* sessions or *dialog replacement* sessions (the "A" stands for "auto-mated" and refers to how the session is handled technically from an engineering standpoint). Usually, dialog replacement is done by the original on-camera performer. However, in some cases (as with a foreign commercial), the original performer's voice may be replaced with yours.

A second type of looping session occurs when a small section of voice-over copy is repeatedly recorded in an attempt to achieve the perfect performance.

Voice-over recording sessions can be for a variety of projects, including commercials for radio and TV, promos, tags, sales presentations, film narration, corporate or industrial video narration, animation, inter-active CD-ROM, books on tape and many others.

COMMERCIALS AND PROMOS

These are basically the same thing. The difference is that commercials typically sell a product or service and air on several stations, while promos sell a radio or TV station's programming and air only on that station. Promos can be of any length and include everything from the short "coming up next" tracks you hear over a TV show's credits, station IDs, 30-second spots for a specific show and longer image promos.

Commercials can stay current for years, while promos usually have a limited life span ranging from one day to several weeks. TV programming changes frequently and even if the program time slot stays the same, TV stations are constantly updating their visual graphics. Most of the time, changes in a program's time slot, or a stations image, will require production of new promos.

TAGS

Tags are used on both commercials and promos. A tag is the last few seconds of the spot during which the final call for action is made. AFTRA defines a *tag* as an incomplete thought or sentence, which signifies a change of name, date or time. For TV promos, it usually begins with a call to action, such as "don't miss," "watch," or "tonight at . . . ," followed by the name of the program, the time and the station's call letters. The exact order of these elements may differ, but the general information is the same. A typical TV promo tag might be:

"Watch Jeopardy weeknights at 7 here on NBC 7-39."

Commercial tags are similar, except they tell the audience where to buy the product or how to contact the advertiser.

"Order your Super Chair today. Only $19.95. Call 1-800 555-7423."

If you are booked for a commercial tag session, you may do dozens of variations. Each tag may have a different address, phone number, or something unique. Each version you read must fit within a set period of time. AFTRA considers each tag to be a different commercial, so if you are doing a union session you are paid the tag rate for as many tags as you do, as well as the one-time session fee.

Types of Studio Setups and Script Formats

Recording sessions come in all shapes and sizes and with a variety of format styles. The following sections describe some of the setups you are likely to experience.

SINGLE SESSION

At a *single session*, you are the only person in the studio. There will be only one microphone, a music stand, a stool, and a pair of headsets. Many recording studios also have monitor speakers in the studio, so that you can choose to wear the headset or not. Let the engineer make all adjustments to the mic. You can adjust the stool and music stand to your comfort.

For a single read, you are the only voice that is being recorded at the session. This does not necessarily mean that you are the only voice that will appear in the final project. Other performers, to be recorded at another time, may be scheduled for different sections of the project, or for the tag.

GROUP SESSION

Multiple-voice sessions are often the most fun of all types of sessions simply because of the ensemble. Dialog copy is usually more creative than single-voice copy, and dialog scripts frequently have a comedic premise where there needs to be an interaction between characters. In some cases, the principal actors and the tag announcer may all be in the studio at the same time — it can get cozy. Each performer normally has his or her own mic, music stand and headset. Depending on the studio, two performers may be set up facing each other, working off the same mic, or on separate mics in different areas of the studio.

A group session is like a small play, only without sets. You will have an opportunity to rehearse your lines and get into character. Once the engineer starts recording, you're "on"! The producer or director may give direction to only one performer in the group, or to the group as a whole.

SCRIPT FORMATS

There are a variety of script formats used in the business of voice-over. Radio, TV, film, multimedia and corporate scripts all have slight differences. Regardless of the format, all scripts include the words you will be delivering and important clues you can use to uncover the three building blocks of any effective performance:

- Who is the audience?
- Who is your character?
- Why is your character speaking these words at this moment in time?

The scripts in Chapters 9 through 12 will give you a good idea of some of the script formats you can expect to see in the studio.

SESSION BASICS

All studio sessions are handled the same. There are two soundproof rooms — the control room and the studio. These are separated by a wall of double-glass and a sound lock with doors between the rooms. The studio is where you will be when you perform. Unless you are doing a group session, you will be the only person in the studio or "booth." In some cases, especially for sessions involving young children, the producer may also be in the studio.

Some sessions are done with a *phone patch*. For these sessions, some or all of the people involved with the session, including the recording engineer, may be hooked up by telephone. An engineer and performer may be the only people at the studio. Phone-patch sessions are also becoming increasingly popular with high-quality national voice-over talent.

With a phone patch, these performers can work from a studio at their home, and connect with producers around the world. They simply record their tracks to digital audio tape (DAT) as the producer gives direction over the phone. The DAT is shipped out that day for next day delivery.

Another variation of a phone-patch session uses ISDN (Integrated Services Digital Network) telephone lines. *ISDN* phone lines are special high-quality lines for transferring digital information in real-time. A studio with ISDN capabilities can connect with a performer on the other side of the world, and treat the session just as if the performer was in the studio, on the other side of the glass.

The producer will do most of the directing for the session. After all, it is his or her vision that you are attempting to create — and it is this person who is ultimately responsible for the project. If you are at a studio that does a lot of commercial production, the engineer may also be giving you direction. If you are on a phone patch, you may receive direction from the person on the phone, either relayed through the engineer or through your headset.

The Session: Step-by-Step

Let's walk through a session from the moment you enter the studio, until you walk out the door. Much of this is review from other parts of this book; however, this will give you a complete picture of a studio session. After reading this section, you will know what to expect and should be able to act as if you have done it all before. Although the studio session process is very consistent, there are many variables that may result in variations on the following scenario. Just "go with the flow" and you will be fine.

Once you enter the studio lobby, your first contact will be the receptionist. Introduce yourself, and tell her which session you are attending. If the studio is in an office building and you paid to park in the building's parking structure, don't forget to ask if the studio validates.

The receptionist will let the producer know you are there. You might be given your copy at this time, or you might have to wait until the producer comes out of the control room. Depending on how the session is going, you may have to wait awhile in the lobby, but it will much shorter than the wait you had at the audition.

The producer or engineer will come out to get you when they are ready, or the receptionist will let you know that you can go back to the control room. Or, someone might come out to let you know that the session is running late. There are many things that can put a session behind schedule. Remember, this is a hurry-up-and-wait kind of business.

When you enter the control room, introduce yourself to the producer, the engineer and anyone else in the room you have not yet met. You can be certain that anyone in the control room is important, so be friendly and polite.

If you did not receive the copy earlier, it will be given to you here. This is your opportunity to do a quick script analysis, set your character and ask any questions you might have about the copy. Get as much information as you need now, because once you are in the studio, you will be expected to perform. Get a good idea of the target audience and correct pronunciation of the product's and client's names. Make notes as to attitude, mood and key words. Mark your script to map your performance so that you will know what you are doing when you are in the studio. The producer or engineer may want you to read through the copy while in the control room for timing or to go over key points. When the engineer is ready, you will be escorted to the studio.

In the studio, you will usually find a music stand, a stool, and the microphone. Practice good studio etiquette and let the engineer handle any adjustments to the mic. Feel free to adjust the music stand to your comfort. If a stool is there, it is for your convenience, and you may choose not to use it if you feel more comfortable standing. Some studios will give you the option of performing without having to wear headphones, but for most you will need to wear them to hear the director. Wait until the engineer indicates that you can put your headphones on.

At the start of most sessions, the engineer records a reference tone for approximately 30 seconds. The reference tone is for setting playback levels later on, and can be very loud and annoying when listening on headphones. Most studios provide a volume control for your headphones that you can adjust, while others must adjust the volume from the control room.

If you wear a pager or carry a cellular phone, make sure they are on vibrate or turned off while you are in the studio. Better yet, leave them in the control room. The beeping or ringing might interrupt an otherwise perfect take and answering a call is disruptive to the session.

The microphone may have a *pop stopper* in front of it, or it may be covered with a foam *wind screen*. The purpose of both of these devices is to minimize popping sounds caused by your breath hitting the microphone. Popping can be a problem with words containing plosives such as "P," "B," "K" and "G." If the wind screen needs to be adjusted, let the engineer know.

When the engineer is ready to record, you will be asked for a *level* or to *read for levels*. He needs to set his audio controls for your voice. Consider this a rehearsal, so perform your lines exactly the way you intend to once recording begins. If you speak softly when reading for levels, and then speak much louder on your first take, your level will be too "hot" and your performance will have been wasted on an unusable recording. You may do several reads for levels, none of which will likely be recorded. However, the producer or engineer may give you some direction to get you on the right track once recording begins.

The engineer will *slate* each take as you go. You will hear all direction and slates in your headphones. This is not the same as slating your name for an audition. The engineer usually will slate, or identify the project or section you are working on, followed by "take 1," "take 2" and so on. Before or after the slate, you may receive some additional direction. You may also hear a low- frequency tone, or buzz, when the engineer is slating the track. This tone makes it easier for the engineer to locate the desired takes when he begins editing. The slate tone is used most commonly on analog tape recording sessions, and is not used as much on digital recordings.

Do not begin reading until the engineer has finished his slate and all direction is finished. You will know when you can start by listening for the sound of the control room mic being turned off. If you speak too soon, your first few words might be cut off or unusable. Wait a second or two after the slate, get a good supporting breath of air, then begin speaking.

As you are reading your lines, the engineer will be watching your level and listening to the sound of your voice. He will also be keeping a written log sheet of take numbers and will time each read with a stop watch. He may also be discussing your delivery or possible copy changes with the producer or client.

COMMON DIRECTION CUES

After each take, you can expect to receive some direction from the producer. It may be that you read too slowly and need to speed up your delivery. Or, the producer might tell you that you have a few seconds "to play with." This means you read too fast, and can slow down a bit. Do not change your attitude or character, unless requested by the producer. Also, do not comment about things you feel you are doing wrong, or ask how you are doing. Let the producer guide you into the read he or she is after. Some of the other direction cues you might hear are:

- **"Pick up the pace"** — You need to read faster, but keep the same character and attitude.

- **"Split the difference"** — An earlier take was either too fast or too slow, and the last take was a bit the other direction. On this next take, adjust your pacing to something in between. The same direction applies to treatment of your character, or on your inflection or enunciation.

- **"Play with it . . ."** — The producer is giving you the opportunity to use your creativity to make the lines work better. Have some fun, modify your delivery, change your pace a bit, try a different inflection and so on.

- **"Three in a row"** — You are being asked to read the same sentence or tag three times, back to back. Give each read in the set a slightly different treatment. The producer is looking for a read that will work best with the rest of the copy. You will frequently be asked for three in a row when doing tags.

- **"Add some smile"** — Literally, put a smile on your face as you read the copy. A smile changes the physical attitude of your body, your mental attitude, and comes through in your read. Smiling makes you sound more friendly, and adds energy to your delivery.

- **"More/less energy"** — Add some excitement to your read, or calm your delivery. Use your body and move your arms to increase energy. Relax and soften your body movement to reduce energy.

- **"Billboard a word"** — This is also referred to as *punching* a word or phrase. *Billboarding* simply means to give a word or phrase a little extra emphasis. The intent is to have that word stand out from the rest of the copy.

- **"Make it conversational"** — Take the reading out of your delivery. Pretend you are telling a story, or visualize yourself talking to your best friend. Talk *to* your audience, not *at* them. Everything you have been doing may be just right, but the illusion of realness may need a little help. Keep the pace and energy, maybe add some smile, and believe in what you are saying. Do this and you will make your delivery more natural.

- **"Warm it up a little"** — Make your delivery more friendly and more personal. Get a sense of what makes you feel warm and fuzzy and use that to shift your attitude to get a warmer delivery.

- **"Stay in character"** — You are drifting in and out of character. Your performance is inconsistent. Something in your delivery is not consistent from beginning to end. It could be an accent or speaking style, attitude or even inconsistent volume. Try to keep your character the same as you read the copy from take to take.

- **"Do a pick-up"** — This means that the first part of a sentence or paragraph was fine, and that the director wants you to continue from a certain point in the copy. They will specify where they want you to "pick it up" from. When you do a pick-up, it's always a good idea to read into the pick-up line. Starting with the last few words before your pick-up will make the phrasing and flow natural, and the engineer's job of editing easier. It's also a good idea to read out after the line by continuing a few words into the next sentence.

- **"Wild line"** — The director or engineer is asking you to do a single line or phrase over. It's not uncommon to do several complete takes, then go back and do wild lines for certain parts of the copy. The director and engineer will be making notes as to which takes they think will work best when everything is edited together later.

- **"That's a buy"** — The three little words you've been waiting to hear! Good job, great take, you're done.

There are many other directions you will be given. Do your best to perform as the director requests. There is a reason why he or she is asking you to make adjustments, although that reason will sometimes not be clear to you.

You may think, and the director may tell you, that you have a perfect take. When the producer gets a good take, you may hear "do it again, just like that," or "one more time for protection." Then there may be several more takes. Each additional take may be slightly different from the one before, or the producer or director may ask for major adjustments, or even make changes to the copy. As you do many takes, you need to remember what you have done before. The producer may say he liked what you did three takes ago. You need to try to duplicate it, even if you don't remember what you did.

Producers usually have a clear idea of what they want, and may not be receptive to your suggestions. Find out what the producer is looking for when you first go through the script. Once in the studio, you should be pretty much on track for the entire session. However, if you get a great idea, or if it appears that the producer is having a hard time making a copy change, by all means speak up. You are part of a team, and part of your job is to help build an effective product. If your idea is not welcome, the producer will tell you.

Recording studio equipment sometimes has a mind of its own. There are times when the engineer may stop you in the middle of a take because of a technical problem, and you may have to wait awhile until it is corrected. Although not often, technical delays do happen. When they do, you need to be ready to pick up where you left off, with the same character and delivery, when the engineer is ready.

If you need some water during the session, let the engineer know and it will be brought in for you. If you need to visit the restroom, let them know.

If you need a pencil, let them know. If you need *anything*, let them know. Once your position is set in front of the microphone (on-mic), the engineer will prefer that you not leave the studio, or change your position. Even a small change relative to the microphone can make a big difference in the sound of your voice. This can be a problem when doing long scripts or lots of takes. If your mic position changes, you can sound very different on different takes, which can be a problem for the engineer if he needs to assemble several takes to build the final commercial. If you must move off-mic, try to keep your original mic position in mind when you return to the mic.

Keep your volume consistent throughout your session. Changes in dynamics may be useful for certain dramatic effects, but, generally, you will want to keep your voice at a constant volume. If your performance does call for minor changes in volume, try to make sure they occur at the same place in the copy for each take. This becomes important later on, when the engineer edits different takes together. If your levels are erratic, the changes in volume may become noticeable in the final edit.

You know what the producer wants. You stay in character. Your timing and pacing are perfect. Your enunciation and inflection are on track. Your performance is wonderful. The producer is happy. The engineer is happy. And, most important, the client is happy. That's it! You're done, right?

Not quite.

Wrap It Up

Before leaving the studio, make sure you sign the contract for your services. If you are a union member, the producer will probably have a contract already filled out for you. Read the parts of the contract that apply to your session before signing. If you were booked for one commercial, and the producer had you do three plus tags, make sure the changes are made on the contract. Also make sure you call your agent and let him or her know about the changes. If you are unsure of anything on the contract, call your agent *before* signing the contract.

For union work, send your AFTRA form to the union within 48 hours of the session to avoid any penalties. The union form is the only way AFTRA has of tracking your work, and making sure you are paid in a timely manner. If you are working freelance, make sure you are paid before you leave the studio, or that you have a signed invoice or deal memo. You've completed your part of the agreement, and you are entitled to be paid. It's up to you if you agree to have your payment sent to you, but keep in mind that you take a risk of delays or not being paid if you do this.

It's good form to thank the producer, engineer, client and anyone else involved in the session before you leave. Keep the script for your files, if you like. If you think your performance was especially good, you can ask the producer for a copy of the spot when it is finished. Always ask for a DAT, a one-off CD, or a reel-to-reel copy, but don't argue if all you can get is a cassette. Audio cassettes and reel-to-reel copies will usually be sent to you or your agent, often at no cost. But there may be a charge for a DAT copy, CD, or videotape copies of a TV commercial. If distribution of a commercial is via audio tape, it's easy for the engineer to make an extra copy of your spot when making dubs for radio stations; however, sending tapes to performers is not a high priority. In this digital age, finished commercials are increasingly being distributed via ISDN networks directly from the studio's computer, or via one-off CDs. The commercial you performed in may not leave the digital domain until it is aired and you may find yourself waiting several weeks, or even months, before you get your copy.

Once your session is over and the paperwork is done, you are free to leave. Your job is done, so don't stick around for the rest of the session or to talk. The producer and engineer have lots of work ahead of them and your presence can cause delays, costing time and money. After you are gone, the process of assembling all the pieces of the puzzle begins. It may take from several hours to several days before the final audio track is complete.

If your session is for a TV commercial, the completed audio will often be sent to a video post-production house where the video will be edited to your track to create a final TV spot. In some cases, just the opposite occurs — the video may have been edited to a scratch track, and the purpose of your session would have been to place your voice-over against the preproduced video. Once mastered, a number of copies are made and distributed to the radio and TV stations scheduled to air the spot.

Follow-up your session with a thank you note to the producer. Thank him or her for good directing or mention something you talked about at the session. Be honest and sincere, but don't overdo it. A simple note or postcard is often all that's necessary to keep you in the mind of the producer or director and get you hired again. If you haven't already, be sure to add their names to your mailing list for future promotions you send out.

References and Resources

Voice-acting is part of show business. It's a lot of fun, but it does take some effort and dedication to become a successful voice-actor. Self-marketing is one key to success even if you have an agent. It is also important to stay tuned into the trends of the industry so that you can learn new techniques and adapt the ones you have mastered.

There are numerous books and resources on this subject that either contain some things I have not included here, or discuss them in an entirely different manner. Of course, I encourage you to refer to this book often as you pursue your adventure into the world of voice-acting. But I also encourage you to study the works of other authors, read the trade magazines, and take classes — lots of classes. Authors and instructors write and teach in many different ways, and you may find that you learn more quickly from one particular style. I encourage you to experience many different instructors and styles to find those from which you can learn most efficiently.

The following sections contain a few resources for your continued education in this exciting business, many of which have been discussed in this book. This list is certainly not complete, but it will give you a good starting point. The page numbers shown below the author's or product names indicate the pages in this book where the item is discussed.

Books on Voice-Acting and Related Subjects

Any book on acting and acting technique will be of value. Here are just a few you might find interesting. Except as noted, these books can be obtained from your local bookseller.

Alterman, Glen — *Two Minutes and Under*; Smith and Kraus, Inc. (1993)

Male and female monologues useful for building skills in character development.

Beaupré, Jon — *Broadcast Voice Exercises,* First edition (1994)
NOT in bookstores — This book is available for $9.50 (plus tax and shipping) from the publisher: Broadcast Voice Books, Ltd., 474 Crane Blvd., Los Angeles, CA 90065-5053 (telephone: 213 223-6287).

A good introductory book of voice exercises and copy. Although much of the book is intended for performers in broadcast radio and television, there is a lot of useful information for the voice-actor.

[pp. 63-64]

Berry, Cicely — *Voice and the Actor*; Macmillan General Reference, Simon and Schuster (1973)

[pp. 56-58]

Blu, Susan and Molly Ann Mullin — *Word of Mouth,* Revised edition; Pomegranate Press, Ltd. (1992)

Bruder, Melissa, Lee Michael Cohn, Madeleine Olnek, Nathaniel Pollack, Robert Previtto, and Scott Zigler — *A Practical Handbook for the Actor*; Random House, Inc., Vintage (1986)

Clark, Elaine A. — *There's Money Where Your Mouth Is*; Backstage Books (1995)

Cooper, Morton — *Change Your Voice – Change Your Life*; Harper and Row, Publishers (1984)

A useful guide to improving the quality of your voice and developing good breath control.

[p. 41]

Joseph, Arthur S. — *The Sound of the Soul*; Health Communications, Inc. (1996)

Breath control is vital to good voice-acting. This book is about breathing and using your breath to achieve Vocal Awareness to improve the sound of your voice.

[pp. 40-41]

Personality Types

Understanding your individual personality makeup and the various characteristics of other personality types will help you when it comes time to give life to a character contained in the words in a script.

Baron, Renee, and E. Wagele — *Are You My Type, Am I Your Type*; Harper, San Francisco (1995)

[p. 77]

Brinkman, Dr. Rick, and Dr. Rick Kirschner — *Dealing with People You Can't Stand*; McGraw-Hill (1994)

[p. 77]

Keirsey, David, and Marilyn Bates — *Please Understand Me — Character and Temperament Types*; Prometheus Nemesis Book Company (1984)

[p. 77]

Advertising, Marketing and Self-Promotion

There are literally dozens of books about marketing and business. The following three cover the basics and include lots of ideas and marketing techniques. Although these books are primarily intended for a small business, many of the concepts can be adapted for the independent voice-actor.

Crandall, Rick Ph.D. — *1001 Ways to Market Your Services — Even If You Hate to Sell*; Contemporary Books (1998)

Putnam, Anthony O. — *Marketing Your Services — A Step-by-Step Guide for Small Businesses and Professionals*; John Wiley and Sons (1990)

Slutsky, Jeff, and Marc Slutsky — *How to Get Clients*; Warner Books (1992)

Tongue Twisters

Tongue twisters are a great workout for developing clarity, good articulation and breath control.

Karshner, Roger — *You Said a Mouthful*; Dramaline Publications (1993)
[p. 65]

Seuss, Dr. — *Fox in Sox*; Random House, Inc. (1979)
[p. 65]

Seuss, Dr. — *Oh, Say Can You Say*; Random House, Inc. (1979)
[p. 65]

Other Resources

Neti Pot^{TM} —

A useful tool for maintaining clear sinuses, the "Neti Pot" is inexpensive and easy to use. It is, perhaps, the best way to apply a nasal wash. You can obtain yours by contacting the Himalayan Institute at:

Himalayan Institute   Toll-free: (800) 822-4547
RR1, Box 400   Direct: (717) 253-5551
Honesdale, PA 18432-9706   Fax: (717) 253-9087
E-mail: Himalaya@epix.net
Internet: www.himalayaninstitute.org

[pp. 69-71]

Voice-Over Guide

The *Voice-Over Guide* is a quarterly publication by Dave & Dave, Inc. The guide features a listing of Los Angeles voice-over recording studios, talent agents who represent voice-over performers and the current AFTRA rates for Los Angeles. Additional information for Dave Sebastian Willams' Voice-Over "Workout" Workshops, demo production and cassette duplication is also included. Subscription cost is $5.00 per year. Contact:

Dave & Dave, Inc.   Phone: (818) 508-7578
1770 North Highland Ave.   Fax: (818) 508-5830
#H-648
Hollywood, CA 90028

The Agencies — What the Actor Needs to Know

This is a monthly publication that includes current information and up-to-date listings of SAG and AFTRA talent agencies in the Los Angeles area. It also includes tips and advice for auditions, and lists what some agents are looking for. The cost is $10 per issue or $50 per year. Also available in Los Angeles and New York performing arts bookstores. Contact:

Acting World Books
P.O. Box 3899
Hollywood, CA 90078

Theatrical Reference Books, Voice-Over Books and Other Materials

Samuel French, Inc., is an excellent theatrical bookstore. Check the reference section for a book titled *The Agency Guide*. This book includes a brief description of every franchised agent in the Los Angeles area, how long they have been in business, the types of talent they represent, who to contact at the agency, and a wealth of other information. Samuel French also carries preprinted address labels, which can save you a lot of time later on, for the Los Angeles talent agencies. Contact:

Samuel French, Inc.   Phone: (213) 876-0570
7623 West Sunset Bl.,
Hollywood, CA 90028

The Voice-Over Checklist

Jim Staylor is a professional voice-actor who has performed internationally as both voice-over and on-camera talent for hundreds of commercials, corporate projects and CD-ROM/video games. His Voice-Over Checklist covers all the basics from preparing for the session to what to do afterward. His Internet web site contains a considerable amount of useful information for both performers and producers. A laminated pocket-size version of the checklist can be obtained by contacting:

Jim Staylor
Staylor-Made Communications
12065 World Trade Drive, Suite 2
San Diego, CA 92128
E-mail: info@staylor-made.com
Internet: www.staylor-made.com

[p. 207]

Cassette Labels and J-Cards

For a free catalog containing information about hundreds of labels, including blank sheets of labels and J-Cards, ready for printing on your home computer, contact:

United Ad Label   Toll Free: (800) 998-7700
650 Columbia Street   Direct: (714) 990-7700
P.O. Box 2216   Fax: (800) 998-7701
Brea, CA 92822-2216
E-mail: c_s@ualco.com
Internet: www.ualco.com

You can also find blank labels by Avery at your local office supply store.

If you have access to the world wide web, you can find a tremendous amount of other information on acting and voice-over by logging on and searching for the keyword *acting* or *voice-over*. Most major bookstores also have internet sites, including Amazon.com, one of the largest internet bookstores.

Focal Press (the publisher of this book) has a large catalog of books on subjects related to voice-acting. If you are interested in learning more about the technical and performing aspects of television, film, multimedia and live performance, you can obtain a catalog by contacting them at:

Focal Press   Phone: (781) 904-2500
225 Wildwood Ave.   Fax: (781) 904-2620
Woburn, MA 01801-2041
Internet: www.bh.com/focalpress